Born to Win

Born to Win

Joginder Singh
Former Director, CBI

Kaveri Books
New Delhi –110 002

Title: Born to Win
Author: Joginder Singh

First Published in 2002
Edition 2026

ISBN-13: 978-81-7479-055-2
Price: Rs. 850.00

Published by

Kaveri Books
4832/24, Ansari Road, Darya Ganj
New Delhi - 110 002 (India)
Tel.: 011-47072321
E-mail: kaveribooks@gmail.com
web: www.kaveribooks.com

Typeset by: Delta Book World, New Delhi

PRINTED IN INDIA

Foreword

This book is a post retirement autobiography spanning over nearly three years of active life lived by Joginder Singh. He and I were colleagues in the Ministry of Commerce in 1980s and I have fond memories of a close association with him. Joginder was active and full of life then and he continues to be active now. People as a rule wither and decline with age but Joginder seem to have defied this law of nature. He has grown younger with years. His imagination, creativity and humour have not diminished with years nor have they lost their flavour.

Joginder has been one of the country's distinguished IPS officers, who has done well in any job entrusted to him. In retirement he is as active as he was in office and doing so well that some of his colleagues are also looking forward for an early retirement. To him retirement is liberation from bondage, a kind of elementary freedom and not an opportunity for withdrawing into comfortable isolation drawing monthly pensions with increasing dearness allowance.

This book is not a catalogue of events. It is much more than a mere chronicle. Its narrative form makes it a run away piece of writing whose energy makes events explode off the pages. The narrators voice won't letyou go. It engages readers in understanding characters and situations. In this book Joginder has some acute observations to make on life itself.

He has a robust faith in imagination and hope which triumphs over apathy and skepticism. It is for nothing that mankind's great visions were conceived in times of worst adversities. Without nurturing illusions about life Joginder celebrates the passionate accomplishments and the great opportunities which life provides to fulfill one's dreams and ambitions.

Life is not just a series of days lived. For every individual there are some fixed parameters within which life is spent. There are extraneous factors beyond one's control influencing the personal destinies of man. But Joginder would not like any one to surrender one's destiny to the decisions of others. The future, he thinks, is not pre-determined. An infinite number of choices are there and one should exercise one's free will to pick the one which one prefers. It is weak people who feel secure obeying someone who tells them what to do. Joginder strikes such men with savage strokes. Living according to him needs to be modified with continuous efforts elevating it to higher and more purposeful forms of life. The process of improving, learning, reforming and introspection should be an on-going process of living. He strongly feels that life ultimately offers us what we seek from it. In its inexhaustible depository it has everything. It is our commitment which makes us what we become. We are all authors of our lives. Stars are born and stars get burnt out. The habit of introspection and viewing ones own role in a detached manner helps in self-regeneration. It is in the mirror of self-examination that one sees ones true-self. At any moment of life, one should feel that one can face the world and look into its eyes. By one deeds, lifestyle and thoughts one can find ones own path of adventure and when the end comes one can stand up to say I have dared to live.

In this complicated and subtle world of human affairs every bit of work done honestly, every intention rightly conceived and each step taken in the right direction produce spectacular results, though at times we might not be able to see them happening instantly.

Joginder has been one who has continuously tried to identify himself enthusiastically with national tasks. Doing them with a sense of excellence and a sense of pride without appropriating other people's achievement is his characteristic style. I wish we had more people like him to enrich the profession to which he belongs. The readers will enjoy his book. My good wishes are always with him in all his endeavours. His is a case of a junior surpassing his seniors. I see him in that relation to me.

Abid Hussain

Former Commerce Secretary,
Former Member, Planning Commission,
Formerly High Commissioner
for India in USA

Preface

Life is a continuous flux and flux itself is life. There is no continuous joy-ride in life. It would be dull and uninteresting, if there were no obstacles. More than half the pleasures in life are of overcoming difficulties. It shall be deceiving ourselves if we believe that we are indispensable and the world cannot do without us. That we can do without the world, however imperfect it may be, is also a fallacy.

Life runs on a definite pattern. It is for us to detect that pattern, and use it for our best advantage. A lot depends upon our, pluck, more than our luck. Being a part of the bureaucracy, I have moved along with it, sometimes influencing, sometimes being influenced and sometimes observing and at times being observed.

It often happens that somebody else's words express implicitly our own feelings. Here I would like to quote a few apt lines from Yeats:

Nor law, nor duty bade me fight,
Nor public men, nor cheering crowds,
A lonely impulse of delight,
Drove to this tumult in the clouds.

I have tried to portray in this book the contemporary society, how people behave in the best and the worst of times.

This is a record of over three years of life after my retirement. There is an interesting story or an episode on every page. May be, you had a similar experience or a worse or better one. I feel that life is like a battlefield, with constant conflicts between our actual inner selves and our outer portrayals, between the heart and the mind, between the innate and the acquired. But what we should not forget is that if life is a battlefield, we have all been born to win...

Joginder Singh

Contents

End of the road or a new turn?

Many people wonder as to what retirement means? Is it the dead end of an active life? Is it only waiting for death, for the retiree? On my saying that, despite retirement, I have no time to do all the things I have wanted to do in life, I notice a look of disbelief in my friends and acquaintances. Even my retired colleagues are reluctant to believe me. I felt that I must pen down all events, some eventful and some uneventful, in my life, if possible, every day. Truly speaking, this is not my life story. It is an account of the behaviourial interaction of others amongst themselves, as well as my reactions to events and people. Time is a limited commodity, and a conscious effort is required to prevent it from going waste. It is essential to have a routine, so that one can allocate time for the things one considers worthwhile. A lot of my time, in fact, over 75 per cent is spent in writing. It is not something, which can be delegated to a private secretary. Otherwise, he would be the one, doing all the writing and would be an eminent writer himself. Incidental to writing, there is a lot of other routine work, like sending letters, writing addresses, taking the computer print-outs and occasionally going to market, to replenish the writing material. I prefer a male secretary, as he can do all the leg work, go to the post office, get reservation for travelling and sit late if necessary.

Sometimes, daywise events are written, and some-times they are clubbed together to give a coherent presentation, instead of a disjointed view. Each day is a small story in itself. It carries a message or observation for the readers and myself. It is not exactly a chronology of the day or the days. It is how others view me and what my perception is about them. Sometimes, I have been brutally frank. At other times, I have been over charitable. On other occasions, I have not tried to ruffle feathers and have attempted diplomacy. Unlike Khuswant Singh, a prominent columnist and journalist I do not believe in murdering men and their reputations, through my pen. But the effort is to convey what I feel. One advantage of retirement and of not taking up any job has been that one can work at one's own pace. One does not have to do the over-kill, and prove to self or others. In Service, the effort is always to indulge in one-up-man-ship game, and go on proving that one is indispensable. This urge fades with retirement. The bureaucratic system has become too complicated and too large to govern the country. Rules and laws are framed, with a view to make profligate the bureaucracy and its powers. The Inspector Raj, and not only the Police Raj, has managed to entrench itself, and is there for all times to come, unless the elected rulers see through the fraud that is being perpetrated in their name and for the so-called good and welfare of the common man. But five generations or five decades have passed, since India's independence, without any perceptible improvement in the situation. Rules and procedures, drafted two centuries ago and out of tune with the present-day requirements, take precedence over the common sense and welfare of the ordinary man. I have heard people saying that it is a sin to be poor and without influence.

Free from chains

My first day after retirement was just like any other day. I knew that I was not going to be in a rush to run anywhere. So

I had a leisurely walk and came back. My wife went to her office, which was close by at Patiala House at that time. I did not feel any change. I still had a number of visitors and pressmen telephoning me. But my first priority was, to sever fully and finally all my connections with the Government. I was still in a Government house, which was in my name. It had to be transferred to my wife's name. She was very much entitled to one. I had to get my pension payment order and some more terminal financial benefits. The office of the Accountant General, Bangalore, was very prompt in sending me the Pension Payment Order. I had decided to draw the pension paid to me by my parent State of service at Jalalabad, which still is my permanent address. I had already opened an account in the State Bank of India, Jalalabad, and communicated it to the A.G. Bangalore. The A.G. Bangalore, authorised the Accountant General, Punjab, Chandigarh to pay my pension and raise the debit against him. The AG Punjab issued a separate order to authorise the payment of the pension at Jalalabad. The rules are that an IAS/IPS officer, even after retirement, has to be looked after by the State of his allotment. It is they who have to pay the pension. Each All-India-Service Officer, which means the IPS/IAS and now Indian Forest Service, is given a State of allotment. It may not be his native State. On allotment, he or she has to learn the local language, laws and rules. In the absence of passing departmental examination, there is no increment or promotion for the official. Willy nilly, one has to know the local language, which in my case happened to be Kannada. I had passed the state examination in 1963. My getting through was courtesy of the examiner, a Divisional Commissioner, than on merit. He did it to save me from any financial loss. But he said, I should be able to read and write like a native. I thanked him for his suggestion and told him, that I had set up a kind of record of learning a Dravidian language, in one year. He appreciated it.

There is a lot of post-retirement correspondence required to get your dues. It is inescapable and unavoidable, as the pension paying authorities are to be intimated as to where the final amount should be sent. I had learnt typing out of compulsion, in 1984, as my handwriting is practically illegible. So I did not feel totally helpless. I realised that I would have to give three months to settle my affairs and start a new retired career. Another colleague who retired before me was not that lucky. He had to pay for a number of pilgrimages to pension sanctioning authorities, as well as give a "Nazrana or Mammool" before he got his pension payment order. Unfortunately, anybody can hold you up, as long as he has the authority to give what actually are your dues.

A number of businessmen and organisations approached me, with handsome offers of a salary of six figures a month. I did not want to accept anything and be a subject to the frowns and smiles of my new bosses. The Government rules require that before taking up any job, within two years of retirement, Government sanction is required. I did not want to have anything to do with the Government or its bureaucracy. So I warded off all offers saying that for two years it was not possible to take up any job. I realised that the reason for the offers was not my competence, but the possible influence, which went with the former job of a CBI Director. Without being impolite, I made it clear that I was not available for sale to any bidder. I was clear that with the pension, the land income, my house rent of Rs. 25000 per month at that time from Bangalore and the interests from the Government dues and commutation of the pension, I did not have to look back. It was sufficient for my life-time, to maintain the same standard of living that I had before retirement. Moreover, the demands on one's time and activities can be reasonably controlled, in the absence of a job which ties you down for a fixed number of hours.

Avoiding the Government connection

Since my wife was still in service, with four years to go, till her retirement at 58 in 2001, and now 2003 with the increased age limit, I immediately had a private telephone installed in my name. It was to ward off any criticism of hers that she was allowing her husband to misuse the government facilities specifically sanctioned for her. I had to make a number of STD calls. Even if she had paid for them, on my account, it would confirm that her telephone was being used by a non-entitled person. Having been a lawman all my life, I felt that it was better to be Mr. Private, than still hang on to the trappings of my wife's office. In fact the private telephone arrived ten days before my retirement.

While in service, one was moving from one place to another and there was an easy access to the telephone. I have also added a personal cellular phone to my assets, for the sake of always being accessible to my family. This has enabled my family to be in touch with me anywhere in the country. Of course, the telephone companies do not earn any fat revenue from me, as I do not have even five calls to make. Most of the time, it is to return the telephone calls. I do not have to run to answer any phone call, as all calls after four rings are programmed to go automatically into the answering machine mode. I have been getting a lot of calls to make recommendations to government officers, on the strength of having been the Director of the CBI. This is something I never did while in service and I do not intend to do so in post-retirement.

Making the house habitable

The Jalalabad house, where my father has been living since 1955 had been in a state of great despair. It was almost falling off. After the death of my father, I was an irregular visitor to Jalalabad. Since I was the President of Giani Gurbux Singh DAV College, I had to carry the legacy of my father.

During my visit, I would live in the run-down house and keep postponing the repairs and white-washing of the house. I had kept one set of my old and out-of-fashion clothes for use during my bi-monthly visits to Jalalabad. Once when I went there, I found that rain water had spoiled every single item in the house. I used to lock the house and take the key with me and open it only on my arrival. I was upset to find out that even one room was not safe for living. I decided to spend some money and put, Om, my man Friday to get the house done up. The old roof had to be replaced by a new one. The bathroom too had to be repaired. My mother had decided to stay back and supervise the work. It took six months to get the house into a reasonable and livable form. My father, when alive, did only the minimum essential repairs to keep it from crumbling. I was hardly interested, as my wife and daughters were in Delhi. The Agriculture operations required my presence, periodically and so the habitation was a picture of neglect. When the house was being repaired, my uncle, Mahant Harbhajan Singh remonstrated that the house could have been repaired at a much cheaper cost, if I had got it done while in service. I replied that it could even have been rebuilt had I wanted, at no cost. I did not want to be accused of having used my position in service, so I did not even get the house repaired, while in service. The house stands in reasonable shape. I still use the car of my late father which he purchased a few months before his death in 1995. It has run less than 20000 kilometres in five years. My visits to Jalalabad range between one month to two months. The visit in the month of January is almost fixed as I have to be there for the Bhog or the end of recitation of Path on the death anniversary of my late father on 23rd January. My wedding anniversary falls on 19th January. Normally my wife and I have been going to Jalalabad on 20th of January, so that we could reach there in time for the commencement of the recitation of the Path on 21st January. The Path is kept in the

Library of the College named after my father, as Mahant Kartar Singh Memorial Library.

Small office, home office

With no official back-up, at any health emergency or even any accident, immediate communication is of the utmost importance. It was difficult to get used to a life, without the facilities of a government, like an official vehicle, a PA and other fringe benefits. To fill in the need, for replying to the ever increasing correspondence, I engaged a part-time private secretary in the first month of my retirement and also a full-time driver. I was quick to adjust and felt that I must get used to a new life-style. Government service is not the be-all and end-all. I started enjoying life more, as I realised that I was not a slave to anybody. I did not have to bother about being answerable to anybody, except myself. Being answerable to oneself is more painful than being answerable to anybody else. One advantage of retired life was that I did not have to sacrifice my morning walk for anybody or any meeting, except when I had to catch a plane or a train. I received invitations to address meetings on the general conditions in the country and on corruption. Since my retirement, I have visited Ooty, Goa, Daman, Bombay, Cochin, Bangalore, Mysore, Lucknow, Jaipur, Indore, Gwalior, Chandigarh, Ludhiana, Ambala, Jallundhur, Amritsar, Ganganagar, Nepal, and London, on invitations to address meetings, conferences and seminars. All the trips have been fully paid, along with boarding and lodging. Apart from that my fortnightly column has been appearing regularly in 'The Dainak Bahaskar' and 'The Pioneer', and a number of other newspapers all over the country.

Trying hand at fourth estate

I convey myself by writing. The following are the books which have been a bridge between me and my readers since 1996.

1. Make a Way Where There is None
2. Ways of success and happiness
3. 50 Days to Top

   (These three books are on self-development)
4. Some Untold Tales

   This contains humorous pieces pertaining to everyday life. These books are published by Har Anand Publications Pvt Ltd, New Delhi.
5. Without Fear and Favour : An Autobiography; it was an instant sell-out and the first edition is already over. It is published by Kaveri Books, New Delhi.
6. The Indian Kaleidoscope. It depicts the present-day scenario in the country in various walks of life. Jawahar Publishers and Distributors, New Delhi, published it.
7. Inside CBI; One of the top best sellers in India as assessed by The Hindustan Times (The Top National Daily) in January 1999. This book is on the investigation and the high profile cases handled by the agency, the Central Bureau of Investigation. This agency is equivalent to the FBI of the USA. The author was the Director of the CBI (Head of the Agency). It is published by Chandrika Publications, New Delhi. This book is also published in Hindi by the same publisher.
8. Outside CBI; It is published by Gyan Publishing House, New Delhi. It is a book on events.
9. Inside India; It is published by Indian Publishers Distributor, Delhi. It suggests ways and means to improve the country.
10. Be The Best: It is published by Indian Publishers Distributors, Delhi. It is about succeeding in life and excelling in one's field.

I used to keep a regular record of all relevant news paper clippings, a practice discontinued as my study is running short of storage space. However, my faithful computer keeps a record of every single word I have written. My getting hooked on to the computer is the result of an accident and a combination of circumstances. Initially, I did not believe that a computer could do all the things, claimed on behalf of it. I had learnt typing out of a necessity, in 1984, when I joined the Indian Institute of Public Administration, for doing a nine months course in Advanced Programme in Public Administration, called APPA. It was immediately after my five and a half year deputation, from 1st January, 1979 to June 1984 and it conferred an M.Phil. degree on all those who completed the course successfully. My real purpose of pursuing the course was to spend another year with my family in Delhi and prolong the stay. Most people join this course even now, after two decades, only for this reason. As a part of the course, one was required to write a dissertation of 200 pages on any subject of public administration. I scribbled it and gave it for typing. The typist threw his hands saying that he could not read what I had written. I tried my hand at reading and was equally unsuccessful in deciphering what I had written. So I decided to join a typing school near my house and learn pounding the type writer so that my output could be legible. I can type now, with the added advantage that the computer key board is the same, as that of the type writer. It is much softer than any type writer's.

Occasionally, I watch TV, while working on the computer. But I hardly pay any attention to it, like millions of shop-keepers or house-wives, who leave the TV on for an occasional glance. Worth commenting are the dresses of hostesses, especially girls on the music channels. Every day, they are becoming more and more skimpier reaching a point of embarrassment. But perhaps the hostess gets paid for this. All this is being done under the mistaken impression that such dresses and flippant styles attract more and more viewers. This impression is based on the fact that in the early nineteen fifties and sixties, most people, even those who did not know a word of English, went to see English pictures for a few semi-naked or baring scenes. In fact, some of my illiterate friends saw such movies a dozen or more times. What was a taboo in the 1960's, is an outdated fashion now. A girl making two plaits of her hair was considered ultra modern. The actresses in the black and white films were considered fallen women and non virtuous. It was a problem to get girls play even the role of Sita in Ramayana. Quite often, boys dressed as girls portrayed the characters. Women wearing the veil was an old custom and quite common till 1966. When I got married, my mother insisted that my wife veiled her face from my father and grand father, that is father-in-law and grand father-in-law. Surinder, just fresh from the Punjab University after her M.Sc. replied that it was a queer logic that she was to hide her face from those who would come to her rescue in case of need. But there was no restriction on her being spotted and seen by the criminals and rogues. This was a logic to which there was no reply. She removed the veil at the nodding of my grandfather whom I had asked if there was any objection to the veil being removed. Modern generation would be aghast at the fact that at one time, young girls had to cover their face from their elders. The veil has its origin from the time of invaders in 539 AD, when any woman, if good looking, was seized by them to satisfy their sexual urges. The winner would not only take the spoils and properties, but also the women they could lay their hands on. Values change, approaches change and people change. This is the way of life. Every generation likes to make its own mistakes and learn from them. God has given such a short life-span that no man can do all the things he wants in his life time. With over six decades of existence on earth, I can say with confidence that Shakespeare was dead right, when he said that all the world is a stage and we are all actors and actresses. The trouble is that we like to occupy the centre stage, even long after our show has ended and our innings are over. It is great wisdom to realise that when our innings are over, we should bid good-bye and make room for somebody else. I have been visiting Jalalabad and dividing my time, between various lecture assignments, meeting people and writing. The death anniversary of my late father, Mahant Kartar Singh, had been observed in the Giani Gurbux Singh DAV College, Jalalabad on 23rd January every year regularly. This project was very dear to his heart and is a tribute to his contribution in the development of the small town, where he settled after being uprooted from the areas, which form Pakistan now. I must confess that the irreparable loss of death of even the dearest mellows down with the passage of time. The trick is to keep the memory alive and continue the good work done by the previous generation. It is the only way posterity can remember and recall the work good or bad done by us.

I did not bother about personal conveyance in the past. The government rules permitted the officers to pay a token amount and use the government vehicle for private purposes up to 300 kilometres per month or pay for more mileage. I committed the mistake of purchasing a second-hand Esteem car, in February, 1998, which was reported to be in a good condition. I regretted having purchased a second-hand car. I beat a hasty retreat and sold it off almost at the same price. I thanked my stars that I did not have to visit repairs shops and garages to get the car tended for replacing the old worn-out parts. With a heavy heart, I decided to invest in a brand new car, with the unwritten assurance that it would be a trouble-free investment, for at least a few years. The expectation has not been belied for the last three years at least. The moral is: buy brand new stuff. Never go in for second-hand goods. They will rarely be trouble free.

House hunting

Under the government rules, it is possible for the house occupied by one spouse to be transferred to the other. I had not shifted to the Bungalow meant for CBI Director to avoid the hassles of shifting a house. Since 1979, I have shifted from Moti Bagh, to Rabinder Nagar, to Curzon Road, to Kaka Nagar, Bapa Nagar, Lodi Estate and then Tilak Lane. The last five changes from Kaka Nagar have been in five years. I was assured by the ministers, and the secretaries to the Urban Development Ministries that they would go by the rules and transfer the Tilak Lane house to my wife, who was eligible for it. Even after the Urban Development Minister passed orders to make a uniform policy to transfer the houses to the spouses, if they were eligible, the matter was kept hanging. A lady bureaucrat saw to it that despite various pleadings and the orders of the then Minister, Jethmalani, nothing moved, except a few notings on the file. I do not like to go on pleading again and again. Despite assurance from the office of the minister that things would be sorted out, I decided that enough was enough. I was charged the market rent for two months, that is a total of Rs. 30000 or Rs. 500 a day, as against the normal rent of Rs. 500 per month. I sent the cheque and shifted to the new house, allotted to my wife in a lower category to Bharti Nagar. I felt that I had been a lawman all my life, and I would go by the orders of the government. The lady bureaucrat was also shifted from the ministry. I can only presume that a total impression would have been the cause of the bureaucrat shifting, including perhaps the housing policy. The moral is that there is such concentration of power in the bureaucracy, that it is not difficult for them to frustrate any one, at any level including a Minister. Ultimately the minister's orders prevailed and others got the benefit. I had my peace of mind and self-esteem, that the trips to the ministries and ministers were over, for being allowed to stay in Tilak Lane, so as to avoid shifting.

It takes a few months to settle down to a new, changed life style. It is for this reason that bureaucrats do not take to retired life kindly. I had to divide my time between Jalalabad and Delhi to get my late father's house repaired, to change the bank accounts to my mother's name and to decide about the cultivation of land. Being Chairman of the local management committee of DAV College in Jalalabad, I also had to be involved in the educational affairs of the town. General elections were round the corner, after Gujral lost his job as Prime Minister with the Congress withdrawing support to him, in 1998 February. A lot of rumours were floating that one major political party would ask me to contest elections to the Parliament. The newspapers also announced me as a BJP candidate from Ferozpore. But nothing finally emerged, and the rumours died a natural death. I have friends and foes in all parties, as I never obliged anybody at the cost of my duty. In Singapore, the ruling party seeks the best candidates for the jobs of members of Parliament and Ministers. But in India, it is your past services rendered, and loyalty, which secures you any office. I have never hankered after any office or job and hence no disappointment at any happening. The post-retirement jobs, given to the government officials, are directly in proportion to the services rendered or the services which might be rendered. It has nothing to do with merit or competence. In fact, it will be unfair to criticise the politicians for such appointments. The serving bureaucrats pick up their friends, cronies or supporters and send up their names for the political master's signatures. It is a mere formality, as the ministers somehow feel that bureaucracy is the repository of all wisdom. Whatever it proposes, must be all right and it goes through Delhi.

My mother, when she gets bored in Delhi, goes to the ancestral house in Jalalabad and vice versa. I make it a point to telephone to her, at least once in two days. She attends to all calls herself. This is her way of being in touch with all those who want to speak to her. Most of us make the mistake of having calls attended by others. When somebody calls up, he/she wants to speak to the person, he/she has telephoned and not to the PA or Secretary. PA's and Secretaries are good for filtering the calls. But they cannot substitute the boss. Occasionally, my mother places the phone wrongly on the cradle, keeping it permanently engaged. Once I had to tell our neighbour, Dr. Tilak Raj to tell my mother to have the phone properly placed. I used to lose temper with my mother, at small lapses. I have stopped doing so now because in her old age, I do not wish to add to her problem of having lost her husband and my father. I used to be a fire-brand. But the fire is under control now.

Entertain to be entertained

I often get friends and relatives, who have to be entertained. It is basically a return hospitality. Delhi being a city of distances and a city of babus, it is just not possible to invite friends or relations for a meal, without adequate notice. Even with one week's notice, it is just not possible to be sure, that all the people on the guest list would turn up. When I have to entertain one or two guests, I make it a point, to take them to India Habitat Centre for a lunch or dinner. It saves the hassles of getting raw items to the house and having them cooked. The guests also like a proper meal rather than a lavish high tea, or coffee. This way I can regulate and save enough time for my writing. In fact, I prefer to invite or be invited for lunch, as it is always possible to have time to rest after the meal. It also prevents late nights and upsetting of the routine. The lives of most of us are built around routine and we feel upset, if it is disturbed. I even prefer to take my daughters for lunch. Left to myself, I would avoid eating food from outside. My stomach gets upset when there are too many condiments or chillies or when the food is stale. One cannot guarantee that these contingencies will not occur when eating outside. Once in a while, I run into a few Ministers like Jagmohan and Arun Jaitley, in the India International Centre, where they too drop in for meals or tea.

Without fear or favour

I had seen many ups and downs in life. I had decided to make rough notes of several incidents, which had happened to me. I kept on polishing them from time to time so that, at some time or the other, I could publish my autobiography for the benefit of the younger generation. I wrote and completed a book in 1984, during my study leave and the nine months course in the Indian Institute of Public Administration. Being in service, I could not publish it, as some portions were critical of the functioning of the government system. It would have been a violation of the rules of conduct. Having been a law-enforcing man all my life I did not wish to do anything wrong and get into trouble, I kept the self typed manuscript with myself. Mr. Rakesh, and Anil Jain of Kaveri Books agreed to bring out my autobiography in February, 1998. It was brought out as " Without Fear and Favour", and was almost an instant hit. My only regret is that I did not have enough time to polish it, nor did the Editor of the book spend any time on it. But then, what is perfect in life? It was a hurried job, for which I needed six months more. It was brought out in the record time of one month on 5th February, 1998. The excellent response to my autobiography was a source of encouragement to me. It sold more than 1000 copies under the heading " Without Fear or Favour". I had asked my friend and colleague D.R. Karthikeyan from my cadre to formally release the book. I was brutally frank in portraying men and events. I also made fun of myself, as to how I as the bridegroom was left behind, by my marriage party, who was more keen to see Chandigarh than attend my wedding on 19th January, 1966. It is an interesting account. I have presented myself as an ordinary Indian, which I happen to be. I realise how life ebbs away. We have too little time to do all that we wish to accomplish. My Publisher, Rakesh, though of low profile, put in his honest effort to promote the book and was responsible for an excellent production. I am glad that I finished and published the book, as it removed many misconceptions about me. It portrays the real me, a simple, non-public school product, with no pretensions of any kind.

My life in 1998

During 1998, I was able to compile a book on the conditions in India. It was named, *The Indian Kaleidoscope* and published in October, 1998. The professional Editor did an excellent job of joining the disjointed portions. I still consider it as one of my best work, which portrays the conditions of contemporary India. Publishing a book is not enough. It is also essential to launch it properly and give it good publicity. Here somehow, my publisher did not exert himself to do the publicity. In fact, at his instance, I had requested a Minister to launch the book, to which the then Minister agreed. But the publisher did not even send a written request and did not take any steps to push the sale of the book. I realised that it is equally important to write a good book, and also to publicise this fact. *The Indian Kaleidoscope* has a Foreword by a former Cabinet Secretary, who criticised me for almost being a sanitary inspector in finding fault with the existing conditions in India. He also praised my work, which he felt should lead to the starting of a public movement for a better polity.

I had announced on transfer from CBI on 1st July, 1997, that I would write a book on the CBI, which would expose the political corruption and the hypocrisy of the so-called moralist politicians, including the then Prime Minister, Inder Kumar Gujral. It was bound to be controversial, as it would have been a first book of its kind on the CBI by a former Director. I was approached by a number of publishers, including a foreign one. One even brought a cheque of one lakh, and eventually got scared and backed off, not daring to publish any controversial book. The second one felt that it was too critical of the government and felt that if he published the book, the government purchases of books published by him would be stopped. The third one dilly dallied and again gave the excuse of being busy with other works. Ultimately, it was a young publisher, Sanjay Jha, a novice in the trade, who took up the challenge and in the first instance itself published 5000 copies, out of which 4000 were sold in the first few months. The book was released on 25th December, 1998. It was an instant hit and came in the best-seller list. Publishers want to see which side of their bread is buttered and they wish to eat only butter and not the crumbs. Why only blame the publishers, it is the universal trend? Nobody is in the business or trade to make losses. He or she is there to make some money. It is for this reason that I carry no ill will against anybody and I am on the best of terms, even with my enemies or the persons who might have suffered because of my actions while discharging my duties.

I used to send articles to all major dailies including the Hindustan Times, Indian Express and the Pioneer. They were published. Most papers wanted me to write exclusively for them. I decided to stand by the Pioneer, which had stood by me, both when I was in and out of service. I have excellent relations with all publishers and all Editors. Only one Editor told me that his proprietors were not happy with his publishing my articles, as the paper belonged to a particular party. The proprietor wanted to enter the Rajya Sabha and the publication of my articles in his paper would earn only minus points. I stopped sending any more articles to that paper to avoid any embarrassment to the Editor. I felt that I have to be fair to myself too as whatever I write has to be from my true self.

To Nagpur RSS headquarters

I had a totally unexpected invitation to preside over the annual Vijay Dashmi celebration on 1st October, 1998 in Nagpur, of RSS. It is a prestigious simple function, where young Rashtriya Swayam Sevak Sangh volunteers have a march past, salute the Chief Guest, the RSS Chief and Dy. Chief. The Chief of the RSS is called Sarsangh Chalak. I am not a member of any political party. It was a tribute to my method of working that I was chosen for this signal honour. I promptly accepted the invitation. I had started making arrangements for my train/ air journey, when the other surprise came in the name of an intimation that RSS would arrange for my ticket as well as boarding and lodging. I had made arrangements for my stay in one of the guest houses of the government, as I did not want to burden the organisation with looking after me. I was informed that arrangements had been made for my stay at the house of one of the active members of the RSS, Laxman Singh Bankoti. I was earlier facing a moral dilemma, that if I stayed in the government guest house, the officer who had booked the government accommodation, might get into trouble for accommodating me. I did not want to put anybody in trouble. I thanked that officer who had come to receive me, and conveyed my reason for not staying with him. He appreciated it, and went back. Straight away from Nagpur Airport I went for the function, meeting and dinner with the Sikhs of Nagpur. The function ended at 11 P.M. I slept at the top floor of the house of my host. I had to be ready next day at 6 AM to take the salute of the volunteers at 6.30 AM. I got up at 5 AM and made my own tea with the kit I carry and reached in time for the parade. Sarsangchalak, Prof. Rajender Singh and Dy. Sarsangchalak Sh. H.V. Seshadri were already present. I joined them in taking the salute and later addressed the public meeting. It was one of the most disciplined gathering I had ever seen. I was told that the discipline of the RSS is not from any badges of ranks, but is inculcated from within, apart from nationalism, loyalty to the nation and basic Hindu values. As a youngster, I had attended some of the programmes of the RSS. But I was too young to comprehend the importance of these things.

I praised the fact that RSS was engaged in character and nation building, which was the utmost need of the hour and of the country. I felt that this should be the universal ideology of the country. I suggested that fight against corruption should also become one of the cardinal edicts of the RSS. I also visited the RSS headquarters in Nagpur, which is not guarded by army, or police. It is a simple structure, where the inmates live a very austere life. Nobody has any worldly possessions. Even the Chief, Prof. Rajendar Singh, who travelled with me back to Delhi, did not have more than a few sets of personal clothing. It cannot be said that any RSS functionary has any wealth of his own. They are literally Sadhus, devoted to the cause of building a strong India. It has become fashionable to dub the RSS as a fascist organisation. But a visit and discussion with the top brass would dispel any such illusion. They are only pro-India and pro-Hindu. There is nothing to be ashamed of being a pro-Hindu, because basically every Indian, whatever be his present religion had Hindu origins. If Indians are not going to be pro-Indians, the British, Americans, and other countries are certainly not going to stand for us. Pseudo intellectuals have given different values to the country and one of them is that in the name of secularism, you can condemn anything 'Indian'. If a Hindu speaks for Hindustan, he is dubbed as a communalist. If anybody else speaks for his religion, he is only considered defending minorities. It is good to be liberal and respect everybody. But there is no sin in respecting yourself and your country above others. One does not have to completely agree with the host. It is also not necessary that the host agrees with the guest, as long as there are broad points of agreement on the basics. This approach alone can keep the country together. India has been under foreign rule, because the inhabitants did not work or live or speak with a single voice and a single authority. Anyone who stands for India, is an asset for the country.

The RSS is a socio-cultural organisation. It is not a trust. It is not registered. It does not pay income tax and , moreover, it has no members on its rolls. The RSS is a 'faceless organisation, "With regard to finance, the RSS is an auto-financing set-up. The RSS does not have a list of its members, though the number of swayamsevaks, of the RSS, runs into several lakhs nation-wide. Anyone attending a shakha is a swayamsevak. There is no register to record his name. There are no membership fees. Anyone can become a swayamsevak and continue be one all through his life. The swayamsevaks are known to the heads of the shakhas, by their faces. About donations to the RSS, no one will ever know, how much others have contributed, since there is no record for an individual contribution.

The RSS is run by donations, called "gurudakshina." Again, there is no account of what each member pays. Every year during Gurupurnima, a thali is placed under the RSS flag, called "Bhagwadhwaj." The swayamsevaks then make their donations and contributions to the flag and on the thali. "In this way, no one knows, what is the individual contribution, of a swayamsevak. Every year all the top brass of the BJP, including the Prime Minister, gather at some place and make their donations to the dhwaj on the thali.

Officially, no one knows each one's contribution, since everything is mixed up. The RSS also does not have to pay taxes, since the donations are not shown as income. It is not income. In a temple one does not pay taxes on dakshina : The question arises then how the money is spent.The amount collected by each shakha is sent to the executive body of the RSS. It then decides on disbursement of the amount on various "social projects." Not much money is required as the RSS has hardly any expenses. Even the shakhas do not need much fund. At the most, each shakha would buy a football or some such stuff for the swayamsevaks to play since it's a physical training session.

Bangalore beckons

My tenants in Bangalore, Madura Coats, a multi- national company informed me that they had decided to vacate my house, as they had down-sized their operations and staff. They were excellent tenants and I offered to reduce the house rent, so that they could continue there. They again informed me that they had nobody, who could be eligible for the high rent they would have to pay. They had been my tenants for the last 18 years. There was not a single occasion, when they either delayed the rent, or any other payment. They had maintained the house and I had no complaints whatsoever against them. The rent paid by them to me was less than half paid by others, for a similar accommodation but I was contented that the house had paid for itself, and the government loan. I did not wish to stretch or try my luck further. I decided at once that if I could not get a proper tenant, it would be best to sell off the house. Getting stuck up with a bad tenant is like marrying an ugly woman deliberately. You are stuck up for life, with no escape route. When one is in government service, there are occasions, when you can combine personal work with duty and save on air fare. Since the same tenant had continued for the last 18 years, there was no particular need for me to go to Bangalore to look after the house. Now as this problem had arisen, after my retirement, I had no way except to go at my own expenses. I did not wish to travel by train, as this would have meant more than 48 hours either side or 96 hours of total journey. If you include the waiting time, the total time might come to five days. This would have meant less time available for disposal of the house. I had enrolled myself as a member of the Flying return programme of the Indian Airlines and Air India.

If you travel by any of the members of the programme, you can earn some points or miles as they are called. When the accumulated mileage reaches a certain limit, then you can encash to get a free ticket for journey both inside and outside the country. I discovered that I had enough points to earn a free return ticket by the Indian Airlines. I went and spent fifteen days in Bangalore, in search of a good prospective tenant or an outright purchaser of the house. It appeared a futile wait. The advertisement in the papers did not help, nor did any police connection, or knowing senior officials. My brother-in-law had come to Bangalore and we went to see a mutual friend in Vijaya Bank. I came to know that the Bank was on the look-out for a permanent residence for the Chairman/ Managing Director. I was told that a committee would go around and decide, after I had responded to their advertisement to sell my house. I had no option, but to wait for something to turn up. It is just not possible to rush such matters, as the next step depends on somebody else. I only wanted to get the worry of renting out the house off my chest. Things do change after retirement and I was aware of the changed circumstances. After fifteen days of waiting, meeting various property dealers, and answering some red herring calls, I came back to Delhi. I also sent an offer to the Bank, offering my house for rent or sale as desired by them, and at the price fixed by them. There is a lot of work to be done, if one wishes to sell one's house. The taxes have to be up to date, and a clear legal title to the house is required. After two months, I got an offer from Vijaya Bank, which was much below my expectations. I accepted it readily, as instead of getting returns, I was spending on the house to maintain it. I discovered that I needed certificates from my Delhi income tax officer that I had no dues against me. My last return was not enough. The certificate had to be in the prescribed proforma. I also needed a certificate from the competent authority that the valuation of the house was fair and it was not being undersold to avoid payment of the income tax. This was notwithstanding the fact that the house had been sold to a public sector bank. Fortunately, I got an invitation to address the police officers under training in Mysore. The invitation almost coincided with the finalisation of the sale of the house. It could not have come at a more appropriate time. Finally on 5th September, 1998, at the end of my visit to Mysore, I sold my house to Vijaya Bank with a heavy heart. This house had been built with love, care and attention to even the smallest of details, as to where the telephone or the TV would be kept. I was not destined to stay in it, even for one day. But that is what life is all about. A wag has said that fools build houses and wise men live in them. The sense of insecurity, on not owning a house is dispelled, if one has enough money to fall back on. For me the sale of the house was like a wind fall and winning a lottery. An investment and a building built with the government loan had left me enough to live comfortably during my life time. In any case, I had a place in Jalalabad to live and also a place in Delhi. In fact, the basic requirement in life is only one good big bed room, with an attached bath room. There is no end to the items, we tend to collect. Most of them remain in lock and key and clutter up the place.

Fast track pension, no speed breakers

Pension is one attractive feature of the government. It has been made more attractive with 50 per cent of the last salary, being given as pension. With this comes a handsome package of commuting 40 per cent pension. Commutation means that one gets 125 times the amount of pension in a lumpsum and draw 40 per cent less pension for the next fifteen years. After 15 years, if one is still alive, one gets the full pension. This amount enables a retiree to fulfil his family obligations, like the marriage of his children or settle down to a new life style. Money is always a confidence-builder. Financial security is the best security. One senior official belonging to the audit and accounts service told me of the massive corruption in his organisation in authorising pension. I told him that nobody dare ask me any money, though I had retired. I challenged him and felt I would be proved right. In all fairness to the AG's organisation, I got my dues in time. I invested them so that I could live off the interest, along with my pension. This is what most pensioners do. I am no exception. Most visitors who come to me after retirement want to use my name and contacts for getting either government jobs or some other help from the government. I merely listen and let the things as they were.

About Khushwant Singh

April 01, 1999, the forenoon was spent in meeting Khushwant Singh, the famous writer, with Sanjay Jha, my publisher, who presented my Book 'Inside CBI' to him. Sanjay was keen to get some kind of review from him. I was non-committal and did not request that he give his views on the book. All authors are conceited. Very few are generous to appreciate others as they believe that they have produced something remarkable, unrivalled in the past, and are unlikely to be surpassed in the future. Khushwant is too old with an equally aged wife. Khushwant writes from his heart and that is why his writings reach out to so many. He does not mince words and does not believe in sugar-coating them. The best thing is that he has eighty titles to his credit and all written in long hand. He said that he does not use the computer. In his case, the age shows. It is a case of willing spirit but weak flesh. It is true, for everybody, in the seventies and above. We talked about Bhindranwale and his methods of writing. He told me that the only way to treat fundamentalists of any religion is to treat them with contempt. He has a board outside his flat, which says, "Do not ring the bell, if you are not expected". In other words, nobody without an appointment is welcome. His house is littered with books and papers. Khushwant did not offer us even a glass of water or a cup of tea. May be, he feels that, if he started offering soft or cold drinks, people would linger on beyond their welcome time.

In his column of 23-9-2000, published in The Hindustan Times and some other papers under the Heading "Malice towards all" he made the following observations about me. "One evening I was in Lodi Garden sitting on a ledge below the Bara Gumbad mosque. It is my favourite spot to take a short rest between my perambulations. It has become my chosen resting place for two reasons: the dome of the Bara Gumbed is the most sensuously perfect of all domes I have ever seen; and from where I can see people striding along the paved footpath without them noticing me.

That evening I saw a family of three break away from the stream of walkers and head across the lawn towards me. As they got closer, I recognised Joginder Singh, retired head of the CBI, with a lady he introduced as his wife and a young girl as his daughter.

Joginder Singh had a walkman dangling on his side. Taking out the earplugs, he talked to me. I assumed he was listening to the evening prayer rehras or a kirtan. To make sure, I asked him what he was listening to. I am listening to my recorded speeches, he replied unfazed.

Listening to your own voice? I remarked dumbfounded. His wife, who heads the Publication Division, came to his rescue. Yes, they are full of wisdom. He reads lots of books, gets the best out of them and puts them in his speeches. You should listen to them sometime.

I did not rise to the bait. My lady companion diverted the dialogue to another topic. Are you writing another book? She asked. Yes, replied Joginder Singh in a triumphant voice. Bofors! You'll see I will reveal everything about it. He continued.

On my way back home, I recalled another man who was in love with his own voice. This was the late A. S. Bokhari, who was Professor of English at Government College, Lahore. He was a great wit; his Patras kay Mazaameen, a collection of humorous articles, are still widely read and acclaimed in Urdu circles. He was also an excellent after-dinner speaker and was applauded wherever he spoke.

Bokhari became Director General, All India Radio, then of Radio Pakistan, before he joined the UN as head of the Department of Mass Communications. He had the world as his audience. Wherever he spoke, he won the loudest applause.

Professor Bokhari died in New York. Though he had a family, he lived alone in a spacious apartment attended to by an elderly woman housekeeper and cook. My friend Shafqat Mohmood, a retired Pak diplomat, who also lived in New York and was a regular visitor was informed. He immediately went to Bokhari's apartment and, as instructed by the late professor's family in Lahore, proceeded to make an inventory of his belongings.

"When he had finished with the main rooms, the housekeeper told him of the attic where the professor spent his evenings and did not allow even her to enter it. Shafqat went into the attic. He was surprised with what he saw. There was a hi-fi the professor's speeches. He spent most of his evenings in the attic sipping his Scotch and listening to his own voice. It was a kind of vocal narcissism. Can you suggest a more appropriate word for a person who is in love with his own voice"?

The writer's bug has bitten K.S. Bains, my batchmate. He wanted to know how to write. I had invited him for lunch along with, Sanjay Kapoor. Sanjay is an experienced journalist and was the head of Bltiz Bureau in Delhi. Now he is a free-lancer. Sanjay and I discussed about the project of a book on the Police. May be, someday I might collaborate with him for the book. I can be generally careless at times. This is a common frailty I share with fellow human beings. I do not eat betel or paan, as I am likely to spoil my clothes. I spilled Coca-Cola on my white pants of safari suit. I got it washed to avoid permanent stains. The guests wanted to linger on. But I literally pushed them out, by 3 P.M. I do not miss my siesta, unless the heavens are falling. Probably on the day of death, if it happens to be after 1 P.M. I might have to tell the Yamraj to please come after I have had my sleep. After the siesta, I went for a meeting with Dr. Jain of Jain TV and Chandan Mitra of The Pioneer for possible assistance to keep the financially strained paper afloat. It went on till 6.15 P.M. I visited Khan Market for getting the Microwave oven repaired. A visitor, Rajesh Handa, whom I had not met at all earlier, came asking for help in acquiring a job as a pilot. My suggestion to him was not to lose heart and perseverance. Later in the day my repaired Esteem car was delivered. It met with an accident on 29th March. Surinder was travelling in it. I sent the other car, the small Maruti 800 of 1996 vintage, for repair and replacement of its mudguard. I was too tired. I watched the news that Jayalalitha would pull the rugs from under Vajpayee. My favourite programme, Chat Show at Movers and Shakers, took another 45 minutes. I had been busy doing nothing. It dawned on me not to have more than one programme a day.

Honouring all religions

Today (02 April 1999), it was a usual beginning of a day. I read plain man's prayer in three volumes. They are the finest set of brief prayers, for each day of the month. There is a separate prayer for morning and evening. By turn each day, I read one non Sikh scripture in the morning. No non-Sikh religion has been left uncovered. I have read Buddhist teachings, Jain's scriptures, the Geeta, the Quran, and the Bible. Of course, the Granth Sahib is read every day and my effort is to complete reading of the holy book on the birthday of my three daughters, Randeep (born in 1969), first January, Gagandeep and Harveen on 12th July, (born on same day but in 1972 and 1977) Surinder on 7th November (born in 1943) and myself on 12th October (1939). My late father was not sure of the date of my birth. He said that it was written with the intention of getting admission to a school, as otherwise I would not have been eligible for admission to the primary class. There was a rule, which required children not to be less than five years old before admission. My mother feels that my age as shown in the records is exceeds by one year. She is not able to recall the exact date or time. The result is that I do not have any Kundli or exact date of birth, indicating the configuration of stars. It does not affect me though. But it foxes all the astrologers. My mother told me that I was born on 15th Maghar or Magh. My father passed away on 23rd January 1996. I was the Director General of the Indo-Tibetan Police Force then. I have added completion of one path or full reading of the holy Granth on his death anniversary. The reading of the holy Granth is after the morning ablutions and a bath, or whenever I have time.

Kannadigas honour as a great son of Karnataka

I had to spend an entire forenoon withdrawing cash from the Vijaya Bank, located on Barakhamba Road. Fortunately, my private driver is there to take care of parking the car in the overcrowded areas. It is almost impossible to find a safe parking place in Connaught Place or other markets like Khan Market, Lajpat Nagar or South Extension in Delhi, unless one is game for some dents, scratches, mischief or fights. The other option is to find a less crowded low end market, where all that you want may not be available. Another half an hour was spent in getting the cells replaced in my Palm Top Computer. I use a computer, whenever I get a chance. Some guests from Jalalabad, Inderjit Singh, and Om were there till 2 P.M. when I had my lunch of boiled vegetable. I served them with food, full of curry and ghee. I have gained at least four kilograms despite my best efforts to diet. The tight pants, which fitted a few months back, amply reflect this. The option is either to reduce or face other medical problems. Indiscretions in eating have bloated me beyond my own acceptable limits. The fight to keep the weight down has been going on for the last 40 years. Sometimes, I succeed. More often, the temptations win. I have been subscribing to health magazines and buying books, on reducing weight. Like millions of fellowmen, I lose the battle. I go on gobbling tempting food, whether hungry or not. I try to get rid of all sweets in the house. But it is a losing battle.

I went for the annual conference of Kanada Sangha in Karnataka Bhavan. Mr. Vittal, Central Vigilance Commissioner, spoke in English. It is an organisation of the Kannada speaking people in Delhi. I have been an adopted Kannadiga, as I have served in the Indian Police Service Cadre of Karnataka from 1-6-1961 to 31-10-1997. My pension is being paid, by the Government of Karnataka. I had been requested to speak in Kannada. I uttered a few words in Kannada, with Punjabi accent. Perhaps many did not understand my Kannada. The rest of the speech was a recollection of my pleasant memories of service in Karnataka, and how some kind of system still works there, despite all-round deterioration in the country. Gokak, Secretary of Fertiliser department regretted the Anti-English Policy of Government of Karnataka, which might shut the world window of that State. The Editor of Kannadiga publication, Mr. Samaga, despite the constraint of the budget and without even a telephone, in his paper office, or in his house, has been able to galvanise Kannadigas living in Delhi, thereby proving once again that money is not everything. I was honoured as a great son of Karnataka in the public function, along with Sh. Vittal, Central Vigilance Commissioner, Gokak and others. At 8 P.M. I went for the wedding of Vikram, son of Arun Bhagat, a batchmate in the IPS and a classfellow. All social occasions for me are an excuse to meet people with whom one loses contact either due to lack of time or inclination. I met quite a few batchmates and was lionised by many, for my writing and TV appearances. I scrupulously avoided food, as all hotel food is full of a heavy dose of oil.

By the time I returned it was past 10.30 P.M. I had hardly any time left except for writing this piece. I was pleasantly surprised to find that the programme "News Break" on Zee India TV starts with my picture at 10.30 P.M. every Saturday.

A life long-time links with Karnataka

My morning started with a visit to the Gurudwara Bala Sahib, a shrine built in memory of the 8th Guru Hari Krishan whose mortal remains were cremated there. Before my IPS interview on 22nd December 1960, I had visited this Gurudwara for the Guru's blessings. Since then, if I happen to be in Delhi on a Sunday, I make it a point to re-establish myself with the Guru's blessings. Rarely have I gone to other Gurudwaras in Delhi, unless they are on my way. I feel that whatever I have got in life, I owe it to the blessings of the 8th Guru. Not that the other Gurus are less important or less holy. It is simply a question of one's faith in one incarnation of the Guru. Before becoming the Director CBI, nobody ever took notice of me in the Gurudwara. It suited me to go anonymously and come back. But the TV, the media and newspapers have enabled, some people even in the Gurudwara to recognise me.

It gives the benefit of a smile from the visitors and the priests. After the visit, I went for the DAV function of celebration of Mahatma Hansraj's birthday. There the heart warming fact was the affectionate welcome from the Governor of Madhya Pradesh, Bhai Mahavir, Acharya Swami Ji, late TR Tuli, President of the DAV Managing Committee and Padam Shri GP Chopra. It was a wonderful function which made one feel proud of being an Indian. I could not stay for long, as I had to go to Karnataka Bhavan to receive the honours of having done proud to Karnataka in administration. I was touched at the honour conferred though I had retired more than one and a half years ago. It was also a function to make Kananadigas proud of their heritage, culture and the unity of the country. I was mentally, emotionally and physically a part of them. Kannadigas are the most liberal and tolerant citizens of the country and this has made my ties everlasting with them. In fact, even now I subsist on Karnataka. It pays me my pension of nearly Rs.15000 per month. It has given me a huge lottery from the sale of my house built with a loan of Rs.120000. My contacts are all in Karnataka or from Karnataka.

I watched TV for about 45 minutes while sipping tea. I do not devote any exclusive time to watching TV. It is combined with some other activity, which is mechanically performed. It is only some interesting programme that gets my exclusive attention. But it is rare. In the evening, Mr. Sareen and Mr. Azad, TV Producers, dropped in to discuss the project of a serial on the Kashmir situation. Ultimately it was produced and a span of eight episodes was required for it being telecast. I compered each episode. Later, my nephew Titu (real name Jaswinder) and his wife dropped in. Unless I regulate my time, I am left with no time to write any article or any book. My mother, Lajwanti, who had gone to my sister Sarla's house for ten days returned along with Titu and his wife "Rosy".

A piece of advice

In my post-retirement dictionary, starting the day's routine before 11 AM is too early. Getting up or going for a walk before 7 AM is an unearthly hour. While mentally I decide to get up early as it is said that only the early bird catches the worm, yet in practice I wait to catch the worm late in the day. I went and addressed about 125 prospective entrants to the civil service, who had cleared their written examination. It reminded me of my interview on 22nd December 1960 for the IPS. I exchanged my impressions and how to go about being interviewed. I told them that in answer to a question as to why I wanted to join the Indian Police Service, my answer was that I liked the service. I was asked on this reply the reasons for my liking the Indian Police Service. It was a tricky query, and my selection or rejection depended on my reply. I said "Liking is something, which cannot be explained in terms of reasons. When you look at a flower, you cannot pinpoint, whether the liking is for the colour, or smell or petals". The reply made my day. I also had a word of advice for the ladies, eager to join the service. I told them that unless they catch, or get caught young, by their service colleagues they might miss the bus and remain discontented "Misses" all their life. On the return journey, I purchased some non-vegetarian snacks from Gole market. It used to be my favourite haunt with my daughters Machu and Choosie, during their non-vegetarian days. Under the influence of their mother, they have become vegetarians. I suppose, the followers of Radhaswami, are required to be vegetarian. Although a non-vegetarian, I can manage being vegetarian, most of the time. I suppose, as you age, the food no longer remains a great attraction. One can no longer find the latest Dhabas with exotic food attractions. I feel that chicken or cheese is merely chicken and cheese. The actual taste is by the stuffing or condiments sprinkled on it, above it, under it or inside it. There were times when for the sake of tasty food,

I went to all kinds of filthy areas to eat unhygienic food, in slums. It is not so now. Five star hotels serve their food in good vessels by liveried bearers. Most of them, though, do not deserve any mention. These days, to compensate for over-eating spicey and fatty foods, I try to eat totally fat-free and only boiled vegetables. Dinner has almost been given up, unless unavoidable.

Racing in life

By the time I returned home, it was well past 2 P.M. After eating some vegetables I slept off till 3.45 P.M. I left for the race club where I am an Honorary Steward. The word Steward gives the impression of a headwaiter. But in the racing terminology, a Steward is both a judge and umpire to ensure that no rigging and no fixing takes place there. I spend about two hours a day on this activity per week. It is amazing how people bet their life's savings on the one horse's capacity to come ahead of others. Probably, the people (Punters in racers language) betting are from the category, who can lose a few lakhs without feeling any pinch. Running a race club requires co-ordination with the horse breeders, trainers, jockeys, punters, judges, local administration, and above all, the bookies who accept the odds and bets on horses.

I returned home feeling tired. The only way I know how to overcome tiredness is to have a hot water bath. This is an instant cure for overcoming dullness and tiredness. I have been having a bath, both in the morning and evening, for instant freshness. Ajit, my chum, had invited me for dinner. Surinder does not like to go for programmes, later than 9 P.M. She gets up at 2 or 3 A.M. for her Radhaswami routine. She reluctantly agreed to go to Ajit's place. We were the first to arrive. Ajit was the Defence Secretary, when the former Naval Chief Vishnu Bhagwat lost his job. He has moved now to Industry and later on as the Finance Secretary of India. A typical bureaucrat, but totally upright and not amenable to any out-of-the-way recommendations, is the best choice for the Chairmanship of the Foreign Investment Promotion Board. His house, thanks to his Foreign Service, Secretary-level wife, is a masterpiece of interior decoration. Curious items from all over the world, convey an aesthetic taste. Moses and his wife, both from the IAS, also joined for dinner. There was an instant rapport, in the entire group, as Moses and his wife, are from my former cadre, Karnataka. Mohan Das Moses, now retired, like me, was in the State Finance Department, when I was the Director of Youth Services. I used to chase him frequently for sanction of sports and youth programme proposals, sometimes to the point of harassment. Ajit, his wife Kamlesh, and Achala are of 1964 IAS Batch. Their conversation turned to the usually familiar topic of their Mussoorie academy and training reminiscences. Since, I too knew some of the characters, being dissected and with oral jabs and vibes, I did not feel out of the conversation. Achala, glorified herself, as an author, and an astrologer. I am not qualified to comment on that, because neither have I read her works, nor do I believe in the hocus-pocus of astrology. I believe, if something good is going to happen to me, let it come as a pleasant surprise. If something adverse is in store, why should I know it in advance, and upset my peace of mind? Quite often, such dooms-day predictions are self-fulfilling. The mind tends to bring about what it believes. By the time we came back it was 10.45 P.M., too late for me to work on the computer.

Over security

Delhi government has constituted a jumbo sized committee of 147 persons to chalk out a programme of the tri-centenary celebrations of the birth of Khalsa. I, as an, invitee being a member of the above committee, decided to attend a programme where Sonia Gandhi, the Congress President, was to be present. Being a special Protection Group Protectee, it is almost impossible to go to any function where she or the Prime Minister of the day will be present. It took me forty-five minutes, to reach near the old Secretariat. The Police stopped the traffic at least 4 kilometres away. People had to foot it out, and there was no parking place within a radius of a few kilometres. At the top of it, the strict security checking had generated half a kilometre long queue, for entry to the venue. I felt it was not worth it to go through the hassle. Even if I decided, to go through all the obstacle course created by the over security, the function was likely to be over. So I just drove back, after having spent one and half hours in my air-conditioned, Esteem car. I utilized the time in reading and scanning the newspapers.

One organisation called National Akali Dal sent me a fax message conveying their decision to confer on me the title of Panth Rattan. It is a flattering title, to be conferred in a Gurudwara. There was another function of a sports goods industry today. But having spent the entire forenoon for journey to the old Secretariat, I decided that I better pack my stuff for going to Gujarat tomorrow.

Flying visit to Gujarat (7-4-1998)

I got up at 3.30 AM to catch the flight to Baroda at 5.50 A.M. I make it a point to avoid the inconvenience of a journey, where my morning exercise and walk is affected. For me, the morning walk is that dose of medicine which adds quality to my life. But as there is no other flight, and the train journey would have take over 13 hours, there appeared to be no option but to catch the morning flight. Bleary-eyed, and short of sleep, I travelled to the airport, by the vehicle arranged by Gujarat Narbada Fertiliser Corporation, Bharuch. An officer Punia, who had attended a seminar addressed by me in Cochin, was instrumental in arranging my address to Bharuch Management Association. I reached Bharuch at about 9.30 A.M., in an air conditioned Maruti Esteem car, the same brand which I have. With just enough time to change the dress, I rushed to the corporate office of the Gujrat Narbada Fertiliser Company to meet and address the senior officers on management and vigilance. The MD, AM Bhardwaj and his team of officers, were sharp and brilliant and asked searching questions. I was overcome by tiredness, due to lack of sleep. After lunch with Mr. Bhardwaj, IAS and MD of Gujarat Fertilisers, I slept for one hour 38 minutes according to my stopwatch. I make it a point to time every activity, so that I can get the best out of time and regulate my programmes. One often tends to linger on, to pass time. I never had any problem of passing time. Writing books and writing for newspapers and magazines keeps me amply occupied. I have to write at least two pieces every week. After I got up, there was a horde of local pressmen, wanting to speak to me. My views and speech adverbatim were recorded for the local Bharuch TV Channel. After them, the local MLA, Iqbal Patel called on me, for a few minutes. With a quick visit to Punia's house to say "Hello" to his school going daughter, son and his wife, I rushed to the venue of my address. I spoke for forty minutes, followed by eighty minutes of a question-answer session. The question and answers session is a battle of wits. I came out as a winner in this. A formal dinner with the management committee and a courtesy call to the house of Mr. Bhardwaj ended my visit. Mrs. Bhardwaj is a talented lady, who at one time, was on to making TV serials. At present she is busy promoting, a cultural exchange programme of the visit of children, to Turkey. I left at 10.15 P.M. for Baroda, known as Vadodara in Gujarati. I spent the night there and boarded the flight at 7.45 A.M. on 8th of April. I could have travelled from Bharuch in the morning. I avoided it as it can be dicey, with a traffic jam or a flat tyre or a recalcitrant vehicle.

Two dinners, one defamation and a small tiff

There was enough work to be done on 9-4-98 for the defamation case filed against me by Jagannath Misra for publishing in a book the charges mentioned against him in the case chargesheeted by the CBI in Patna. He is trying to avenge my orders of chargesheeting him in the fodder scam case, so that it deters the future directors in taking any action against any corrupt politicians having nexuses with the dishonest officers. I have refused to comment or talk on TV about the matter, which is subjudice and is based on the cases filed against Jagannath Misra, whom I have never met in life. There is no personal angle or animus. In the evening there were two dinners, one hosted by the Dabur Chief Burman and the other by Dr. Madhav Mehra, Chairman World Quality Organisation and head of the Institute of Directors. At Burmans party, I ran into my batchmate Tejinder Khanna, who was unceremoniously removed from the post of Lt. Governor of Delhi, due to the change in the Government at the Centre, He was succeeded by another batchmate Vijay Kapoor. I make it a point to attend all parties, not to eat, but to meet people for building up the data bank, for my books and articles. Interaction with fellow human beings fills the reservoir for penning one's ideas, reactions, and feelings. Though I enjoy meeting and interacting, I time, to the minute, I want to spend and then take leave of the hosts. Nobody minds disappearance from big parties. In fact, some of them expect you to disappear. I make it point to be back by 11 PM. A delay in one day has a snowballing effect on next day's programme. I make it clear to my hosts about the time I can spend, and after that I walk out. It enables me to socialise and work as per my schedule. In this way, I manage to find time for everything and everybody, by being a time quantity controller.

I had a tiff with my daughter Bibban over occupying the bathroom for a longer period, thereby delaying my using it.

Since I was wrong, I apologised and made up. Though as headstrong as I am, she is a good daughter. The fights essentially are a reflection of the generation gap. It requires time, for the older generation, to get used to the ways of the younger generation, their jabbing on telephones endlessly for hours together, wearing shabby and crumpled dresses, in the name of fashion, endlessly late night parties, senseless 'dog music' and taking for granted sometimes, that things will work out for them as desired by them. I had my publisher dropping in to discuss certain matters for "Inside CBI", my book. He left before my lunch and siesta hour. In the evening another visitor dropped in to recommend somebody's transfer in the Police and another wanted Police help in the recovery of 90 lakhs advanced against documents. I am treated as one-man consultancy, as well as recommending agency, by ninety per cent of my visitors. Where I am convinced about the genuineness, I send written requests to the concerned officials. Otherwise it is a plain straightforward 'No". My friends tell me that I should be more diplomatic, now that I am retired. I tell them that now it is too late for me to change.

In the night, I went for accepting the Panth Rattan Award from the National Akali Dal, in Mansrover Gurudwara. It took me over one and half hours to locate the place. It was flattering that people recognised my stand in anti-corruption fight. Spending one and a half hours to find your way for a distance of 15 kilometres, though, was too much. I have decided that in future, unless I am totally familiar with the route, I would insist on people inviting me, to send an escort, so that I do not waste time in the frustrating, aimless and fruitless search.

Visit to city beautiful and back to hot Delhi

One morning I left for Chandigarh with Surinder by Shatabdi Express at 7.30 A.M. to attend the Bhog ceremony on the first anniversary of the death of my late mother-in-law.

It is a fast train and covers 250 kilometres in three hours. Even by car, it takes 4 and a half hours. The executive class is very comfortable, with excellent breakfast, or lunch, as part of the ticket. The supply of newspapers is another plus point. The train was late by 50 minutes. The Bhog was a family affair, confined only to the close relatives. It was a wise decision, as nobody has time or inclination to join death ceremonies, unless it is that of a close relation, or under official obligation. After one year, the sting of death is also not as sharp as felt in the initial months. In any case passing away is a relief for old people. It is better to die early than to live longer at the mercies of others, both physically and financially. It was pretty hot in Chandigarh. But still, after a post-lunch nap, Surinder, and I visited our vacant house in Mohalli. It is a one Kanal or 500 square yard house. It was initially purchased by my mother, for Rs. 14000 paid over a period of 10 years from 1969 to 1979. It was built during my posting to Chandigarh in 1988. My late father wanted to purchase a new car, to replace his 1986 model car. I suggested to him to invest the money in building a house, rather than in replacing his two years old car, which was doing only 8 to 10 kilometres a day, in just going and coming back, from the field in Jalalabad. The house had paid for itself, during the lifetime of my father. I have not rented it out, on the ground that it would be a dead loss, if the tenant does not vacate it, when we need it or if the tenent does not pay rent. I will have to rush to the Court and even then, the possibility of justice during my own lifetime would be remote. We returned in the evening by Himalayan Queen in AC first class coupe. Surinder slept the entire journey, and I used the time to work on the computer.

Next day was the hottest day in Delhi of the season with the mercury crossing over 41°C. Except for visiting the Gurudwara Bala Sahib and buying snacks in Lajpat Nagar market, I did little. Traditionally, I like to rest on Sundays, though every day is a Sunday for me, as a retired person. I spent sometime working on the computer. In the evening, my daughter Gagandeep and her husband Gunveer dropped in for dinner. Both are well versed with the computer than me, who always need a helping hand around. Their visit always helps in getting my computer problems solved. Occasionally the computer threatens, that I have performed an illegal action and it will be shut down. I yield to the threat and shut it down myself. It seems to forget and starts operating all right, after a few minutes.

Heavy food-a prelude to lethargy

The standard routine of walking, sipping tea, bathing, prayer, and breakfast consumes four hours of my time. By the time one is free, one feels tired. In the past, my wife and I would take a nap, after a heavy breakfast. A heavy breakfast leaves you unfit for any work for at least two to three hours. A light breakfast keeps me fit, and I can plunge into work straightaway. Somehow, we tend to overeat, as if there would be no next meal. A psychologist says that it is due to an inbuilt instinct, from the ancient times, when man used to hunt for his food. Man did not know whether he was going to get the next meal, or starve it out. It is true of me, in any case. Good food attracts me like a magnet. Regretfully, I go on stuffing, till I am full to the brim, despite my desire to stay slim and trim. The result is a constant battle with the bulge. Both sides win occasionally and the fight continues. Today was no different. After assigning sufficient work to the PS, I went for inaugurating the upgradation of the hospital facilities of Guru Nanak hospital in Roshanara Road, headed by MM Goldi. The machine had cost Rs. 1.45 lakhs. The money was raised in my presence from various transporters, showing that generous people do exist, who care for the underdog. I joined them for lunch or Langar, consisting of three tanduri rotis, dal and cauliflower vegetable. This is one universal feature of Sikhism, to ensure equality amongst all classes of people. We eat the same food, sitting or squatting as the place permits. The Roshan Ara Road is a crowded place, with almost prayers on one's lips, to spare the new car from dents and bumps.

Meeting my former boss and Prime Minister

In the evening, I met HD Devegowda, the former Prime Minister, and had a brief chat with him on the political situation. He was worried and was not clear on the election/government scenario. He is also a Prime Ministerial hopeful, as hope springs eternal in human breast. He has been both good and kind to me. I call on him, lest he feels ignored, now that he is no more in any worthwhile position. After the usual routine, I start a simple paath to be completed on the birthday of my daughters. They share a love-hate relationship. Both accuse their mother, of being soft to the other. But they make it up quickly, and there are no permanent hard feelings. Abassi my eldest son-in-law, was also present at the time of Paath. Scriptures of almost all religions are not in the common man's language, except some portions. But nobody says anything, for fear of being excommunicated. But in the case of the Granth Sahib, the hymns of 9th Guru are not only clear, but are remembered by all. The Muslim scripture-the Quaran in its original form, is in Arabic. The result is that very few understand it. My advocate Vipin Gogia had come to see me yesterday but, I had missed seeing him as I was with Mr. H.D. Devegowda. We discussed in detail later on the defamation case filed against me, in Delhi High Court. I have left it to him to take any line he wants to take in the case. The case is of literally the category of "*chor kotwal ko danteey*". "It is the thief reprimanding the policeman". Based on the court case and the confession of one of the accused, I mentioned the role of one Jagannath Misra, in protecting the scamsters. He wants Rs. one crore for the defamation. He is already facing a criminal trial in the court of special judge of CBI, Patna, on the same charge. I have written the book with a view to expose criminal elements. Criminals are a curse on polity. My book is, at best, a minor exposure and my colleague Biswas, IG CBI told me that what I have written is only 'vegetable' and not 'meat'.

Khalsa's Birth (13-4-1999)

It is the three hundredth birthday of the Khalsa or the Sikh religion, as it is known and seen in the world. I believe that one's relationship with God is extremely personal. Man is often a beggar at the door of Lord Almighty. For the Sikhs, the holy book the Granth Sahib, is itself the Guru. I have it in my residence since 1967. So I do not feel a need to go to a Gurudwara on any occasion. I do visit Gurudwara Bala Sahib whenever; I am in Delhi on every Sunday. However, when on tour, I do not miss a chance to visit any historic Gurudwara, or any other religious place of other religions, if it happens to be nearby. Surinder had a splitting undiagnosed headache affecting her mood too. I spent my entire day in the air-conditioned room. I had the satisfaction of seeing my article on the birthday of Khalsa, as the leading piece in The Pioneer supplement. The *Punjabi Digest* and *Punjab Today*, the two leading Punjabi magazines also carried my pieces on Khalsa.

Petty pin pricks

When one is in government service, a few things like prompt service of other government departments, like the municipality, CPWD and others like hospitals is taken for granted. One does not have to interact with them personally. The personal staff takes care of the details one takes for granted. After retirement, I noticed that it is impossible even to get a leaking tap repaired. Our newly renovated bathroom's tap has been leaking for the last two months. Even though I have personally spoken to the Executive and Superintending engineers, the tap has remained leaking. It is silly to speak to the Minister or Chief Engineer to get something done, from the staff, for which they are paid. Effectiveness is glaringly missing in the administration. Another racket, worth mentioning, is the maximum retail price. I wanted to purchase a ream of paper for my printer. The price for the same brand varied from Rs.133 to Rs.180. The mark-up on the maximum retail price is not less than 50 per cent. By sticking labels, any price can be charged. The ultimate sufferer is the consumer, and specially those in the fixed salary group. This is one reason for need-based corruption. Ultimately I ended up paying Rs. 110 for a ream of paper, where the maximum retail price printed was Rs.155.

Bypass to by pass future problems (16-4-1999)

William Shakespeare said it is divinity which shapes our ends. Man of course has to continue planning for future development and progress. There is, however, something called an invisible power, which always guides us. Without this guidance nothing can move. No man can work, or achieve anything, without the command of the Almighty. One may call the divine power, the will, intuition or suggestions coming from within.

Let me share a personal experience I had on 16th of April, 1999. I went for a walk at 8 O' clock in the morning. I felt uncomfortable, for a fraction of a second, after one hundred metres of walk. I thought, perhaps, it was due to heat. I asked a co-walker, Gurmeet Singh, if it was really hot, or only I was feeling so. He confirmed that it actually was very hot. I commented that henceforth I would start coming for a walk earlier in the morning, before it becomes hot. I completed my usual quota of 4 kilometres of walk in Lodhi Garden in 50 minutes, which comes to a speed of about 5 kilometres an hour. I had not had anything since morning, except two cups of tea and a glass of juice. On reaching home at about 9.20 AM, I told my wife Surinder of the discomfort. Both of us attributed it to heat. After my wife left for office, a lingering doubt however remained in my mind. I shaved off my chest to facilitatc cventual ECG. I consulted her and she agreed that I should go for a check-up. At about 10.30 AM, I spoke to my retired batch and college mate cum friend, Shri R K Takkar, Managing Director of Apollo Hospital. He said that he would fix up for a check up. I also rang up my cousin Dr Pradeep Babbar in Faridabad, who said he would join us in Apollo directly. My wife and I went to Apollo. Dr Pratap C Reddy, Chairman of the hospital, was there. His Secretary Raji had been brief by Shri Takkar, MD to take care of me.

I was taken promptly to Dr Vipul C Roy, the interventionist cardiologist. It again was a divine guidance, my going to Dr Vipul Roy. Dr. Pradeep later told me, that he felt, if ever an angiogram was required, it should be done by Dr Vipul Roy. He was, however, happy as to how destiny had led me to Dr Vipul Roy, who he thought was the best interventionist cardiologist. Dr Pradeep is the son of my maternal uncle, J.R. Babbar. Next to my parents, I have been close to this family. All the children of my uncle are well educated and well placed. What is more important is that they have kept intact the human values. Dr Pradeep's presence gave me a moral boost. I was touched by his concern, and attentiveness to details. I felt confident that I was in the pink of health and after an angio, I would be able to go home. I was however proved wrong. The angio indicated that three of my main arteries were blocked, one 100%, the others 85% and 65%. There were other five blockages. I was told that I was carrying a time bomb in my heart and chest. There could be a heart attack any time. I was, therefore, advised an immediate heart bypass surgery. A bypass does not prolong life, but improves the quality of life. The doctors told me, that with the preventive by pass, I could control the condition, before it became explosive. A bypass done on an undamaged heart will give a better quality life, rather than when it is done on a heart, which has been damaged by the heart atttack. Having been used to an active life. Being on tour outside Delhi, at least twice a month, I did not want to live with the fear of having an attack, at any time and restrict my mobility. Further any small stomach ache, headache or ache in any other part of the body, would give rise, to the feeling that it must be the onset of a heart attack. I decided, therefore, to go in for a bypass.

Another factor that helped me to make decision in favour of a bypass was the story of Dr Vipul Roy. He told me that he himself had a hole in the heart. He first had to get his heart operated, before he could be a cardiac expert. I thought, if Dr Roy could survive well over 25 years after his heart surgery, why could not I ?

After the decision was made for the bypass, I came in contact with Dr I S Virdi. I was greatly impressed by his cheerful disposition, immense patience and reassuring manner. He put me at ease and I felt I was in good hands, rather, the best in the country.

Apart from the good reputation, Apollo enjoys the services of three top heart surgeons, Dr.Virdi and other doctors, as well as other heart specialists in Delhi and India. Other two doctors had gone to America to attend an important cardiology conference, with the result that there was hardly any cardiologist in Delhi during the week and hence hardly any heart operations. As per Karma's chase, the timing of the operation, doctor and hospital were all the doing of the divine hands.

Dr Reddy, Chairman, Apollo had told me that they have a system of fast track surgery, which was available in Chennai only. I said to myself, life and death is in the hands of God. Nobody can give you one breath more and nor can anyone make you die before the destined hour. However, we humans have to try, as per the wisdom given and I firmly believe that God helps those who help themselves. God creates conditions, which leave only, that option open, which He wants us to opt. Here God had beckoned to me and indicated the direction. I was already 59½ and any delay in keeping the heart in good condition would have been fatal.

Dr Virdi told me that, with all the modern amenities available, the bypass operation had a success rate of over 95 per cent. I was in that 0.4% per cent of people, who had volunteered to undergo an operation, to avoid the contingency of a future heart attack. Like all other decisions made in life, I decided within 10 minutes after the angiography to take the plunge. My wife Surinder, a devout woman herself, was in full agreement. My next request was immediate operation, if possible on the same day, though for a few seconds I felt that it be done on Monday, the 19th of April. It was probably an inner desire to postpone the operation for two days. Then my mind reflected on the quotation "Do the things you fear and the death of fear is certain". I did not know anything about the surgeon Dr. Virdi. I only felt that whatever happens, would be the best. Dr. Virdi dropped into my room and told me to be ready the next day, to be wheeled into the operation theatre, at about 7.15 A.M. Dr. Virdi, an endearing, competent and charming person, had spent over ten years in Australia and was the elected fellow of the Royal College of Surgeons, a rare honour. Umpteen times, blood had been sucked from my body with several syringes by dozens of technicians, for the tests about which I knew next to nothing, even till today. I took it in my stride and wanted everything, to be over soon. It is not the event that affects or scares us, but it is the waiting or anticipation of it.

Heart surgery and a new life (17-4-1999)

I got up as usual at 6 A.M and was ready for the "D" Day. A wheel chair was brought and I had to use it. I volunteered to walk down to the operation theatre, but was overruled. I was wearing an ill fitting pajama and a shirt, with totally shaved off hairs from every part of the body. Even the body had been washed with the disinfectant. An injection was given in my neck at about 7.30 A.M. and that is the last I remember of my earthly existence. When I next got up, in the intensive care unit, the watch showed the timing at 10. I wondered as to how soon the operation could be over. It was pointed out that it was 10 P.M. of the next to next day. I found my body strapped to all kinds of machines, with innumerable tubes jutting in and out of my body. All the efforts of the doctors and nurses were aimed at helping the helpless, paining and aching patient. One did not mind the pain, except the severe backache, caused by lying straight. Fortunately, Dr. Virdi said, I could turn sides, though some other doctors totally forbade it. Machines and monitors were monitoring all bodily functions. It is a miracle that man can see, what is going inside the body of another fellow human being. It was almost perfect snooping and spying of what was inside the skin and how a particular organ was behaving. It was almost too complicated for a layman like me. I left it to the better sense, wisdom and medical knowledge of the professionals, for giving me as many pricks and concoctions, to join together, almost my chest cut across, foot long wound on both legs and one arm, where the blood vessels had been taken out, for grafting to replace the diseased arteries feeding blood to the heart. Not that I know anything about the heart and its internal constituents; it is what the doctors and the medical journals have told me. After excellent care and all efforts at reducing the bodily pain, I was allowed to leave the hospital on 26th of April. My wife Surinder and daughter Harveen accompanied me. It was a nice feeling to be out of even the best of hospitals. It immediately made me forget my worries and pains.

Back to dear home

I returned home after spending the time from 16th April to 26th in Apollo Hospital, where I had left my earthly existence for nearly thirty hours to be revived after a triple bypass heart surgery on 18th of April. Home-coming after paying my respects and homage to eight Guru Harikrishan's last mortal resting place, was itself a moving experience for me. It was an instant decision, approved by Surgeon Inderjit Singh Virdi. I felt that I was given a second life, God only knows, for what and for what purpose. Any surgery, especially a bypass compels you, to lie flat on the bed. In the bypass surgery, it is more so, because the entire chest and collar bone, is cut to take out the heart for repair. This was a major problem. Normally, I do not make any fuss about any difficulty, as I believe that if God gives a problem, he provides a solution too. The only thing is that, as short-sighted mortals, many a time we tend to overlook the obvious solution in front of us. There was no energy left. Even talking on the telephone was exhausting. There were innumerable and tons of medicines to be consumed at regular intervals, breathing and lungs exercises to be done, apart from the inhalation to be done three times a day, along with pushing three balls up with the strength of the lungs. Inadequate body strength and no energy to do the normal things, like being able to be get out of bed, makes one peevish. Every little activity consumes energy, which is what is required to live well. I had a court case coming up against me, in Delhi High Court, by one of the accused persons in the fodder scam. I spoke into the mini tape recorder and asked my wife, Surinder to correct the replies typed by my efficient Secretary Jeetendar Kamoj. My sister Sarla, my publisher of Inside CBI, Sanjay Jha, Inderjit Madan, Om Parkash and Seth Madan Lal dropped in, unannounced, putting aside my plans to avoid visitors. One has to be civil to anybody, who comes to the house. Some people come for sympathising, some come for commisserating, some to find out how you have survived, and how near you are to death, and some come for genuine concern. In any case, some social chit-chat always cheers one up. Quite often, a chit-chat, repeating the same story as to how it happened, becomes exhausting. Life after a bypass at least for a considerable time, is only a story of taking medication, and rest so that the incisions can be healed. In my case, both my calves and left arm have deep incisions, though fortunately the chest cut where the sternum bone was cut has healed well. One does not know or cannot work out the right ratio proportion, between rest and activity. Too much lying down gives backache whereas too much of activity tires one out. Life is a long series of lying in bed, moving in the lawn, and ambulating between the bath room, dining room and sitting in the study. Even entertainment TV is of no interest, as it is the repeat of old antics, the same jokes, the same gyrating movements, the same violence and the hero and villain getting thrashed regularly. One of my Bombay friends, sometimes, sends me funny videos, which cheer me. Three dozen or so TV channels are glutted with advertisement. The result is no uninterrupted programme. But the TV channels also have to make money to stay afloat. TV, music, exercise are the only activities, which a teetotaller like myself can or would indulge in.

I have nothing against drinks. My grandfather, late Mahant Natha Singh, could beat any drunkard, in any competition. My father used to have an occasional drink. I saw to it that whenever I went abroad, I got the finest Scotch Whisky for him. Somehow, I never liked the stink or smell of liquor or even that of beer. I also rationalised that with my limited salary, it would be impossible for me to offer drinks. If I accept anybody's drinks, then I would have to offer the same to those, whose hospitality, I enjoy. Of course, some colleagues to whom I posed this question, shrugged off by saying that you do not have to return the hospitality of the rich and famous. You can help them out. When I pointed out that this was nothing but indirect repayment in kind and amounted to corruption, they laughed at me saying, "Everybody is doing it". I said, " If this were to be accepted as a valid explanation, then God save the uninfluential and the unconnected".

Postoperation days

Today that is Monday, 03 May 1999, The Pioneer carried my article dealing with corruption. The Day After, a fortnightly magazine carried two of my articles in today's issue. It is a matter of great satisfaction for any writer to see his writing published. Writing is an author's baby. It is good to see it in the form of a publication. Feeling good cheers one up, and makes one forget the constant nagging pain, which continues till the operation cuts are healed. It is a good therapy to keep one self busy, within the limited energy one has. There are no quick-fix solutions to the healing. Only time heals. I was told by my cousin, Dr. Pradeep, that a lot of cholesterol would be used up in my surgery. Cholesterol is, what binds the body cells. So I have to alternate between rest and work period. Even meeting visitors or answering phone calls appears to be a strain, some time. Except for 15 to 20 minutes of walk, I generally stay in the house. Only once on the 5th of May, I went for my check-up by Dr. Inderjit Singh Virdi. My ECG was taken along with the X-ray. The ECG as interpreted by the machine was abnormal. When I asked my Cardiologist, he replied that, since the sheath (Pericardium) in which the heart is enclosed was removed, the ECG will always be interpreted by the machine as abnormal. Otherwise, I was in a better shape than was expected within two weeks of my operation.

Again, on 5th May, I went to a TV Studio for the recording of a programme on Doordarshan which was telecast on 6th May, 99. The host wanted to know from me whether there was any political angle in the prosecution of a former foreign minister for requesting the Swiss government in slowing down its co-operation in Bofors case. I replied that I had been a professional police officer for over 36 years. The sanction for prosecution was in response to a specific request sent by me for a particular offence. It will be incorrect for me to involve myself in any controversy.

The Doctors had warned that getting conditioned to the "Re-engineered" Joginder Singh would take time. One thing is certain, that after a major surgery like the one I had, one has to rekindle, one's interest in life. One way is by reading and doing positive things and accept the limitations of the body. It looks as if in a jiffy I have crossed the threshold of sixty. But I still tend to look upon my daughters as small children, needing protection, guidance and help all the time. The style, the process, the method and approach of every generation is the same. Even working on computer tires me out. I have to keep my legs at a higher level, so that the circulation of blood is speeded up. After every work or sitting down for two hours, I must rest for half an hour. But I am reminded that "Even this shall pass away" after a few weeks. Then I would have probably forgotten the trials through which I am passing now. It is like the sicknesses of the previous year, which we cannot even recall. The attitude of taking life as it comes is the only remedy for living well. It is several phases of life one passes through. In the last few weeks, the daily record has become a combined collection of events and persons. Days and events are merged. Because during the convalescing period, one is only waiting to be fully all right. On the 7th of May, I had my first social outing of the evening, to attend a function to honour HS Nirula, as the Asian of the Year. The NRI Institute of which I am the Chairman had organised this function. Mr. Jagmohan Singh, the Secretary General of the organisation, had an impressive gathering of guests. I stayed only for about fifty minutes and did not eat anything. I did the customary presentation of the bouquets and made a short speech.

For me it was only a testing water, as this outing was done, within just three weeks of the open heart surgery. If one does not go out, one is constantly thinking of what one has been through. There are ups and downs in recovery. Too much, either of rest or activity, is tiring. The trick lies in striking the golden mean. Everybody has to discover his or her own threshold of rest and activity. It is very important to keep occupied, to get a feeling, of being normal. It is impossible to go on watching the TV, all the time as almost the same films, are shown on all the channels. All channels present shooting, beating or singing of inane songs, which are not possible in real life. Humorous or funny films are few. The humor is not the 'in thing'. The fat free diet makes me hungry. Lying on the bed for hours together gives backache. In any case, in the post-retirement age of nearly sixty and above, the body will have some problem or the other. One has to learn to live with whatever falls to one's lot.

From the 22nd of May, I have started going for a walk to Lodhi garden. It was my first visit after five weeks. At least, I have been able to do about two kilometres in thirty minutes. Meeting HK Dua, a top journalist, now posted to Denmark as an Ambassador, was doubly useful. He had undergone a similar surgery. His tips and advice was very encouraging. On Tuesday, 25th May 1999, I had lunch with a young progressive NRI, HS Nirula, who with his initiative and enterprise, from Rs.5000 has created an empire of over $ 800 millions. His business extends over all four continents including India, the UAE, the USA and the UK. He has done proud to his family and the Sikhs. When I asked him about the secret of his success, he said that the secret was perspiration, and some luck. Another thing was that he never hesitated from trying for fear of failure. He has been adjudged as a top Asian by the NRI Institute.

I have been going off and on to Appollo hospital for the check-up of my left arm, which has not healed. Dr. IS Virdi, a very competent and excellent surgeon and now a friend, has been very encouraging. Whenever the pain becomes unbearable, I remind myself; "Even this shall pass away," like every good and bad thing in life. It is my computer, which is my constant companion. I can let off my joy, my happiness and my frustrations by scripting them.

My daughter, Bibban, a good child, often gets angry at the restrictions, I impose on her, like not watching movies, in the cinema theatre, from 10 P.M to 1 A.M. Every generation regards the previous ones as ancient and old fashioned. It is basically the inevitable generation gap. The older generation goes by perceptions, which may not necessarily be of the present generation. There is nothing, which can be done about it, except to live with the situations as they arise. My wife, Surinder, that way is more in tune with the modern times. May be, my daughters share their feeling with her more than they do with me. Surinder has been more than my wife. She has been a support, saviour, doctor, and nurse in sickness, and during and after the heart bypass surgery.

There is a steep decline in the level of energy. It comes back, gradually, may be at the rate of 30 to 40 per cent every month. But by today, that is Sunday, 30 May 1999, I am able to amble around, for about 25 minutes in the morning and for a similar period in the evening in Lodi Garden. There is no substitute to patience in the entire healing process. My food is bland and totally fat free, unless the cook, contrary to instructions, has been using oil. From day one of the surgery, I have been on sleeping tablets, as the last thing in the night. Doctors recommended this, on the ground that undisturbed sleep accelerates the process of recovery and healing. But even that dose has been reduced by me to half. The trouble with the sleeping pill is that it makes me drowsy, during the day time also.

Putting misery behind/Looking in new directions

Today, (Saturday, 05 June 1999) there is a distinct feeling of being better than in the past. It is also due to the fact that today it is the end of the seventh week after the operation. Scabs on the two legs and the left hand have fallen off. The healing of the open wounds is nearly 90 per cent over. But the bony part of the chest takes between eight to twelve weeks to heal. I am still on half sleeping drug Zopicon or Valium. These drugs act both as pain killers and induce sleep. Sleep plays one of the most important parts in the recovery of health, apart from the medicine. I can walk a distance of over two kilometres in Lodi Garden. *Day After* magazine carried my two articles in the June issue. Punjab Kesri, a daily in Hindi, Punjabi and Urdu has been carrying some of my articles, almost every fortnight. Hindu carried my Central Piece on 26th of May, 1999. It is a matter of great satisfaction for me that, even when not cent per cent fit, I can write coherently. My Secretary asked me today why I do not work full time. I told him that my needs in life are so little that I can manage very well with whatever I have earned lawfully plus my pension. I have worked for thirtysix and a half years for the government. I do not want to work for a private person and give him the satisfaction that he has the former Director, CBI, working for him. When people hire you, after your retirement they are not hiring you for your competence. They are hiring you so that they can trade your influence and former position in the government. In fact, I had an offer of a fat salary, ten times more than what I last drew, to work for a company. I politely declined. The head of the company thought that I was declining due to inadequate emolument. He said, "You name the figure for working for us". I said, "Thank you. But I do not wish to work full time. I want to be master of my own time, and not be bound by any routine of rushing off at 9.30 P.M. and worrying about getting late, due to traffic jam, or whether the boss will be annoyed, if on some days I do not come to the office".

He said, "You are the first official to have declined my offer. Otherwise, retired people run after me, for post retirement jobs, even at a much smaller salary". I said, "They are not Joginder Singhs", and the matter ended there.

From type writer to computer

I must confess that, despite my handling or mishandling of computers since 1993, I am still substantially a computer illiterate. I had such a low opinion about the computers that for years together, I stuck to the good old manual typewriter. Necessity teaches you every thing. So, by and by with the help of my daughters and wife, Surinder, I got hooked on to the computer. Still, I feel that for me the old models, may be four years old, are good enough for writing articles and books. In fact, the more complicated the gadget, the more confusing I find it. There are so many functions in modern-day computers, that an average user like me is hardly able to use, or understands how to use just 5 per cent of it.

For the first time, I managed to sleep from 11 P.M. to 6 A.M. without a sleeping pill. I have been on sleeping pill since 16th of April, when I was admitted to the hospital for my bypass surgery. I must have slept for sometimes as I was not groggy this morning when I got up. Lunch was in Oberoi hotel, courtesy a senior colleague, Abraham Verghese. Verghese has been both my senior, boss, friend, cadre mate as well as a service mate. Now both of us are retired. But I always show deference to him and Mr. Haralankar.

Not Bharat Rattan, but Dilli Rattan

Today, (Saturday, 24 July 1999) I was conferred the award of 'Delhi Rattan', by All India Intellectual's conference in the YMCA tourist hostel. Judge Ashok Desai of Allahabad High Court along with Sh. Bhisam Narain Singh and Krishnamurty conferred this honour on me. Earlier, last week, a group of the hosts led by Sh. B.N. Sharma, Advocate, had called at my house to communicate their decision to confer this award and solicit my confirmation. It was a good function without any political leanings. Amongst others, I met my friend Karthikeyan. He is a dedicated official, who has literally put his neck on the block, by supervising the investigation actively, and effectively of the Rajiv Gandhi assassination case. He is a marked man for life. I mentioned to him that governments have a habit of using officials and discarding them. He is the one person who deserves the highest security all his life. LTTE are a much more dreaded group than the Sikh or Kashmiri or Naga terrorist. The morning walk gives me a free evening to work on my book. The only danger is that I have to save my time from being used by others or being wasted in dinners, and lunches. I force myself to write, to discipline myself. The ringing telephone breaks the continuity. The telephone is both a blessing and a curse. With automation, it is impossible to speak to any official to complain about a dead phone as an automated, lifeless tape gives the answer that you are in the queue, or the lines are busy or this number does not exist. It is a progress from the 1950's, 60's or 70's, where it was impossible to get across to anybody except on a lightning call basis. One should be grateful in life for small mercies. I have solved the problem of ringing telephones or inconvenient calls. When in service, there was always somebody to take the calls, but after retirement, the telefax with answering machines works as my secretary. When I am not at home, the caller can always leave a message for me. My machine can take forty messages. It also helps me to screen the telephone messages and respond to those I want to and ignore the ones I do not wish to reply. In any case there are not more than half a dozen calls every day. It also safeguards against mischievous and threatening calls.

Last night I went for a dinner to a restaurant hosted by a friend. It took two hours of my time, and one page of writing in terms of work. But it is good to go out, and be in circulation. Spending two hours outside the house, on small chit-chat, means putting your article back by two days. In the formal lunches and dinners, for teetotallers like me, except for inane conversation like the weather or adding to weight or further promotion in service or increase in business, there is nothing else. I avoid late dinners, as they upset my schedule. I am an early eater and early riser. I avoid dinners and if I have to go, I excuse myself early.

Counting days

It is sixteen weeks since the bypass surgery. I find myself a new man with a new zest of energy. In fact it is much more than in the past. The walk is much brisker. Bypass gives one a sound heart for another fifteen to twenty years, unless one is careless with food, leading to fresh blockages of the arteries and heart problems. The heart is what sustains life and circulation of the blood. I received an offer from a fellow morning walker, to head one of his companies. I told him that I would not like to do any full-time job. The temptation of money holds no lure for me or the offer to charge expenses for my staff or the vehicle. I told him that I have enough for my needs during my life time and I do not need anything more. I have been clear in my mind that I would not work for any private person, after having worked in the government. He was rather disappointed. Even the offer to be on the Board of Directors of the Companies, was put off by me. I had almost left for London/Birmingham on the 6th of August on the invitation of the Indian Cultural Association. Even the ticket had been received. Just one hour before the departure by the Swiss Air, the organiser telephoned from the U.K. to say that they had postponed the function, for one month. I had declined the invitation and the free ticket. But only on his insistence, I had agreed to proceed to London. It was good in a way, as the Swiss Air flight would have first taken me to Zurich. From there I would have to board another flight for London. The nine hours journey would have been stretched to thirteen hours. A visit to Europe or England does not fascinate me, as I have been abroad at least forty times. To me, all European cities appear alike. All buildings and departmental stores are of the same design with almost the same goods. The only difference is that you pay for the goods in the local currency. I have engaged a young boy as my driver. I noticed his absence from the car, when I came out of the bank yesterday. He lied that he had a quarrel with somebody over non payment of the parking and that is why he was delayed. In the evening when I went to a function of Ivory coast national day at the residence of VP Punj, the Honorary Counsel General, I again noticed his absence. He again lied that he was there with the car. I had taken a round of the parking area. Only when I had almost sat in somebody else's car, I found that the driver had returned. I had to pull him up. He still denied his absence. I came to known next day from my servant that he had brought the Esteem car home. When I confronted the driver, he said that he had come home to put coolant in the car. I asked him " why did he not check water, coolant or air the first thing in the morning"? He had no answer. I told him that he had lost all my trust in him.

Biting the hand that feeds

Considering the conduct of the driver, I devised my own strategy. Yesterday, I went for lunch at the invitation of a friend to Taj Palace Hotel. I asked him to park the car and give the key to me. Today, again when I went for a function of a film, I made him park the car and pocketed the key. He had taken the car yesterday to sell petrol from it. About five litres from the full tank was stolen or sold by him. The government drivers sell petrol frequently. Some other drivers might also be doing so. One has to safeguard one's own interest. Even the maid servant, who accompanied my mother last month to my sister Manjit, stole Rs.6500 from my mother. My mother has a poor eye sight. I make it a point to give her Rs. 10000 per month to spend the way she wants to. It is deliberately done lest she feels that after the death of my father, she has to stretch her hand. Her income is much more, and it is her own money she is getting from me. She is in the last stages of her life. Well, this is what she has been telling me for the last ten years. I want her to be happy. As long as my father was alive, it was his responsibility, to look after her. After his passing away, I want her to feel that she is still cared for. The only trouble is that she has not changed with the times, unlike my father. It is not her fault. It is the limited exposure and unwillingness to learn, which comes in the way. All of us, including her, feel that our knowledge of men and matters is the best and we know how best to deal with any situation. Nobody and nothing is perfect in life. Even those of us, who claim to be perfect have their weak points. With minus and plus points we muddle through life. This goes on till the last minute and last day, till it is time to say adieu. However there is a constant endeavour, to improve it. But in the eyes of the people, we wish to please, we sometimes fall short in our achievements. All of us have problems, which keep us worried. The poor worry about their next meal. The rich have the problem of controling their weight, diabetes or blood pressure, all the result of over-eating. The big hotels and restaurants run on the purses of those who can afford to throw Rs.5000 or even more for one meal. What the men earn by toiling, their ladies spend. Kitty parties in five star hotels are mute witnesses to the bloated, over-fed, belching ladies of the super rich, in constant search of new avenues of excitement and variety. Many five star hotels serve meals, which regretfully are the left-overs of the previous meal.

A year of body dissection

I visited Jalalabad, from 16th to 20th of August 1999 and returned on the morning of 20th August along with my mother. I had a severe stomach-ache and could not sleep for the whole night. I was diagnosed, as having an inflamed gall bladder with stones. I underwent an operation on the 26th of August. Fortunately it was what is called laparoscopy. Four holes were made in the stomach and the gall bladder was abstracted. From 21st to 28th August, I was in the Appollo hospital. Dr. Kriplani along with Dr. BML Kapur performed the stitchless surgery. I seem to be the most operated person, with almost every vital part of the body, cut or repaired or added. I had a piles operation in 1971. Two cataract operations on the eye in 1994 and 1996, a heart bypass in April 1999 and a gall bladder surgery in August 1999 and an appendicitis operation in 1959. One has to live life, as it comes and make the best of it. Any amount of lamenting is not going to improve the situation. My prescription is that we accept the inevitable, and make the best out of it. The silver lining is that after an operation, that particular disease is off. The defamation suit by one of the fodder scam accused, a former chief minister of Bihar, came up on 30th of August. It has been adjourned to 21st January, 2000 with a stipulation that I must file my written statement in eight weeks. My column appeared in The Pioneer every alternate Monday in August,' 99. It is good to note that one's views are publicised without much editing.

The only trouble with hospitalisation is that every trip means more medicines, a change in one's life style, restrictions and near absence of physical exercise. As one ages, such episodes are inevitable and one has to accept them gracefully. In Jalalabad, from 15th to 19th August, my time was spent in sorting out land, pension, and college matters, as usual. In Jalalabad, it was chicken everyday for lunch. My mother, who had gone to visit my sister Manjit also returned. Though she has all the facilities in Delhi, she has hardly anybody to talk to. There is nobody of her age group in Delhi, with whom she can share memories. She was more than busy in Jalalabad. Aged 85, she has hardly any eye sight left. Her own entertainment is meeting people and talking, as she can hardly see. There is a special TV installed in her room. Mostly her maid servant and visitors watch it. An air conditioner installed in her room is sparingly used in Delhi and Jalalabad.

Teething trouble

It is a natural tendency to postpone facing a problem, till it is unavoidable. It happened with me last week and also this week. Hardly had the doctor pronounced me fit, after the gall bladder operation, my teeth and gums started giving problems. The pain had become intense and unbearable on the 4th of September. I had to consult the top dentist Dr. L.K. Gandhi. Dr. Gandhi has the best dental clinic in Delhi. Undoubtedly, he is the best in his profession. He advised me to take the painkiller Flexon or Combiflam. It helped me but not much. Even the sleeping tablet could not induce sleep. This continued on to 5th of September. In the morning I consulted the doctor, assigned by Dr. Gandhi. Dr. Amrita Gogia did root canal treatment. It has given some relief. But due to the toothache, I dread to eat anything. Modern medicine tries to keep the body going, and the parts are forced to drag on. Perhaps, longevity has its drawbacks. My late friend Chaman Lal committed suicide in Bombay probably because he was fed up with bodily diseases. Money can add on years, but rarely quality replacement of the body parts, which have outlived their life. Every disease, which afflicts any body, at that particular moment, appears the worst ailment. All the efforts of modern medicine are to relieve pain, so that a person can engage himself in his avocation with full heart and concentration. A doctor may declare you fit, in respect of the problem, or the part treated by him. But there is no guarantee that some other part of the body will not give any trouble.

This morning again, Tuesday, 07 September 1999, at 1 A.M. the toothache was acute. It was so intense that I had to cancel my Bombay visit for recording the programme of 'Movers and Shakers', by Shekhar Suman for Sony TV. A heavy dose of the expensive antibiotic augmentin, each tablet costing Rs.35 with Flexon, a pain killer and the application of Borax Glycerine provided some relief. Dr. Amrita Gogia is trying her best to save a rogue tooth. The unbearable pain continued. In the evening, I visited the airline office to get the ticket revalidated and also the office of The Pioneer. After the evening walk, meeting five visitors and the dinner, there was hardly any time left for work. For the next three days, I had to visit the dentist for tooth fixing. Any pain, which afflicts you, is bad and seems to be the ultimate in suffering. The computer on which I work decided to take a holiday for two days. No amounts of coaxing had any effect on it, till its doctor, a computer engineer Babli persuaded it to start working, as per the commands. It has been recalcitrant off and on. My walks have been regular. My walking companions, different every day and at times none, provide enough material for my stories and articles.

Inside CBI - The Hindi version

Today Friday, 10 September 1999, a visit to the dentist consumed the entire forenoon. The afternoon was spent having lunch, siesta and then at the Hindi launch of "Inside CBI". Mr. L.M. Singhvi, M.P. and former High Commissioner of India and to the U.K. launched it with Mr. Chandan Mitra, Editor, Pioneer presiding over the function. As I am nearing sixty, I have to take adequate rest. Not much time is left, for serious working, due to the dental trouble. I have been visiting the dentist regularly. The treatment itself is painful. The doctor has to work, in the most sensitive area and it is done with the help and co-operation of the patient. Even the anaesthesia prick is painful. But the relief is possible, only after the teeth have been tinkered with. One has no peace often but to live with aches and pains.

A number of visitors come to see me, and to persuade me to make recommendations. I have never believed in making or accepting recommendations. So most of the time I say No. This is affecting my popularity but it is difficult to change one's life style and way of working after such a long stint. Everybody in the government talks about liberalisation and simplification of procedures, but precious little has been done, to demolish the barriers created, during the permit and quota raj regime.

Two rogues go

Yesterday (Tuesday, 21 September 1999), was another eventful day in my life. I had to have two teeth extracted by Dr. Seth at Dr. Gandhi's clinic. I, like others was scared of the pain of extraction. I braved myself saying that it is better to undergo pain once for all, than to suffer constantly. Dr. Seth gave two injections, which according to him, would be no more than two mosquito bites. They were much more. But I reminded myself of my philosophy that what cannot be cured should be endured. Modern life has introduced painkillers. They do not exactly kill the pain, but they bring it within tolerable limits. The local anaesthesia, given through injections, killed all the pain at the time of extraction. I came to know of the extraction only after the doctor told me that both the teeth were extracted. There was almost a continuous flow of blood from the root of the teeth till late in the night, when on the advice of a visitor, I drank cold water and kept a cold pack on the gap. The painkiller Flexon along with Novomox, an antibiotic, has to be taken regularly for another three to five days. The Pioneer of 20th September carried my article on "Be not good, Be good for something". This year almost from the beginning, has been a maintenance year for me. I had to constantly visit doctors, hospitals and the CGHS dispensary. I have not made any fuss about it, or even talked about it. Everything flows from God Almighty. One cannot adopt double standards in praising the Almighty, and not accepting his will. Man has the capacity to see good, if he wishes to see, even in the worst of circumstances.

Those forgotten martyrs

Last week, I attended a function of Martyr Bhagat Singh to celebrate his birthday. The British secretly hanged Bhagat Singh, an agnostic Sikh, along with Raj Guru and Sukhdev. Except for one organisation in Baljeet Nagar, a slum area adjoining Patel Nagar in Delhi, nobody in the country remembered that 27th September was his birthday. It was a well-attended function, in which the Shaheed Bhagat Singh Krantikari Organisation, presented me an award for my services to the Nation. The area has narrow streets, non-existing water supply, and erratic electricity. The place is no better than a village. The authorities concentrate all their attention on New Delhi and other VIP areas only. Earlier in the day, I attended a cricket tournament match, a competition in Delhi Public School, R.K. Puram. The traffic and parking position has become so bad that it took me nearly 45 minutes to cover a distance of 10 kilometres and find a parking place. One outing from the house consumes an entire forenoon or afternoon. I see most of the people wanting to meet me only at 5 P.M. so that at least in the forenoon I can work. Sometimes, my batchmates drop in or I run into them. Just yesterday, three of them Miss S. Mozumdar, K.S. Bains and Manmohan Malhotra met me. We exchanged old time notes. My other cadre and batchmate Colaso met me in the morning. He was on his way to Simla. His son Sunil has moved to Delhi from Bombay. FTR Colaso, has always been "Father Colaso" to me. He is now reconciled to my always calling him "Father" in front of his wife, son, daughter-in-law and grandchildren. He believes that "I am incorrigible, as his earlier protestations against my calling him Father had no effect on me". He has been a very good friend, a good host. He retired as Director General of Police, Karnataka State. I had been offered the job earlier by the then Chief Minister of Karnataka, Devegowda. Colaso had asked me not to come back to Bangalore, till his retirement in October, 1995. I had dodged the request of the Chief Minister, and so Colaso became the DG. I have never held any great love for any job. Colaso came for dinner with Sunil, his wife, Manju and two granddaughters, Rhea and Maliaka. He stayed for an hour and a half. We chatted about everything and I presented him my book "Inside CBI". I slept at 12.20 P.M. and got up to be in time for the Annual General Meeting of the shareholders of The Pioneer. The paper had made a loss of over Rs.16 crores before the present management took over. Now the losses stand at Rs.2.8 crores. Hopefully the losses would be wiped off soon. One of my lower teeth is wobbling. It may have the same fate as the previous two, which have been pulled out. Surinder has been very busy with her office work. She has to tie up for a major function, for which the Prime Minister is coming on 2nd October, to release a multi-media CD which will contain 55000 pages of the works of Mahatma Gandhi, 15 minutes of his voice, photographs and movies made in those times. For any function involving a VIP, one has to keep one's fingers crossed. Even if the smallest thing goes wrong, the head of the organisation is held responsible and sometimes the head rolls.

The best walk is in the Lodi grave yard

I have changed my routine and finished reading all the Delhi English newspapers, before going out from my morning walk to the best walking place in Delhi, that is, the Lodi Garden. When Ibrahim Lodi built the garden he did not imagine what his graveyard would do for the Delhites. The English added the present lay-out and the graveyard has become the finest lung place in Delhi. In fact, the best gardens in India are around the graveyards of the Mughals or other rulers. Whether it is Agra or Delhi, the central place is some kind of a tomb of an eminent person, with a lot of open places around. Some places, like the Galib's tomb, have been encroached upon. The area has become a slum. In some other tombs, people have opened commercial establishments, or are using them as residence. It is true both in life and death that what matters is the Station in life. Obviously, the tombs of the rulers are better maintained the tomb of a poor poet, however eminent he might have been.

Even the cremation grounds of former Indian Prime Ministers and in some cases even the son of a late Prime Minister are being maintained by the government. This is apart from converting the government houses, where they resided in their official capacity, as their memorials. Except for Nehru, for whom many other Indians and myself have a genuine regard, most people do not care for such memorials. But it has become a fashion. The governments of the day have bought peace by conceding all kinds of demands. My forenoon was taken up, by going to the Bank for withdrawing money. My second left floor tooth is dangling and cracked. I got the cracked portion taken out, as it was inevitable.

My computer is still my best friend. It has become an addiction. If I want to express my feelings, I do the same through various files opened in it. I am not techno savvy. But this complicated machine is something, which is more brainy and intelligent than myself. It carries loads of files, more than any human can. My daughter Randeep was to come from Assam today. She cancelled coming to Delhi because her son, Danish, just one year and five months old is not well. She would come, when he is all right. I must confess that I am looking forward to his coming to Delhi. He is my first grandson. Machu tells me, that Danish does not like to be cuddled and carried in one's lap. It is a treat to see the young child, if he or she is a friendly type. I have seen many children of my relations, who are peevish by nature. Danish, like her mother, is a happy child. My son-in- law, S. Abassi, is an equally affectionate person. I do not feel a stranger with him, despite the generation gap.

Sometimes I wonder, how a child so loving and affectionate can become a virago, when he has grown up. One can explain it by saying that after growth and development, the same child has developed and found his own interests and diversion. It is true of all of us, both as children as well as adults.

Surinder praised As Gandhi is compressed in disc

It is the birthday of Gandhiji (02/10/1999), father of the Nation. Publication Division, headed by my wife Surinder, had organised a function to release the CD, containing everything about Gandhi. A disc of the diameter of five inches, weighing less than eleven grams or one tola contains 50000 pages of the writings of Gandhiji. It also has 550 photographs, 15 minutes of his voice and 30 minutes of film footage on him, shot when he was alive and active. It is a marvel of science that so much can be compressed in so little a space. Normally for carrying the above items physically, not in the CD form, would require huge containers or boxes, and manpower which can carry 100 kilos. The PM Atal Behari Vajpayee, the Information Minister, Pramaod Mahajan, L.K. Advani, Sikandar Bakht, Ramamoorthy, Kumarmangalam, all ministers in the Vajpayee government were present. The RSS Chief Prof. Rajendar Singh, had also graced the occasion. RSS had invited me and honoured me, by making me preside over the Vijay Dashmi celebrations on 1st October, 1998 in Nagpur. They had sent the air-ticket and made all arrangements for my stay. As per their tradition, I had stayed with one of their eminent workers, Mr. Laxman Singh Bankoti. The RSS function was a model of discipline, by the participants, as well as the spectators.

I have known Sikander Bakht since 1977, when he was the Chairman of the Board of the Governors of Society for Netaji Institute of Sports (SNIPES), now renamed as the Sports Authority of India. I was on its board. I had a brief chat with all the ministers and a few others. The Minister praised Surinder for her leadership and for bringing out such a compact disc. Inwardly, I had kept my fingers crossed and was praying for the function to be over without any hitch. In one case, two years back, where the President of the country was invited, the head of the organisation, again a lady, was suspended for the failure of the microphone and loudspeakers. A departmental inquiry was held against her. Ultimately, she was reinstated, as she could not be held responsible for any technical failure. The then government of the day wanted to have a scapegoat and the poor lady suffered mental agony for two years before her exoneration. All is well that ends well. The function ended well, with Minister Promod Mahajan heaping praise on Surinder for doing a fine job. After the function, I joined the PM and other ministers for a cup of tea. I did eat a few pieces of cheese and other fatty stuff. This was one of the indulgences I had permitted myself.

A new darling in our lives

It rained heavily and my eldest daughter, Randeep arrived with Danish in the evening. Danish has grown up. When he left he was just two months old, being born on 10th June, 1998. He was the centre of attraction of Choosie, Gunveer, Bibban, Surinder and of course myself. He is expressive and has a way of indicating as to what he wants and what he does not want. The whole house revolves around him. This is his first day, and he still has to get used to the house. He walked down to the bathroom, all the bed rooms and my study. Probably, he was looking for the familiar figure of his father, Abbasi. For a kind of minor celebration, we got the food from one of the restaurants of Pandara Road. Pandara Road has a number of eating joints and our acquaintance with that place dates from 1971, when we were living in type four quarters in that locality. The food prepared is much tastier than what you get in five star hotels, and also at one third the price.

I almost broke my own walking record. I walked with Sanjeev Bhargava, an artist, and husband of the former Editor of Cosmopolitan, Simran. Two rounds of four kilometres were done in less than 38 minutes. Machu and her son Danish got up late. Danish just eighteen months old was cranky. Probably, he is still not used to the new place. Gagandeep and her husband dropped in, in the evening. Choosie (real name of my second daughter is Gagandeep) was angry at being left out for lunch at Bhujia Ram Haldiwala by her elder sister, Randeep and cousins Golu and Jasneet. The four girls, which group includes Bibban, had made a programme to go to Faridabad to see their cousin, Chu Chu who is in the IAS posted there as Additional Deputy Commissioner. Somehow, the children get nicknamed for their lives. All of us have nicknames. But when we grow up in our profession, the nicknames fall by the way in our stuffiness of the position in life. Bhujia Ram's shop was on the way. By selling Bhujia, the Bhujiarams (maker of salty snacks) have made millions, perhaps, billions. Choosie felt that while she had gone out of the way to cultivate her relations and sisters, she is normally ignored at the time of such feastly outings. Incidentally, Choosie is a great lover of good food, and a great connoisseur. She as a child used to enjoy seekh kababs and chicken with me, during my visit to the Gole Market. She has become a vegetarian under the Radhaswami influence of her mother. Machu, (real name of my eldest daughter is Randeep) had to apologise. Choosie gets heated up and cools down at the same speed. Parents or elders have to put up with the demands, needs, and tantrums of their children.

Another companion out

Yesterday, one more tooth finished life in my mouth, and Dr. Seth extracted it at Dr. Gandhi's clinic. Dr. Gandhi has the best clinic in the town with a team of dedicated doctors. Any kind of pain is bad, and it is not possible to classify which is the worst of all. My rear lower level tooth required all the skills, before it could be prised away. It has left behind intense pain and swellings. I am again back to the painkillers and antibiotics to prevent any infection. I visited the Race Course, but only for one last race and attended briefly the Stewards meeting. In the evening I met a Serial- and TV maker Arvind Singh, who wants to produce a serial on crime. He sent me the concept paper of the episodes. I have given him a clearance and agreed to participate in the programme as an anchorperson. I know most of these offers are non-serious and hence this is the only way to call off their bluff. My grandson Danish has slightly thawed in his relationship with me. He responds to my gestures and love. When he is hungry, he is cranky. Everybody keeps on feeding him. Today, he with Randeep and his servant had a feel of Lodi Garden. He liked a dog and took away his ball. The master of the dog willingly parted with the ball to see Danish happy. Other games of Danish include, switching off and on of electric switches of lights and fans. I saw another hopeful for making a serial, P.K.Ahluwalia. I have also given him a nod to make a serial, dealing with corruption and malpractices in the country. What happens in real life is that most people lose their enthusiasm. Less than 50 per cent proposals actually mature. Making a serial, getting it approved, shooting it and presenting it for telecast can take up to one year. If the situation changes, it loses its relevance exactly like yesterday's news, which has no takers the next day.

The toothache caused by the extraction of the lower right side teeth has diminished due to the painkiller, Flexon and Novomax capsules are intended to control infection. It is still not a pain-free day. Thanks to the modern medicines, one can somehow manage to deal with all kinds of ailments. I went to Jain TV, for the recording of an election programme relating to poll violence and the use of money power. It took my entire afternoon from 2 P.M. onwards. It was almost a live programme, with the usual commercial breaks and election results. No TV channel survives solely on the programmes. It is the commercials and advertisements that bring the revenue. The atmosphere on the channel was one of a marriage party. A good thing was that a lot of young people were managing the show. Every age is the age of the youth. It is the youth that can exert much more than anybody else. It is the youth which will find a way where there is none. I had the satisfaction of seeing the programme at my house, as the signal takes half an hour to one hour for transmission and coming back to India. At my request, my advocate, Sanjay Yadav dropped in to discuss the reply to the case filed against me by an accused former Chief Minister of Bihar, claiming Rs. one crore damages from me, for mentioning his role in the fodder scam. The next date of hearing is in January 2000. I finalised my reply to the complaint in consultation with Sanjay Yadav.

Elections, criminals and politics

The gums ache, or ache, as a result of the extraction of the tooth, continued today also. I had to take a painkiller at 4 A.M. in the early morning. Ice pack helped a lot. I was escorted to the Zee News TV channel for a programme of discussion on corruption, poll violence, State funding of elections, criminalisation of politics, from 3 P.M. to 4 P.M. The programme continued till 5 P.M. The iced cold drinks and the drugs controlled my tooth trouble. One has to live with pains and aches, when one has crossed sixty. The truth is that human body, like machinery, gets old and becomes dysfunctional. Machinery parts can be duplicated. But there is no way you can duplicate or find a matching replacement for a human heart, ear, lungs, and other systems. My grandson Danish has become quite expressive and affectionate. He is strong willed, and does what he pleases. Danish saw me on the television yesterday and felt happy at touching my video photo on the screen. We will miss him, when he goes away. I left for Ferozpore in the evening by Punjab Mail, which was late by two hours. I worked briefly on the computer and punched in the events of the day before dozing off, with the help of a sleeping pill to combat the tooth ache.

Jalalabad encyclopaedia

My friend Om Parkash picked me up at Ferozpore. Om Parkash had been associated with my father for a long time. He had his scooter garage and repair shop. He is undoubtedly a very good mechanical brain and a great management expert, without having done his M.B.A. Now he is an estate agent. He is the encyclopaedia of Jalalabad. He has excellent contacts with everybody. Without him, I would be lost. He was the one who persuaded me to repair the old dilapidated house. He stood day and night and got the entire work completed in less than six months. He has made the house liveable. Despite all the expenditure, the plaster and the white wash keeps peeling off quite regularly from the walls and the roof. I intend getting the house white washed only once in three years. There is seepage in the old walls and the nitrate keeps on coming out of the old construction. My uncle Harbhajan Singh came to see me. He is the closest living relation. He had his hey days and flings in his youth. Now he is like an old lion. Most well-off people in Jalalabad have a side mistress. It may be a field worker or anybody else, with whom there has been a kind of occasional contact. It is also due to lack of any other means of entertainment. The subject of discussion was how much money the parliamentary candidates collected for elections. It appears that the candidates of major parties collected nearly a crore of rupees. May be, even the losers have made fortunes. It was also rumoured that lakhs were spent by the candidates for purchase of votes, the cost ranging from Rs. 100 to Rs.1500. Nobody has seen any of the above transactions. But they enlightened me with their opinions and their guesswork. In the evening, I went to the my fields for a walk. During the lifetime of my father, about 400 metres of road was built in the field, in between the eucalyptus trees. This is the best walking area in Jalalabad, with no traffic and no pollution. There appears to be a small army detachment in our land by the roadside. As there is no euphoria about the army, the personnel are left to fend for themselves. In this age of electricity, the army unit was managing with kerosene lanterns. For water, they were using the tube well water from my land.

To pay or not to pay

I had a meeting of the local Management Committee of the DAV College at Jalalabad. It is over a twenty-member body. Just four persons, apart from the staff, attended the meeting. I also noticed that the college authorities told me only that much, which suited them. I had to be outspoken and clear in my views. The entire amount from donations and fees is being spent for the payment of the salaries of the staff. Hardly any money is left for development. The college has over 75 percent students from the scheduled caste and scheduled tribes. It is not receiving any government grant or aid. There is always a demand for higher salaries, whether anybody works or not. This is not true only for the college but for the entire government. Proper management has given way to populism. But it is a fact that unless you pay the right salaries, you cannot get proper teachers. The traffic in Jalalabad, is as chaotic as in Delhi. But for the help of local policemen, I would not be able to drive through the streets, which have all kinds of contraptions, including auto-rickshaws, hand driven cart, donkey driven carts, mopeds, trucks, tractors, scooters, bullock carts and the ubiqtuous Maruti car and the backbone of the economy the old war horse, the truck, which carries goods from one place to another. This is true of all towns in Punjab. People have money and have bought cars. But there is no parking place or roads to run them. The average time taken to cross Ludhiana from one end to another, a distance of six to eight kilometres, can take as long as 45 minutes to one hour. The average speed of the vehicle can be as slow as 10 to 15 kilometres. In the absence of any parking place, public roads and streets are used as parking places, leading to unmanageable congestion. As a nation, we wake up to a problem, only when it hits us across the eyes and face. Hence more electricity and fuel would be needed to run them. A kind of inertia has overtaken us. I visited the house of the young lady Sheila who has served as my mother's companion. The visit was to give a present to her on her wedding on 11th October. Her parents and relations were thrilled at my visit, as they did not expect me to come. I also visited another house of a person who claimed to be close to my father.

Packing to pack off to Delhi

I spent the first forenoon in packing my stuff so that I could leave for Delhi in time. I visited Fazilka for attending a programme, to honour the winners of an essay competition for Khalsa's tricentennary. About a hundred students were there. The two kilometres road of the thirty-two kilometres journey was awfully bad. The air conditioner of the car conked out after about eight kilometres of journey, on the way to Ferozpore. Om explained it by saying that as I had put in an old air conditioner in the car; problems like these were inevitable. The Maruti car has been a blessing. But any accessories added to it somehow do not serve or last as long as the vehicle itself. I finished my morning walk in Jalalabad itself. I got the house cleaned, as it will be locked till my next visit. I make it a point to eat in my house, so that I know what is where and whether all the gadgets kept there, including the fridge, toaster, air conditioner, fans, taps are working or not. When the house remains locked for such a long time, it is essential to get it dusted, cleaned at least once in two months. My class-fellow, Kishore Chand has a bakery shop. He baked two kilos of flour biscuits for me. The flour or atta biscuits, though not of symmetrical shapes, are very tasty. The train left Ferozpore in time. Earlier, I had arrived one hour before the departure of the train by car. The horn of the car stopped working on the way. It is one of those things which can happen. But in the night-time, it can be problematic.

Some Movers and some Shakers (Monday, 11 October 1999)

I arrived in Delhi at 5 A.M. I had hoped that the train would reach late. But it was in time. AC first class, my abode for the night, was quite comfortable. I had my usual morning walk in my favourite Lodi Garden. There was just enough time to get ready for addressing the meeting of India International Friendship Society. I gave away the society award along with Bhisham Narain Singh, a former minister and governor. The major view point amongst them was the U.P. Assembly Speaker, Mr. K.N. Tripathi. Others included the deputy speaker of Rajasthan assembly and the Education Minister of U.P., another Tripathiji. Like two months back, the driver had disappeared. Mercifully, unlike the last time, the car was still parked. I had started the practice of taking the key from him. But in the last one week, I had come to realise that he had become responsible. Obviously, he had not changed the old ways. He went for lunch not to return in the evening. I drove to the racecourse myself to watch the last two races and attend the stewards meetings. It is sickening to notice that some jockeys trainers and possibly owners-cum-trainers, play foul and deliberately lose the races so that non-favourite horses win and make tons of money. This obviously is shared. As stewards, drastic action like suspension of licenses, debarring from races, are a few unpleasant decisions, which I along with others have to take. As the meeting continued quite late, the next engagement of All India Qumi Ekta Committee was missed by me. In the night, I drove down to the residence of Ram Vilas Paswan to congratulate him, on his victory in the elections. I saw my programme of Movers and Shakers at the house of Paswan. It is a humorous programme and started with a reference to Ram Vilas Paswan. By the time, I could sleep it was past midnight.

I turn sixty (12 october 1999)

As per my certificate, I complete sixty years of my earthly existence today. But according to my mother, my birthday falls on 15 Maghar. She does not really remember either the day or the day. For all-purposes, I treat 12th October, as my birthday. I complete a Path of Granth Sahib on this day. It was done in the presence of Machu, Bibban and Danish, my grandson and Surinder. For me this day has been just another day. In the evening, for the first time, I took all my three daughters Randeep, Gagandeep and Harveen for dinner. Surinder and Gunveer Singh, my son-in-law and husband of Gagandeep and the young Danish were also there. Danish had a free run of the Amber restaurant. A very kind-hearted waiter, Mohammad Yahaya Khan served us and he carried Danish in his lap. Danish expresses his open preference for Gunveer, next to his mother. He does not like to be cuddled. He is a toy for the grown-ups of the family.

Some are lucky in losing bulge (13-10-1999)

My entire day from 10 A.M. to nearly 6 P.M. was spent in visiting Faridabad to address the 64 probationers of all top Financial Services, including the Civil Accounts Service, Postal Account Service, Defence Account, and Railways Financial Services. Mr. B.P. Mathur, Director of the Institute, had invited me for the lecture. Mathur was the Financial Adviser in the Trade Fair Authority of India, when I was the Director, in charge of it in the Commerce Ministry. I explained to them the role that accounts services can play in bringing about integrity and honesty in the administration. It was a two-hour session. My cousin brother, Dr. Pradeep Babbar, came to the Institute and took me to his house. His father-in-law had passed away on the 6th of this month. I offered my condolences to Vandana Babbar. My niece Dipti and Uma Shankar also joined for the lunch. Uma Shankar, as the Commissioner of Municipal Corporation,

Faridabad, has privatised the disposal of garbage. He told me that it is one of the two projects in the country, which has been successful. His wife, Dipti, is the Additional Deputy Commissioner of Faridabad district. She has lost ten kgs of weight since the birth of two daughters. What is impressive is that she has maintained this loss. She does everything with thoroughness, like her father. It is her persistence, single-minded approach, and hard work which enabled her to make it to the IAS. I dropped into their place, for a few minutes, before returning to Delhi. The traffic on the road from Faridabad to Delhi has reduced the speed of even the fastest vehicle to less than 30 kilometres per hour. It makes no difference, whether one is travelling in a Mercedes or any other car. The difference in arrival time will not be more than seven minutes from Delhi to Faridabad or vice versa.

Balancing life

I had accepted an engagement in DLF Qutab Enclave to address a ladies group. Very thoughtfully, I had asked the organisers to send a vehicle to pick me up. It took 45 minutes to go and 55 minutes to come back, on a pot-holed road. My entire day from 1 P.M. to 8 P.M. was spent on the programme and travelling. It was a two hours of interaction with prosperous, well fed, obese and positively over-weight ladies living in one of the richest areas.

Prosperity and riches have a by-product in the form of rich and good food. It invariably leads to a situation of excess weight and then going to health clubs to shed the flab. I tried to motivate them not to put up with any injustice. I doubt whether even two percent of them would take up cudgels for any cause. Only a minuscule number of them agreed with me. I advised them to go as high as they can for getting prompt response to their problems, and any problem they may take up on behalf of anybody else. The problems of the rich are not necessarily the problems of the poor. Occasionally, they are contradictory. There was no time to devote to writing, due to more than four hours, spent on commuting and meeting the ladies group. But it is only by meeting and talking I can motivate people. I have to keep a balance between the two so that I do not neglect either. It is the balance in life, which is important in any walk of life.

No credit cards for me

Living itself wears out life, till a time comes, when one has worn oneself out thoroughly. But the main thing is not to hang your pants, till the last day and last minute. One should do whatever one is doing, as if it was the most important thing for existence. One should work as if one was going to live till eternity and live as if it was his last day in life. Life hangs by a precarious thread. It can snap at any time. I like to keep my bag ready, with no loose ends anywhere. I do all my transactions on cash and carry basis. I never like to be under debt to anyone or even to God, if I can help it. I have been given all major credit cards, on complimentary basis. I have never used even one of them. This way, I know what I can afford and what I cannot. My work place, the air conditioned veranda converted into a room, has all the entertainment items, like remote control TV and VCP, remote DVCD player, remote music system, cordless telephone, cellular phone, lap top computer with the printer, and answering machine with a fax. But there is no time to use all of them. I do not believe in changing my stuff, for the later models. I feel that my stuff may be a few years older. But it gives me excellent service. It will outlast my life time. In any case, if I start using them, I would have no time left to do any serious or even frivolous writing. I like to plan every minute of my day, and every activity down to the last detail. This is the only way to succeed in any venture one undertakes.

Of leisure, of people

The biggest problem with leisure is to prevent others from using it. My time is wasted not in driblets, but in drops. I normally do not meet anybody, unless I am reasonably well dressed. I also dress up formally, when going out. Putting on and putting off clothes takes time. People drop in, at the time of their choice, and not at the time which may suit the person visited. Before retirement, most of the visitors would come to meet me at 7 A.M., straight from the railway station. Now all the time visitors keep on coming. As I use the home as my office also, I have to be 'suited and booted' to meet people. Shakespeare said that "Apparel oft, proclaimeth the man". A well-dressed man makes a good impression. The only trouble is that one does not know when somebody will turn up. I normally meet people only by appointment. I also do not go out to meet anybody, unless it has been fixed in advance. It saves everybody's time. I do not keep anything loose ended. RS Sahay, Director General of Goa, now deceased, dropped in with his wife. He did a commendable job as the Chief Vigilance Officer of the State Trading Corporation. But since nobody likes vigilance, whose aim is to check malpractices, he did not get the required official support in his drive against the corruption.

I attended a condolence cum prayer meeting in one of the congested areas of Delhi, in Karol Bagh. It is one of the zero space areas, where vehicles have to vie, with the human beings, for space. A human being requires, only a space of two square feet either for standing or sitting or passing through. But in the case of a vehicle, the space required is not only for parking but also for manoeuvrability. The number of vehicles in Delhi has crossed 32 lakh mark, which is one vehicle per four persons. But the official parking space available is not even for one lakh vehicles. The Gurudwara, where I went, was located in an equally overcrowded area. When it comes to religion, we draw a line in criticising anybody. The priest was mumbling his recitation of the prayer in an uninspiring tone. It is true of all religions. The invitees for the prayer meeting were there, only for an obligatory presence. It was either a business connection or being present, as the aggrieved had attended a similar function, where their family was involved. It appeared that everybody was keen to see that the condolence Path was over, so that they could attend to other programmes. Except for the relations, hardly anybody felt even a twinge at the death. I heard snide remarks that a great burden was off from the host, as he could now devote more time to his business. It is a reminder that all the homage and praises are for the living. The deceased is forgotten quickly. The Pioneer carried my article "Agenda for the New Government". I have tried to outline the jobs the new government of Vajpayee should concentrate on.

Poor amongst the rich

Today, (Tuesday, 19 October 1999), was a government holiday. For me, it makes no difference, as I do not have to attend any office. Surinder was at home. I accompanied her to a diamond shop called Tanshiq in South Extension. The confident sale girls rattled the cost of the jewellery running into thousands. As far as I am concerned, I cannot distinguish between gold and brass. For me, glass and diamond are the same. When you buy any jewellery, you end up paying a high price. But when you want to sell, the price offered is down the line. I meekly accompanied my wife without reiterating my views, with which she is fully familiar. The sales girls looked on us suspiciously. They were doubtful whether we had the money to purchase even the lowest priced item, which was about Rs.20000. In any case, it was an exploratory visit to purchase something, for either Surinder or the youngest daughter Harveen. We left within 25 minutes, as Surinder did not approve of any item. I was a mute spectator in the precious shop, which had no relation to the existing reality in the country. Most other visitors were stinking with money, whereas we had to count every single penny. I was not impressed with the shop, where the objective was to slice off some excessive wealth from the filthy rich. We drove straight to the house of Dr.K.K.Paul, an IG of Delhi Police. His wife Omita and Surinder are great pals, apart from being in the same Indian Information Service. I accompanied my wife, just as the Duke of Edinburgh accompanies Queen Elizabeth in the U.K. Most people recognised me thanks to a number of TV appearances this month. Some of them said that they had met me. I had to regretfully point out that it was our first meeting. Then some of them recognised the fact that they had seen me on the small screen. Functions like the one held at the residence of Paul couples are an opportunity to meet old friends and renew acquaintances. The Punjab Kesri carried my article to-day, on the foibles of human nature.

Dr. Gandhi, the best

My tooth ache continues. Dr. Gandhi says that he will cure it. He is doing his best to prolong the life of the natural teeth. But my own feeling is that sooner than later the artificial teeth will take over. It is the nuisance of having constant pain which has impelled me to urge for the extraction of any problematic tooth. I have been taking anti-biotics for the last ten days. But there is no relief. I can hardly sleep. My every activity is tooth- oriented. I can hardly eat anything. It is good in a way as I can shed some excess flab. This morning my weight was 75 kgs. It will be wonderful, if I can bring it down to 70 kgs. But this is a wishful thinking of all those who quickly want to become slim and trim over night. Weight loss is in grams, and gain is in kilos. It is a life-long battle against the bulge. God bless the likes of me.

A salute to police martyrs

21st October, is celebrated all over the country as a police martyrs day, to salute all policemen killed in the year. This practice was started when 10 CRP officials laid down their life for the country on, 21st October 1959, in a conflict with the Chinese. I was pleasantly surprised to receive invitation for the commemoration parade. Further surprise was when the offer of a lift to the function. The Police vehicle came promptly at 6.45 A.M. It has happened with the change in the Commissioner of Police. The new Police Chief Ajay Raj Sharma is a go-getter, with an excellent reputation behind him. We have worked together in the Central Reserve Police Force. The Parade had one of the highest responses from the retired and serving police officers. It was a solemn occasion, where tributes were paid to 987 policemen killed from 1-9-98 to 31-8-99. Andhra Pradesh lost 79 policemen, Arunachal Pradesh 1, Assam 63, Bihar 41, Delhi 16, Himachal Pradesh 2, Jammu & Kashmir 176, Karnataka 14, Kerala 4, Madhya Pradesh 38, Maharashtra 16, Manipur 13, Meghalaya 13, Mizoram 7, Nagaland 4, Orissa 4, Punjab 74, Rajasthan 8, Tamil Nadu 1, Tripura 19, Uttar Pradesh 128, West Bengal 14, Border Security Force 159, Central Industrial Security Force 10, Central Reserve Police Force 117, Director General Security 1, Indo-Tibetan Border Police18, National Security Guards 1, Railway Protection Force 29. Considering the solemnity of the occasion, no refreshments or even a cup of tea is proffered. In my view this would be a good occasion to throw open to the public, so that they are made aware of the sacrifices made by the policemen. But the whole programme has kind of too much seriousness about it. Its scope could be increased to give awards, if any due, to the policemen killed either in the current year or the past year. But the problem is that with too much pressure and demand on the time of the police, for them this has become another ritual to be gone through. Due to the parade, my morning started at 10 A.M. I went for my morning walk at 10 AM. I believe in the adage that some walk is better than no walk. The afternoon was spent in the Race Club, where the Air Chief, Tipinis, had come and gave way the Air Force cup to the winner of the Air Chief Cup. For me, it was an obligatory presence, as a steward. This is one of the days, when I could not devote any time to the work. I depend on my secretary. He said, he would come in the after noon, but did not turn up. Neither did the driver, who I presume has found another job. One should not expect any life-long loyalty from anybody. It is not so even from the close family members. The persons working for me are entitled to try and get better prospects in life. Everybody has to look after his personal interests.

Bowing to the inevitable

Nothing succeeds like success. I lost two more teeth. There was a nagging and constant pain in the teeth. I told Dr.Gandhi, Dr. M.Seth and Dr. Amrita that I would prefer to undergo pain once for all rather than suffer constantly. My worn-out teeth appeared to be a case of unconscious grinding. It took nearly one and a half hours including the X- Ray, local anaesthesia and the extraction. The mouth was bleeding and I could hardly talk. I had a press interview and interviews on two TV channels, Zee News and Ennadu on Bofors case. The immediate provocation was the filing of the charge sheet by the CBI against the accused persons, Quottorchi, an Italian adventurer and a few NRI Indians for bribery and conspiracy. The name of the late Prime Minister, Rajiv, was mentioned as one accused, who has not been sent up for trial. From the Congress, it was Mani Shanker Aiyer and from the BJP, it was Mr. J.P. Mathur, Vice President of the BJP. Quottorchi was perceived to be close to the family of Rajiv, whose wife, Sonia, now a Congress President is an Italian. Mr. Mathur appealed to Sonia to advise Quottorchi to come to India and make a clean breast. Mani Shanker Aiyer said that the BJP had politicised the case for making capital out of it. I tried to present the correct legal case that it was a sheer open case of bribery and no motives need be read into it. Later on, I went to Ennadu Television for recording at Jhandewala. It was explaining the Bofors case for the regional channel. By the time I could sleep, it was well past 1 A.M. I had to remain on pain-killers and anti-biotics for preventing the tooth from infection.

Self Driven and still safe (Sunday, 24 October 1999)

It was a busy day for me. I had sacked the driver for the simple reason that he could not be trusted to come to duty on time. He would telephone that he would not be coming for duty. It would leave me in the lurch. All of us are afraid of change and postpone taking any decision, which may be unpleasant. I kept on postponing the decision hoping that he might improve. I engaged the services of a driver, so that I could spend the journey time in reading or doing some other work. This could save me from half an hour to one hour every day. Since I was without a driver, I drove my car to Gurudwara and later on to Paharganj for the quarterly meeting of the DAV management committee. Driving a power steering Esteem car is the easiest thing and it is a pleasure. The car literally flies. There is no problem with my driving. The only problem arises, when it is a question of parking the car in the congested areas. When the driver is there, it is his headache to find a parking place. But the advantage of the self driving is that you are sure that your car petrol would not be stolen and the driver would not disappear with the car. It is a mixed blessing or non-blessing depending on one's perception. I completed my packing for proceeding to Ooty for a Security and Vigilance programme. In between I wrote an article and played with my grandson, Danish. Danish, who is just 16 months old, wants a new game every time. It need not be an expensive toy. He is happy to play with key chains, pencils, bottle corks, photo-frames, trees, leaves, and flowers. He is the darling of the house. I took him to the Bala Sahib Gurudwara with me. A child has no religion. While growing, the ideas of fundamentalism or liberalism are sought to be planted in him. He may choose to profess any religion and still he shall be a part of me.

Air fatigue or Jet lag (Monday, 25 October 1999)

I got up at 5 A.M. to catch the flight to Bombay and Coimbatore, for inaugurating a programme of the Delhi Productivity Council. My daughter, Bibban, who had her classes at 8.30 A. M. volunteered to drop me at the Airport, as her college is only ten minutes drive from there. I could reach at 7.15 A.M. The flight left in time and each one of the seats of the Indian Airline's aircraft was occupied. I reached Coimbatore at 12.30 PM. I was in the aircraft for over five hours. Despite the executive class travel, there was a feeling of being cramped. The IA flight was carrying two commanders and half a dozen airhostesses to Calicut to enable them to operate the gulf flights from there. We have a strange culture of free facilities. For a Railway man, it is free train travel, for a telephone official, it is free unlimited telephone calls, for a person working in the airlines, it is free travel both in India and abroad. It is irrespective of the fact whether the airline is in the red, or white, and is not breaking even. Most of the governments and government organisations exist for their employees. Many state governments are spending their cent percent revenue collections in paying wages to their employees. Some even dip in the central kitty for this. The question of spending anything on the development is far from their mind. One minister of a state government told me that their 70% of the revenue goes for the payment of the wages, 24% maintenance, and only 6% is left for development for 21 million residents of the state. Arriving in Coimbatore, after being in

Delhi and Bombay, looked like, arriving at a well developed village. The airport though small was neat and clean. The drive from Coimbatore to Ooty took over two hours and fifteen minutes. On the way, we stopped for a cup of coffee, and putting water in the radiator of the overheated diesel old road horse, the Ambassador. I normally do not take coffee. But when in the South, I take coffee or make my own tea with the tea bags. It is for the simple reason that either the brew made by the shopkeeper is too pungent, or too strong or there is too much of sugar or too much of milk. I carry my tea-making kit with a packet of tea bag, milk powder, electric kettle and an adapter, so that any power outlet can be used. I like to have tea of my taste. This is the only drink I take. I have a self-imposed regulation of no tea and no coffee after 6 P.M. In Ooty, I was put up in the Hotel Monarch owned by the film star, Mithun Chakarvarty. It is a neat, well-kept, 67 roomed hotel, with courteous and helpful staff. I inaugurated the programme organised by the Delhi Productivity Council on the Security Scenario in the country. It was covered by the local cable TV. Mr. K.S. Maheshwari, the Executive Director of Delhi Productivity Council, has himself been attending various programmes to ensure that quality does not suffer and the programmes do not come a cropper. His programme officer, Mr. Rajiv Mehta, is both ' Jeeves', (A P.G. Wodehouse character, personifying ingenuity with efficiency) and man Friday rolled into one. The leadership and execution level have to work in unison to achieve maximum performance. Unlike in Delhi, where I was using a fan in the night, I had to use the room heater, to keep myself warm. The rains further cooled the weather. There was a call from a lady introducing herself as Yogita, wife of Mithun Chakarvarty, inquiring whether I was comfortable. It was a pleasant surprise call. I told her that I would like to meet her the next day and that I was quite comfortable.

Shrewd investments

I normally have a late breakfast. But I made an exception to join for the breakfast at about 8.20 A.M. While in the South or even otherwise, I prefer to eat Idlis or Upam. The South Indian snacks have a much wider variety to offer than the traditional North Indian Prathas. Since there was still time for my lecture, which was slated at 11 A.M., at my request, I met Mrs. Chakarvarty. She has left the film career and is now a full-time mother and wife. She told me that she drops and picks up her children from school. It is because of the interest taken by her, and her presence on the premises, which keeps the hotel staff on toe. Mithun Chakarvarthy telephoned from Coimbatore inviting me to Coimbatore, where he was busy with a film shooting. I told him that I would meet him on 28th October on my return journey to Delhi. He is unlike other film stars, who have squandered the fortunes they made on wine, women and gambling. He has made wise investments in the hotel industry, which will outlast his film career. I delivered my lecture for the day. Due to the interests of the participants, my talk spilled beyond to nearly two hours. Most hotel food is oily and spice based. In the morning itself, I had ordered boiled vegetables for the lunch, which are light on the stomach and easier to digest. In any case, I use only the right side of the mouth. As many as seven teeth have been extracted from the left and right side of my mouth. Dentures are still to be fixed up, in their place. It is sometimes excruciating to suffer from tooth ache. I had only a twenty minutes walk in the hotel hall, due to the inclement weather. I walked to the market area a distance of nearly three kilometres to make up for the missed exercise in the morning. Language is a big handicap for anybody. It prevents communication and your ability to get the best of the bargain. So my shopping was confined only to language exchange in English and Kannada. I purchased snacks for consuming them at the odd hours. I often feel hungry at mid night.

Toothpain my constant companion

The official and social interaction is only with the group, which is attending the course or at the best with the hotel staff. Hotel living is a world apart. My mouth is minus seven teeth. The left side has five gaping holes. I cannot even turn my side to sleep with the left side of the cheek touching the pillow. Too much speaking is painful. I had to spend three hours speaking to the two groups, on security and on effective working. I made up for the missing of the morning walk by walking in the hotel lobby. I have been living substantially on boiled vegetables. It is something, which I enjoy and which is healthy from all points of view. Only fresh and firm vegetables will lend themselves to boiling and still remain firm and eatable. For mixed vegetable preparations, any soggy old vegetable can be used. Their condition can be covered with spices, condiments and butter. The temperature outside is about 18 degrees. I have been using the room heater to keep the room comfortable. As the weather is cold, I could not drink plenty of water. But I made it up in the evening. Inadequate water in the body makes one sluggish. There is a stitch put in my mouth at the place, from where a tooth had been taken out recently. It caused pain in the night. I took a pain killer with a sedative to catch up on the sleep. This pain has been there. But since I was on anti-biotics and pain killers, it remained suppressed. It has probably caused a headache, which could also be due to the use of the convector heater. Toothache warbles your outlook on the world. This is because neither you can eat properly, nor can get the pain out of your mind.

Film Stars can be gracious hosts

What cannot be cured, must be endured. It is true for my continuing toothache. My characteristic approach has been to ignore it, and quite often it is the best solution. But I have not been able to wish it away. At the advice of a colleague, I applied clove oil and later on kept clove in the sensitive area. I cannot say that it has cured but at least, it has enabled me to carry on. The official programme was over after five days. Most of the people in the group wanted individual photographs with me. I obliged them. I left for Coimbatore to enjoy the hospitality of Mithun Chakarvarty at about 5.30 P.M. after thanking the hotel staff and Yogita, that is Mrs. Chakarvarty. The car journey took two and half-hours. It was my first personal meeting with him. He received me at arrival at his Coimbatore Resort, along with his brother Gautam Chakarvarty. He has involved himself in humanitarian work, along with setting up a chain of hotels and acting in films. He is a practical and a positive man. He was the single largest taxpayer in the country last year, with the payment of Rs.1.35 crores as income tax. He was honoured by the income tax, as a model citizen. He put me up, in his cottage, to stay for the night. The chef inquired, as to what I would like for dinner. He prepared my favourite chicken biryani. All along for two hours, Mithun was with me. I chatted all kinds of cases with him. His film director and some other people from the industry called on me. Mithun will go still higher in the industry, due to the way he dedicates himself to all his roles. His Coimbatore Monarch Resort is spread in a sprawling 20 acres of land and has all the modern amenities in it. It is in Coimbatore and still far away from the pollution, hustle and bustle of the city. It is a home away from home. Mithun has acted in over 300 films and won three recognised National Awards, apart from hundreds of others, some well known and some not well known. He is a perfect host and a down-to-earth person. He told me that he does not keep late nights and sleeps early so that next day, he is able to devote himself to his work fully. In the Monarch Resort, he treated me as a Monarch.

As I had to catch the flight at 10.25 A.M. I got up at 6 A.M. After tea and morning ablutions, I was ready at 8 A.M.

Mithun dropped in to inquire whether I was comfortable. As I was in the bathroom, I told him that I would join him later. After packing up, I joined him near the restaurant. He made my stay both enjoyable and memorable. Mithun told me that his life was one of struggle. In his early life period, he used to earn his living by giving tuition for Rs 1 to Rs 1.50 per month. He was a good football player. He would be paid Rs 5 if his team reached quarterfinals and Rs 10 for the final. Having seen poverty in its extreme, he is ever ready to help the poor and needy. The film industry unjustly called him poor man's Amitabh Baachan. His achievement in life is much more than that of Amitabh Baachan. He started from scratch and has reached the top in his profession. If we had more Mithuns our country would easily beat America, in all development and progress. My flight for Delhi was rather long, nearly 5 hours. I utilized the time working on the computer, and reading all the available newspapers and a joke book. The tooth problem persisted, so I went almost straight from the airport to the Doctor. The long sitting hours in the aircraft compelled me to retire early in the night. My grandson Danish welcomed me, at my arrival home. He has missed me as much, as I had. Little children act like a magnet for the elders. They are the ones unquestionably obeying without creating a fuss.

Bofors again

Whenever I go out, it takes a few days to catch up on my pending communications, going through old papers and getting back to my routine of walking and meeting people. The longer the duration of stay outside Delhi, the longer it takes to get back to the normal routine. One becomes a stranger, in one's own home. A small matter, like the use of a properly softened and cushioned pillow, can affect the sleep. My study has become a passage. With the house full now, and all kinds of requests for interviews, after the Bofors charge sheet, has been filed, there are heavy demands on my time.

Today, I gave interviews to the Indian Express, The Asian Age, and Times of India. Today's lead head line was my statement given to the Asian Age correspondent. Malayalam Channel Asianet had telecast my statement on Bofors. There was a call from the Principal of Jalalabad Giani Gurbux Singh DAV college, requesting that I should agree to give higher pay scales to the staff. As I am the President of the college, I have to make sure that enough money is available to pay salaries. The College is running without any grants as aid. The money is raised either by voluntary donations or from the fees collected from the students. At present, all the revenue is spent on payment of wages. I told the Principal that if you can raise the contributions and donations, I would have no objection. But some money must be available for development. He told me that the staff wanted to go on a strike. I said that if we do not have the means, how can we pay? I told him to get the report of the committee set up to look into the finances expeditiously. From my side, there would be no objection to pay higher salaries, if some way can be found to raise 13 lakhs additional revenue only for the salaries. When he told that the staff was thinking of going on a strike, I told him that I was not the one to be cowed down with threats. I cannot sell the college property to pay higher wages, which the college is not in a position to afford. This stand was confirmed by the acting chairman of the college in my absence.

Repeat interviews and views

The last three days were rather heavy for me as I had to drive the car to the doctor for my dental problem, to the Race Course, to a function of Mt. Carmel School on 4th and 5th November, 1999 at Kamani auditorium. This has meant a driving time of at least seven to eight active hours, which could have been spent by me in reading or doing other work. Appearance on Jain TV on the 4th of November, 1999 took about two hours and a similar amount of time was spent in the

Race Course. Today, the forenoon and afternoon were spent in meeting the pressmen from PTI, Gulf News and appearing on CNBC TV. In the afternoon, Sushil Moodi, MLA and leader of the opposition and Sarju Prasad, MLA in Bihar, dropped in to look me up. It was a repeat story of the 3rd November, when I met the representatives from the Indian Express, Hindustan Times, Times of India and Asian Age. Asian Age carried my statement in its head lines. The school function of Mt. Carmel School showing the Sound of Music as a drama took a better part of the evening. In short I had no time to work even for one hour. The toothache after giving a lot of sleepless nights, was manageable today.

Press license

The Hindustan Times, Saturday, 06 November 1999, carried my photograph on the front page of a story that Rajiv Gandhi had not received any money. It was a truncated story, which was given by me to the Press Trust of India. The Hindu had carried the full story. The newspapers have a license to quote, whatever suits them. It is a part of life to be quoted misquoted and underquoted. In the Vernacular papers, it was the Punjab Kesri and Dainik Jagran, which carried the same news. I twisted my foot and was disabled from completing my walk. I had to depend on the Voveran tablet, massage and keeping my foot in salt water, to get some relief. At 60 plus, these kinds of problems are inevitable and one has to learn to live with them. It was a pre-Diwali day. Visitors dropped bit by bit and at different times. But I had my siesta. Neither am I apologetic about it. I believe that I must live my life on my terms and conditions.

Non-working culture (08 November 1999)

Yesterday, my wife Surinder completed her 56th birthday. We normally have a lunch or a dinner outing on the birthday of any member of the family. But Surinder had sprained her back, while trying to pick up our crying grandson Danish. This incapacitated her and she was confined to the home. A green, mustard vegetable, consumed during the day upset my stomach as well as Surinder's. The doctor said that probably Voveran tablet had contributed to the bloated and a painful stomach. The truth is that life after fifty is a bonus. One has to carry on with a worn-out body, which is dependent on external assistance in the form of medicines. There is a culture and excuse of non-working in the government sector. Today was Vishawkarma day. No electrician despite loose and dangling wires, came to work on the score of that excuse. When I told an official that this is not a government holiday and government is paying full salary, he blamed the present situation on the prevalence of rampant indiscipline. It is true in every sense. In government service, rarely anybody is dismissed for not working. The government has become a kind of 'Pinjrapole', for the invalid and the unfit. All the talk of good governance comes to naught, when the leadership is confronted with the prospectus of weeding out the non-performing dead wood. Nobody wants to bell the cat, by undoing populist schemes, which leave no funds for development. Government work is nobody's work, and hence nobody in government works with dedication, with a few exceptions.

Catch me in kurta pyjama

Life seems to be running very fast and I have to catch the time by the forelock. Any outing for whatever reasons takes two to three hours. My visit to the dentist took two hours and the visit for recording a TV programme on Bofors with Mani Shanker Iyer took three and a half hours. Mani had done his home work and he alleged that the directors of CBI were talking nonsense. Without losing my temper, I contradicted him and stuck to the guns that the action taken by the CBI was correct.

Mani Shanker was essentially aiming at politicising the issue. My stand was that it was a professionally investigated case and the CBI had done an excellent job. The weather has changed and we have totally stopped using fans. Even one blanket is not enough. But somehow, I spend my spare time in banyan and pajama. My wife says that from the fans, I had come straight to heaters. There is a lot of truth in what she says. I have been rather indiscreet in my intake. Diwali season is full of sweets and I have been consuming them galore. My weight which had come down to 74 kilograms has touched a new height of 77 kilos. My eating prathas and puris soaked in cooking oil has a lot to contribute.

All conveying 'ooh'

The Central Public Works Department has been making an almirah in the bed room for the last seven days. The rooms have been full of dirt and dust. There is a clutter of papers in my room. I cleaned some of it. There is a constant battle against the huge quantity of papers, which I have to handle. I find it constraining, but inevitable for my writing work. My computer had a fight with the printer and the printer did not print. A doctor of the machine diagnosed it as a port problem. Another said that the printer software had a virus. Frankly, I do not know anything about the machine. It has taken a lot of tedium out of my work. It was inconceivable that a machine would outdo human beings in all its functions, including correction, grammar, spelling checks and a host of other functions. It can work as a fax machine, internet receiver and get you to speak to foreign lands, at the cost of a local call. The only problem is that quite often it needs handling with kid gloves to give totally trouble free service. My grandson Danish is an expert linguist. With one word "Ooh", he can explain what he wants. He uses this word with facial expressions. It can be the opening of a gate, riding a car, eating food or rejecting something he does not like. He is a happy-go-lucky child, and is constantly smiling, like his mother did, at his age. He moves and turns things upside down. All of us love children for these kinds of pranks.

Nobody dares to rub on the wrong side

Today (Thursday, 11 November 1999) was one of the unusually heavy day. Thanks to the arrival of a new driver, whom I had engaged today, I was able to go to my dentist for the measurements of the dentures of the four cavities. I have got the STD and my roaming facility has been extended on my mobile cellular phone, which is required only for emergencies. It is more so because of the medical problems, like the heart bypass surgery I had in April 1999, and the gall bladder extraction on 26th August. This phone enables me to get in touch with my family, wherever I may be provided there is a cellular phone facility. Later on a visit to the Race Club and meeting important VIP's and dinner with the National Hydro Electric Corporation took the evening. When I tried to use the printer after 10 P.M., I found that the ink had finished. One has to be a perfectionist to keep everything in stock. In Delhi, everything is available at a short notice. My experience with keeping stock of any item has been that when you need it most, it is just not available. It seems to have disappeared in to the thin air. It is better to purchase on a need basis. It so happens that stocked items become a drag. I attended a dinner hosted by the National Hydro Electric Corporation, for the vigilance officers attending the course, to ensure honest functioning and integrity in working. The Central Vigilance Commissioner was present at the dinner informally interacting with the senior officers. I noticed that nobody was contradicting him on the issues, which needed reconsideration according to the private views expressed to me.

I addressed the senior officials in the power sector to sell vigilance as a management function. I got an impression that most of them did not appear keen to face any unpleasant situation. Most of the careerists in service play safe. It is for this reason that there is a tight lid on malpractices, which go on in the government. There is a dictatorship even in the offices. I had a meeting with a Friday group set by Prof. N.K. Singh to *act as a think tank to advise* the reforms to be brought about in the society. It was a stimulating interaction. I had to cut short my stay as I had to leave for Jammu. The trip was cancelled at the last minute due to the non-availability of a seat and the removal of the AC coach. The entire programme for which I was to be the Chief Guest had to manage without me, as even the airline flight on 13th November, 1999 would reach after the function was over. A lot of time was spent in packing and unpacking and making telephone calls to Jammu to inform about my inability to reach there on time.

Musings

For me all days are Sundays. Life and living continues, whether it is a holiday from the work or festival or health or sickness. The day-to-day requirements do not change. One outing for any work upsets the schedule. Yesterday, the entire forenoon was spent in buying trifles like cups and saucers and glasses, going to the bank and collecting medicines for the dispensary. Distances in Delhi and scouting for particular requirements does take a lot of time. It is unlike in small places like Jalalabad, where even if you go out ten times, you can finish all transactions in twenty minutes. An afternoon nap is a must. I can miss it without much of a problem, if I skip the lunch. It is the heavy stomach, which creates heaviness and drowsiness. There is no one way of dealing with any situation. It varies from time to time, depending upon the state of mind and body. Life offers happiness and unhappiness simultaneously. I went to a Gurudwara in Greater Kailash for the last prayer of a relation's dead wife. At the same place, a marriage had been solemnised fifteen minutes before. There is no fixed way to celebrate a birth or a death. It depends upon the pocket of a person and what he can afford. Some convert it into a social occasion to transact business. Others are either solemn or stoic about it.

It is easier to be fat than thin

My daughter Randeep, along with her 17 months old son, Danish left for Gauhati on way to Naugaon, where my son-in-law, Abbassi is posted as Deputy Commissioner. We had come to accept Danish as a household fixture. We had got used to his tantrums, turning the house upside down and leaving behind a mess and wreckage in every room he entered. Till the last day, that is today, he was trustful of us, only in the presence of his mother. We enjoyed and loved his stay. But he is full of energy and would go his own way in poking at every plug, eating medicines or whatever was given to him, except food. There is a need to keep him under constant watch, lest he harm himself by touching any live wire, or eating something which may get stuck in his throat. My sister, Manjit, had also come to Delhi and she left today. She is short and rather fat for her age. I am also far from being thin. I used to advise her earlier to lose her weight and keep her diet under check. But I have stopped preaching, as I myself need to practise it. She provided company to my mother for two days. Manjit is equally strong-willed and outspoken like me. My mother obviously does not like it. My visit to the dentist did not take long. He had prepared a cast of rubber, with teeth, fitted to make a regular denture for me. When I asked him about the possibility of losing more teeth and making a fresh denture of the artificial teeth, he replied that he would attend to the problem, when it arose. Let me see how the new teeth, though artificial, stand by me.

More time in journey, than on work

I had accepted an invitation to visit Phillaur and address IPS officers attending a vertical interaction course. I got up at 3.30 A.M. to catch the train 'Shane Punjab' at 6 A.M. I was ready to leave at 5.30 A.M. There was a call from the Railway Protection Force SI Tyagi, informing me that my intended train was late by five and a half hours. In other words, the train leaving at 11.30 A.M. would take me to Ludhiana at 5 P.M. From there the road journey would take more than one hour. The net result would be my reaching there after the day's programme was over. I requested and got a seat on the Super fast Swaran Shatabdi, which left New Delhi at 7.20 A.M. and reached Ludhiana at 11.50 A.M. I made it to Phillaur at 12.15 A.M. and had my session on ethics in the Police till 1.30 P.M. My friend and former colleague A.A. Siddiqui was the Director of the academy in the rank of Additional Director General of Police. It was a stimulating session for me as well as the participants. As it was nearing lunch time, I could see hunger writ large on the face of the participants. I decided not to prolong the lecture. It is no use casting even pearls of wisdom, when the stomach demands to be satiated. Siddiqui was present both at my arrival and during the lunch. My throat gave up after tne lecture and I had to take the medicines advised by Dr. Mrs. Dhillon, who had earlier worked with me in the Central Reserve Police Force. I rested for one hour and caught up on the lost sleep. It gave some rest to my sore threat. There was just enough time to drop into my friend Mohan Adya's place in Ludhiana and pick up some sweaters. Ludhiana is the place for hosiery and every two years, I manage to get some good woollen stuff from there. The return Swaran Shtabadi train was in time and I could reach my house only after 11 P.M. Sleeping drugs, cough syrups and antibiotic capsules put me to sleep, though the throat behaved and croaked like a broken and torn-out drum.

Another encounter

I missed my morning walk, because of the heavy drugs the previous night. I could hardly talk. It appeared that I would have to miss my walk. The afternoon was spent in meeting people outside the house. I was present at the function of sale of the paintings of the artists for Orissa relief fund. The dashing hero of yesteryears, Vinod Khanna, now a BJP MP, had also come. He is one of my favourite stars along with Mithun Chakarvarty. He did the hat trick of winning the Gurdaspore seat twice in succession in the 1998 and 1999 elections. There was nothing pretentious about the man. He is as straight and as upright as one can be. He is the only film hero, who made a welcome comeback, after dabbling with Rajnish. Rajnish is one of the greatest modern practical thinkers, who convinces you of what he preaches. Without having set eyes on him, but through his audio-tapes, I find him to be of incisive mind and clear thinking. Vinod has left an indelible mark on the film industry. I liked his role tremendously in film Qurbani. I have suggested to the organiser, Editor, to have a jumbo sale of items of art so that a handsome amount could be raised for the Orissa cyclone victims. Vinod told me that he is now acting only in one serial on "Maharana Partap", the legendary warrior from Rajasthan, who fought against the Mughals all his life.

I was groggy at the time of getting up due to the excessive medication given for the bad throat. But half a dozen cups of tea, running into two litres, had washed off the sloth. My answering machine had stored all the telephone calls received in my absence. During my morning walk, I ran into Padmnabiah, my batch-mate. According to the newspaper reports, he was a sure shot candidate for the post of Governor. I could sense the underlying current in him of having missed something. He did not show it. On the contrary, he said that my name was also in the list of probable gubernatorial appointees. My feeling was that it was not correct information.

He said so, probably to lessen his disappointment. I have never met any political leader except when I go into some function or the other. I met the Prime Minister and the Home Minister to present my book to them. I do not have any regional or a caste constituency or a lobby. I doubt it very much, if the above information had any basis. When you expect something and it does not happen, it leads to frustrations and disappointments. Since I do not expect anything from anybody, I do not feel disappointed. It is not a good feeling, to learn about one's failure. Failure is never glorious, or charming. In the evening I met another near successful appointee to the post of governor, Krishanmoorthy, former Election Commissioner. Again the issue of appointment of the governors came up. He said that everybody might not praise my (Joginder Singh) working, but nobody can raise a little finger at me. I do what I feel to be right. I do not hesitate to express my views, on whatever is, against the interest of the common man. My routine keeps me sufficiently busy. It will be hypocritical of me to complain that time hangs on my hands. On the contrary, I have to budget my time between socialisation and work.

Vehicle explosion in Delhi

This morning I went for a condolence function to Punjabi Bagh area in New Delhi. Delhi roads are choked with cars, scooters, auto rickshaws, cycles, tempos and trucks. The average driving speed comes to less than 18 kilometres in the peak hours. I spent two hours in the car and half an hour at the function. Increasing prosperity means more luxury goods and more vehicles. It also means no parking place and the slowest possible speed, even if you have a car capable of cruising at a speed of 200 kms per hour. Delhi has officially registered 35 lakh vehicles and add another one lakh visiting vehicles. But there is no parking space. Like the population explosion, there is a vehicular explosion too. Nobody, nor any government agency, is serious about tackling this problem. The reason is that most very important or important persons live in New Delhi. They have the benefit of police escort vehicles, which somehow make way for them. What personally does not affect you, does not pinch you. The pendency of over one lakh traffic violation cases does not add to the confidence, that in some way, the fear of god and the law can be put into the habitual traffic offenders. The vicious circle goes on. The chaotic traffic conditions, lack of driving sense, no consideration towards others and lack of parking space, make driving or going anywhere in Delhi, a nightmare.

In the galaxy of VIP's (Monday, 22 November 1999)

It was not an unusual day, as I stuck to my routine of morning walk and a simple breakfast of milk and one chappati stuffed with potatoes. It made me feel heavy. My mother Lajwanti is not feeling well. Even when all right, she magnifies her disease. Now she actually is not well. I have heard her praying to God to end her life, because of various ailments. For lunch, I had two idlis, offered by the Jhas, in the India International Centre. This centre is a meeting, eating and living place. It is in the centre of the town and a convenient place to meet and chat. Its membership is at a premium, as a lot of intellectuals, and pseudo-intellectuals spend their time there. In the evening, I presided over a dinner banquet, of non-resident Indian's Institute. It was attended by the Minister of State, Omar Farooqh Abdulla, L.M. Singhvi, former distinguished High Commissioner of India in London and NRI's from the United Kingdom. Singhvi has a sort of record of having served in the same post for over six years. Now he adorns the Rajya Sabha as an elected member. The minister promised that he would put in his best to solve the problems facing NRI's.

Vote bank is the consideration

There really is no time during the day to work. All the visitors and telephone calls come during the day. I had my artificial teeth fitted today. Probably, I could not place them properly and had to take them out in the evening for eating Gachak. The visitors took my forenoon and afternoon. In any work or job being done by the government agencies, the lack of co-ordination and planning is amply clear. The plans do not follow a pattern or a logic. They are based more on the expedencies, the likes and dislikes of the people who matter. There are a number of speed breakers on the road leading to the colony I live in. The road dividers help in preventing crashes. But the parked vehicles on the main road reduce the size of the road, making a four lane road to a one lane road. As no parking place is available, the broad roads become parking places. Nobody in authority really knows how to tackle this problem in a cost-effective way without annoying people so that vote bank equilibrium, is not adversely affected.

Birth day celebrations (Wednesday, 24 November 1999)

I attended the Railway Protection Raising Day parade, on the invitation of HD Rao, the Chief of RPF. The parade timings were at the decent hour, of 10.30 A.M. It suited me, as it did not affect my morning walk. I avoid any and all programmes which affect my exercise regimen adversely. It was the usual parade, like the ones I have attended for the last twenty years. Each copies the good features from the other and one gets to see the same horse, dog, camel and motor cycles shows. But the unique feature of the RPF parade was a good standard put up by 90000 strong force, which does not have proper facilities. The Director General, which I also was briefly, does not enjoy any authority over his force, like the other Directors Generals. I make it a point, to attend all the functions of the Police Organisations I have headed. My entire forenoon was taken by the journey and parade timings. Attending functions like this gives an opportunity to meet the old colleagues of the force as well as other IPS officers. This way one gets to know how many persons are still alive. In the evening I attended the wedding reception of the son of my first publisher, Narendar Kumar, Har Anand Publishers. The former Chairman of the National Police Commission, (now late) Dharam Vira, was also there. When I discussed the need of police reforms, he expressed total unhappiness at the successive governments since 1977 for neglecting his report. Everybody has been talking about Police Reforms, but in practice, Dharam Vira said, nobody wants to give up the control of the police or stop its misuse. After attending the days commitments, I left for Jalalabad by Punjab Mail, which leaves Delhi at about 9 PM.

With familiar faces

Om, my man Friday, received me at Ferozpore at 6 A.M. He had left at 4 A.M. from Jalalabad. He had got the house cleaned before my arrival, so that I was not kept waiting, even for one minute. My uncle Harbhajan Singh came to see me to discuss college matters, and the land management. He along with Om, is managing my land and all other matters. Om is totally dedicated to my interests. It was he who got the Jalalabad house repaired by standing on the head of the workers. It takes time to settle down. But since this house is so comfortable and every modern appliance is available, I feel settled within the first hour. May be, it is the association that my late father lived here which makes it easy. May be, it is the effect of familiar faces and figures around, which makes everything exactly suiting my mood and needs. This is an important factor, which stands in relation to an individual vis-a-vis the place. My denture was not fitting. It was Dr. Tilak Raj's daughter, Anshu a dentist, who made me practise its proper placing. She gave a sensible advice, that denture must be removed in the night, kept in water and the denture space in the mouth cleaned, to avoid recurrence of any disease.

Some introspection

We have unfortunately developed a culture of being soft all the time. Appeasement is the prevailing formula being practised not only at the national level, but at every level. Today, there was a meeting of the local management committee of Giani Gurbux Singh DAV Centenary College. The poor results were the subject of discussion. One member, Khairati Lal Monga, Vice Chairman, expressed unhappiness over the poor results. Mr. Attar Singh Bedi, another Vice Chairman, complained about the high tuition fees charged by the staff, who spent more time on tuition and less on college work. Nobody had a good word to say for the dedication and devotion of the staff. There was a demand of giving pay scale on the same level as given by the Government of Punjab to aided colleges. The Principal, Balbir, a good man, appeared to be in mortal fear of the staff. The financial position indicated that all the money was being spent on the salaries. The Principal being scared wanted status quo, leaving no money for development. I had asked a financial expert, Amrik Singh, to look into the matter and advise. The committee agreed to give the pay scale recommended by the 5th pay commission, though it is not obligatory, as it is an unaided college. I did not agree to spend all the money collected from the fees on the salaries and insisted that at least 20 percent should be kept for development and maintenance. I made it clear that I was not game for appeasement. Those who could get better jobs were free to leave.

My morning walks continued in Jalalabad also. There are more than 5000 vehicles, including cars, scooters, trucks, auto-rickshaws in the town. Tractors and tempos block the bazar. I have been going for my walks to my land. There is a metalled portion of the private road, which is both free from congestion and pollution. I also have a word or two and exchange pleasantries with my farmers. I always have two or three people joining me for lunch. Today, my uncle Harbhajan Singh and my friend Madan Lal Aggarwal joined me, apart from Om Parkash. It was the usual chicken with tandoori rotis from the market. The tandoori rootis were so tasty that I overate. It was further aggravated with the eating of chicken in the company of my cousins Pappu and Tony, sons of Sardar Jagir Singh, in the evening, at the time of dinner. They are always hospitable and affectionate. They are doing well in business, due to unity and commitment. It is a story of success, victory and rags-to-riches story of the two brothers. Their father has been a god-fearing man and a close associate of my late father in establishing the DAV College in Jalalabad. They have set up the business of rice shelling and enjoy plenty of good will. I was uncomfortable in the night. My computer has some disc problem. The computer was on the whole night. But it could not fix its problem on its own, even though it is programmed to do.

Baba Farid's, Faridkot plays host

I had accepted a programme to address a seminar on eradicating corruption in Faridkot. I changed my routine slightly and limited my morning walk to 50 minutes. I left Jalalabad at 9.30 A.M. Om Parkash drove the esteem car with me and Pappu and Tonny as passengers. His driving speed touched 140 km. per hour. It is for the first time, I travelled like millions of others at such a speed. I had to tell him that we would rather reach safe and late, than not at all, or at the best with broken bones and numerous injuries. He has superb control on the vehicle and is a much better driver than I am. Mr. Chandan Mitra, the Editor of The Pioneer, had travelled from Delhi for this programme, which was organised, in the only good hotel of Faridkot, called Triumph Plaza. The hotel is owned by Sardar Harinder Singh, who had taken the initiative of organising the seminar. He is also the chief of a voluntary organisation called Faridkot Heritage. The entire gentry of the district was present. The function, speeches, discussion and questions-answers session went on till 3 P.M. We had our lunch only at 3.30 PM. After visiting two families at their insistence, we drove back to Jalalabad. The seminar on corruption was widely covered and aroused some curiosity and some interest. The results cannot be quantified, as the objective is to change the mental approach and make people conscious of their role in fighting a social evil. I made it plain that there is no magic wand, which can end corruption. People will have to work for it. I had over eaten in the last three days and was feeling uncomfortable. So I stayed on juice, curds, rice and biscuits. Chandan spoke with feelings and impressed the audience with his sincerity and a clear approach. He is a first rate journalist. It is a pleasure interacting with him. The people of Faridkot were spell bound by his presentation. The return journey from Faridkot to Jalalabad took only one hour. As always, I utilised the time in completing my daily self-prescribed quota of Granth Sahib reading. This way, I do not waste my time or lose my temper or poise on seeing unseemly sights enroute. Hoping that Chandan would join for dinner, a chicken preparation had been made. But Chandan could not join us. Fortunately, there were relations and friends who happily ate it up. I feel morally obliged not to waste any food and eat up the left overs, creating problems for myself. I cannot resist non-vegetarian, well prepared food. I know it will do more harm inside me, than in the dustbin. But I just cannot see the sight of something being wasted. I am happy to pass on sweets, which I get on the occasion of weddings or other functions. What is not in front of you does not tempt you. In my own selfish interest, I see to it that all tempting food stuff fattens others, and not me. I left

Jalalabad in the evening and had dinner arranged by my cousins along with the gentry of Ferozpore before boarding the train at 10 P.M. for Delhi. Om, who had received me, saw me off along with Tonny.

Horses make fortunes for punters

Arriving in Delhi at 5 A.M. upsets the sleeping pattern. My new driver Jagdish was there to receive me at the VIP parking. After reaching home, I just lounged in the bed for half an hour, before going for a walk at 8 A.M. in the green surrounding of Lodi Garden. I have accepted to be a judge in the Delhi Race Course Club. It is out of a sense of public duty. Today, the race was attended by the Lt. Governor of Delhi. The Lt. Governor Vijay Kapoor gave away the Governor's cup . A lot of money running into lakhs is bet on the races. It was followed by a lavish tea, consisting of pastry, pakoras, sweets, sandwiches, biscuits and a host of sundry items. In such programmes, the offering of tea with innumerable items is only a show to impress the guest, that no stone has been left unturned to extend to him the best of hospitality. Immediately, after the races were over, I drove to India International Centre, for a panel discussion on a management book written by my friend, Prof. N.K. Singh. It is a well written book, containing all that is best, has been thought and said on the management from the ancient to the modern times. But my regret is that the actual users, those in the government, due to various constraints, including appeasement and taking tough decisions will not use it. Hence the state of the nation will remain as it is and the private sector will thrive by taking a leaf out of the various management theories.

In the centre of Hyderabad

With one day's stay in Delhi, I left for Hyderabad in the evening to deliver the valedictory address of the course of officials dealing with anti-corruption measures. It was a warm and sunny day, with winter around the corner. So I spent a part of the day in Delhi sitting outside. I, as usual, had my nap of one hour plus in the afternoon. The flight arrived at Hyderabad at 10 P.M. It was a one hour drive from the airport to the National Police Academy. I had joined the National Police Academy in October, 1961 at Mt. Abu, for one year's training. I had passed out in October, 1962. I only once returned to Mt. Abu, as Inspector General of Police, in the Central Reserve Police, to deliver a lecture in 1989 when the National Police Academy had moved away from there. The place and building had been occupied by the Internal Security Academy of Central Reserve Police. Mt. Abu is mostly frequented by the people of Gujarat and Rajasthan. Since as probationers, we had to undergo tough training, it hardly left us any time to comment on the lack of avenues of fun, recreation and entertainment. The tough physical training and demanding compulsions of studying subjects like the forensic sciences, law and medical jurisprudence did not leave any time or energy for going out of the officers mess.

There was a proposal of shifting the National Police Academy from Mount Abu, right from the time it was set up. But shifting did not take place till well after 25 years of establishment to Hyderabad. Setting up any institution means of lot of economic benefits for the local people. The staff drawing salaries in a particular place would spend it there. In this way not only local industries, but even the shopkeepers, retail and the wholesalers would have ready-made customers. The shifting of the National Police Academy from Mount Abu, was opposed not only by the local peoples, but also the Government of Rajasthan. This is what democracy is about. Ultimately, as a sop to the people of Mount Abu, the Central Reserve Police Force was asked to take over the building vacated by the National Police Academy and start something there. That is how the Internal Police Academy of the Central Reserve

Police originated. Mount Abu is very inconvenient in reaching from anywhere in India. It is connected by one railway station, called Abu Road, 30 kilometres from Mount Abu. The air connection was not there. So no guest lecturer, unless he was willing to spare 3 to 4 days for one or two hours of lecture, would be willing to go there. The Central Reserve Police realised this and it too wanted to shift in 1989-90. The then Director General had laid the foundation stone of the Internal Security Academy at Bangalore. The Rajasthan Chief Minister again took up the matter, protesting against the shifting of the Academy so the Central Reserve Police Academy stays put in Mount Abu.

The National Police Academy in Hyderabad is located on 400 acres of land and has all the amenities.

Sojourn at ITBP House

Coincidentally, I stayed in National Police Academy in the ITBP Nivas; a guesthouse built up by ITBP, which I had headed for nearly 15 months from 31st January 1995 to 10th April 1996. I had also occupied 59, Lodi Road Bungalow earmarked for the Director General. The ITBP Nivas, in Hyderabad Police Academy, is a very comfortable, convenient and well furnished guesthouse of two bed rooms. Most police forces, including the central forces, have contributed to the development of the Academy, by putting up the guesthouses. I had a walk in the Academy. A new feature added is a photographic gallery, containing the photographs of all the officers who have been trained there. It also contains the photos of IPS officers who lost their life in national cause. Two officers of Bihar Cadre, who met me there referred to the photo gallery as the Rogues gallery. I commented, in all fairness that we have to exclude the martyrs. They agreed with me. The best library of the Police is in the National Police Academy. The National Police Academy is fully computerised. It has a modern auditorium and other latest facilities including an international size swimming pool.

The Director General, Shri Rajgopal, had gone for a Police Science Congress at Jammu. I interacted with the Inspector General, Mr. Prasad, Joint Director Mr. Naik, and Course Director Shri Mahinder Reddy. The course on anti-corruption was attended by 37 officers from the police, bank, public sector and insurance companies. The IPS Academy, for the first time, has thrown open its portals to the public sector for orientation and training for waging a fight against corruption. I did not want to stay a day longer than necessary. So in the evening, I flew back after calling on the Editor, News Time, which is an English version of the popular Telegu paper, Eenadu. My plan to call on my predecessor Director CBI, K. Vijayram Rao, came a cropper, as the driver instead of taking me to his office, took me to the Airport. I turned back to call on him, after checking in for the flight at 7 P.M. Vijay Ram Rao had won the State Assembly Elections in 1999. He is a Minister in the Chander Babu Naidu government in Andhra Pradesh. He was surprised that the National Police Academy driver did not know the location of the seat of the government. I told him that due to the heavy traffic, I would probably end up both missing seeing him as well as my flight. He very thoughtfully advised that I should catch the flight. It was a surprise that the flight was on time today also as it was yesterday. Probably the Indian Airlines is doing its best, to overcome the notoriety, of the chronic delay attached to it. The food served continues to be inadequate and unappetising. The increased prosperity of the country can be judged by the flight being full to the last seat both in economy and club class. I could reach home by 10 P.M. and sleep in my own bed. There is nothing like your home, when it comes to leading a satisfactory life, as your own home runs, as per your convenience, and one can lay hand on one's things in the flick of a second.

Friday group

As I was out of Delhi since the 24th of November 1999, my routine has been disturbed. I finished replying to the correspondence. Since I am still active in the sphere of writing, a number of people had been wanting to meet me. I gave everybody time to meet me at 5 P.M. Experience shows that people are hardly punctual. It suits me not to spread the meeting time, as I had to go for a Friday group meeting at India International Centre. This group has been started by my friend Prof. N.K. Singh, to sensitise the society. I had given a paper, on combating corruption and it was the subject matter of discussion. I had told the group that I had to leave for Lucknow in the night. So I spent only one hour, with the thinly attended group. Last month, when the group was set up, it was decided to meet on the first Friday of the month. It had about 20 people attending it. But today, the attendance was down to one third of the full group. It is nothing unusual. We start many projects with enthusiasm. But the zeal disappears faster than it should. That is the reason the issues do not get the required attention, both from the government and the private sector. The culture of acceptance of whatever is going on is the undoing of many worthwhile projects, proposals and aspirations. Most people lack the sustaining and staying power and hence we are where we are. My train left in time at 10 P.M. My AC first class coupe was quite comfortably heated in the cold weather. I just dozed off and got up after seven hours. Of course, the night sleep of everybody is interrupted once or twice, by the sheer pressure of relieving the bladder, and I am no exception to it.

Commissions and corruption

The Lucknow mail becomes a passenger train in the night. That is why a journey of six hours by Shatabdi train is covered by Lucknow mail in 9 to 10 hours. In a way, it is good, if you have a comfortable berth to rest in the night. Some trains in Europe deliberately run slow and reach their destination at 7 A.M. to give enough time to the travellers to rest adequately and have a full day for work. However, this is possible for a few trains only. Some trains like Punjab mail leave Delhi at 9 P.M and arrive at Ferozpore at 5 A.M. The Secretary of the organising committee of the Seminar on corruption and commissions Mr. Rizvi received me at the Railway Station, along with half a dozen enthusiastic young men. I was put up in Hotel Awadh Clark. This was the only three star hotel, which had come up in Lucknow in the 70s. Lucknow has only one better hotel in the Star Category, Hotel Taj, which was about 30 kilometres away from the venue of the Conference. The time given for starting the seminar on corruption and commissions was 10.30 A.M. I did not want to be the cause of delay and was due on time. To my surprise, I was among the first guests as well as the audience to arrive. The trouble with punctuality is that a punctual person may end up being a lone ranger. I feel uncomfortable if I am not in time. Neither do I want to keep anybody nor do I wish to wait for anybody. The organisers had to wait for one hour for the hall to be filled to some respectable capacity, and the programme started at 11.30 A.M.

I was bitter about corruption in the country. One good point of the seminar was that it acted as a catalyst for awakening people, and making them conscious. The Governor of Uttar Pradesh, who was to inaugurate the programme, sent his regret at the last minute. Another minister of UP Government did not come because of some death in his family. The danger in inviting VIP's is, they are likely to back out at the last minute sometimes with reason and sometimes without one. The lunch was at the place of Mr. Zaheer. In deference to the possible objection of some people, who are vegetarian, food was a purely vegetarian affair. I used the lunch interval to visit the office of The Pioneer, along with Shri Dipak Mukherji, Director and Uday Sinha, Executive Editor of The Pioneer. The Pioneer is really struggling and doing well. The staff is determined to make it a self-paying concern. I tried to motivate the staff to put in their best efforts, so that we can keep the wolf away. I chaired a session of the seminar in the afternoon, and my work was over at 5.00 P.M.

When I had done my day's work. I felt it would be superfluous to stay in Lucknow for one day more, just because the Hotel is good. A hotel is a hotel, and one cannot get the feeling of home there. By an average Indian standard of income, even the Three star hotel like Clark was prohibitively expensive. A cup of tea costs Rs 50. Washing of a vest and baniyan cost Rs 30 and Rs 40, which is the cost of a new baniyan. Everybody coming to serve you, either with a cup of tea, or for collecting laundry, or bringing a basket of fruit expects a tip, which sometimes turns to be more than the cost of the goods and service. I have never tried to pose as a millionaire. I will never pay Rs 5000 just to stay for 10 hours which was what the organisers were charged for my stay in the Hotel. I decided to leave for Delhi by Lucknow mail after having my dinner at Mr. Zaheer' place. I carry a cellular phone with an all India roaming facility and can contact my wife and she could contact me to know my latest programme. More than that, a cellular phone with contactability anywhere in the country is a confidence booster. Any help can be summoned, without the fear of the lines being down. The charges, for the local use of the cellular phone, the various facilities available would be Rs. 10 per minute. In any case the number of persons to be contacted is few. It is worth the charge.

Lucknow also has its share of road congestion and obstructions in the form of processions of marriage parties, hawkers and roadside sellers. For me and for that matter, for anybody who has any work, the city means the place of work and back to the place of stay. I had visited Lucknow earlier as a student in 1959 to participate in an Inter Collegiate Debating Contest. Later on, the next visit was in the year 1976 to advise the Government of UP, to start a Sports and Youth Programme. I was a state guest of the UP government at that time, where I had come from Bangalore, at their invitation. Later on, I stayed in Lucknow for seven days, as Inspector General of the Central Reserve Police Force in the year 1990 during the Ayodhya problem. I had seen all the monuments and the tourist spots in Lucknow. There was really no need for a repeat visit in 1999. The previous visit to this was in the year 1997 as Director-CBI, to review the case pertaining to an ayurvedic scam of Uttar Pradesh government. The case was monitored by Allahabad High Court and I wanted to satisfy myself, that CBI had left no stone unturned to give its best. The organisers must have felt relief, at my decision to leave Lucknow the same day after my participation in the discussion. I had nobody else to meet except my retired batch mates in the Police, who were not available. It is strange that except the official contacts, an officer has hardly any friends or acquaintances, beyond the officials he comes in contact with. The train journey from Lucknow to Delhi was spent in sleeping most of the time. Two nights were spent in the train and the daytime was utilized in Lucknow.

Tea Addict

The Lucknow mail was late by one hour in arrival at Delhi. The only thing missed by me was my morning tea. I made it up by getting tea from Ghaziabad railway station. Tea for me is a toner as it is for most other people. I really do not feel fully awake unless I have consumed at least 1/2 litre of tea. I have seen people, who do not take tea. I used to be one of them before I joined the service. I cannot recall when I slipped into the habit of taking tea but it is there for the last three decades. Some people may not approve of my taking tea, as it necessitates frequent visit to the bathroom. But it is better than liquor, which I have never consumed, touched and tasted so far. Sunday and Monday were spent in catching up with the old readings.

I had agreed to inaugurate the Student Union of Atmaram Sanathan Dharam College, Dhaula Khuan, New Delhi. After seeing the audience, I felt that there was no point in talking philosophy or matters of corruption or good governance. I felt that I should talk something which could touch their hearts. I reminisced my college days and told them that they are living in better times than we had. My speech was an instant hit because I mixed Punjabi, Hindi and English language. I realise that all undergraduates cannot understand English.

In the evening, I was invited by Star News to discuss the murder of a student by her lover and a former friend. While holding brief for nobody, I made it clear that the law as it stands gives one the benefit of the doubt. The result is that thieves, robbers, murderers and rapists get away. Scot-free I pleaded that there is a great need to change the laws. It was live news. The Information and Broadcasting Minister Mr. Arun Jaitley and Jaipal Reddy, former Information Minister were also present but for the different News segment. Everybody was trying to defend his political turf. Television is a great medium by which you can reach millions of people and present them your side of the issue. It is strange that Star News has no takers in the North and Zee has no takers in the South. Delhi of course has people who see both the channels.

Body maintenance is like car maintenance

My schedule was upset, as I had to meet a number of visitors. There was one interview with Star TV at 12.30 PM and another live recording at 6:15 PM and a visit to Zee studio at Noida for another TV programme. The matter did not end there as the last engagement was to attend the 25th anniversary dinner of Shri Gurmeet Singh at Babar lane near Bengali market. The two channels have their studios in different directions. The journey takes an hour and a half in coming and going and one has to wait for the live interview at the News channel. There was a series of blank calls in the telephone answering machine. The use of fax cum answering machine has enabled me to filter the calls, and spend my time fruitfully. If I am not careful I can hardly find time for myself. In between, I had to visit Indraprastha Apollo Hospital for the check up of my wife Surinder, as the doctor had suggested a cardiological check up, for missing some heart beats. They took her ECG, echo, and cardiogram and put her on holter. I also dropped in the room of Takkar, Managing Director, Apollo, who was my batchmate in the service. After retirement, he has taken up this job. He also had undergone the cataract operation of both eyes. The fact is that human body after sixty years needs repair and maintenance, more often than a young man's body.

Reliving the heart surgery

Time has to be guarded zealously. It has a tendency to leak, and at the end of the day, one can hardly explain to one self, as to what one did, during the course of the day. My routine is so long, of taking tea, reading newspapers, going for a walk, meeting and chatting during the walk, taking a bath, prayers, that it takes me four hours to get ready. In between, if there is any phone call, it has a multiplier effect, as one has either to send a letter or make other phone calls. In the cold winter, which is now, there is a temptation to laze in the sun. I am trying an experiment of eating only when really hungry. Most of the time, we go on eating at the fixed time, whether we are hungry or not. Food times are fixed, after taking into consideration, our working schedule, sleeping or waking habits. They have nothing to do with the body requirements or needs. After a number of years, I have reached the conclusion that it is better to be full, rather than hungry. Of course, care has to be taken, not to be full with junk, fatty or too fried or other type of unhealthy food. I try to vary my breakfast, sometimes with fruits, some other time with corn flakes. At the end, I must have something saltish. I saw the video cassette, given to me by Dr. Virdi, to show what goes on in a heart bypass surgery. It was an eye opener for me to know what I had gone through. My chest was cut with an electric saw, heart arteries repaired with the veins and arteries drawn from the body and chest closed with steel staples. Of course, now after a long period after 17th April, 99, the only reminder of it is the scar I carry. Hats off to the doctor for cutting open my body, with a view to give me a better quality life. I again visited Apollo hospital to meet Dr. Vipul Roy for his opinion on the various reports about Surinder's check up. He suggested another check up before deciding, whether my wife needs a pace maker, or not. I also visited Connaught Place for window shopping. It is for generally seeing what latest electronic items are available in the market. The day starts shortening after 21st June and the shortest day is 21st December. Either it is too cold or too hot and one is at a constant fight with the weather. I have to keep on adjusting my programmes to the length of the day.

It is Modi Nagar, not Moti Nagar

My routine of visiting the Gurudwara of the eighth child Guru, Guru Harikrishan every Sunday, when I am in Delhi remains unchanged. I go quietly and come back at a time when the day's programme is over or most of the devotees have visited and gone away. I am not one of those who like to go early in the morning to the place of worship. It is because I take my own time of finishing my routine and, as an afterthought, perhaps, it is not fair to disturb the Gods also, by intruding on them very early. God's existence must at times also be annoying to himself, that of being worshipped and deified and all the time confronted by the demands of worshippers for goodies of life. I am saying this, because of the limited human intelligence, which cannot see God or Gods as other than glorified and magnified human beings. I had accepted an engagement, supposedly at Moti nagar which is in Delhi. But it turned out to be Modi nagar, which is 87 kilometres away from Delhi. I wanted to back out, but left it to the divine forces to guide. Most of my life's decisions have been made by the higher power which has guided me, at all steps in my life. I mean that God does not come and drive my vehicle, or sits by my side and tells me to do or not to do something. He speaks to me, through the advice, or action of fellow human beings, and I instinctively know that a particular course of action is the best for me. The journey took over one and half hours. I felt it was a bonus. I used the time in reading. On Sundays, there is a lot to read, in the nine newspapers which I get everyday. Quite often, it is a repetition of the same stories. Modi nagar is a small town. It has 17 thousand cable connections, indicating that every house has a TV and a cable connection. The function in the Gurudwara, was to pay respect to the 9th Sikh Guru Tegbahadur, on his martyrdom day. Guru Tegbahadur, along with his followers, was executed, on his refusal to convert to Islam.

The Sikhs, following his tradition, do not do any breast beating. They practise and adhere to their faith, which believes in universal brotherhood. Later, I attended the programme of a Human Rights Organisation and inaugurated its office in Modi nagar. I am its National President while the State President is a well-off gentleman, Sh. Santosh Aggarwal. I emphasised that for work we have to look to ourselves, and not point lapses elsewhere. I suggested that a few items be permitted to be taken up, for effective implementation. It could be minimum wages for labourers, keeping a tab on non-financial banking companies or chipping in our efforts to save our homes from garbage being strewn around. Our need is to have pressure groups, which should have concern for our cities and show initiatives in dealing with the problems as they arise. There are no easy solutions and no easy answers to the problems facing the country.

Computer on strike

Today, (Monday, 13 December 1999), my computer expressed its annoyance, by not opening and preserving what I had written. It showed some visual basics, which are of no use to me. Even the computer doctor could hardly do anything about it, in spite of his spending four hours on cajoling it. I had a heavy schedule of meeting people. It hardly left anytime for serious working. I feel upset when I cannot work for at least two hours on the computer. I missed the marriage of a colleague's daughter, because my P.A. did not make proper entries. I was also at fault, in leaving the engagement diary to him. He admitted his mistake. But this did not help, as an important function has been missed. It is a lesson often repeated, that one should not depend on others. Cross check and check again and again, it is necessary.

Life and death co-exist

I had missed sleep in the night. Half a tablet of Zopicon, my sleeping pill, helped to catch on it. I take a sleeping tablet once in a while. My sleep was disturbed last night by my mother who keeps sleeping during the day, who complained that she was not getting sleep. She had hers, but I could get mine only after taking a tablet. I tried finishing reading the newspapers in the bright sun. The bright sun in the cold winter is an aphrodisiac and I indulge myself in the warm sun. In the afternoon, I attended a condolence meeting, on the death of a business acquaintance, Sunder Vachani, whom I had known for over thirty years. Vachani was heading the Western Group, which had seen better times. He never fully recovered from his heart bypass surgery. My visit for his condolence meeting was to convey to his family that I held the senior Vachani in great personal esteem. The top gentry of Delhi including the Lt. Governor of Delhi, Municipal Commissioner and other officers were present. The real loss is however felt by the members of the family alone. Others go only to mark attendance. I had not met him for two years, as like true businessmen, he had written off all his retired acquaintances. He had neither seen me nor invited me to any of his programmes which was the opposite extreme of his past behaviour.

I, on principle, neither ring up nor meet any serving officer, unless he happens to be a personal friend. Once in while I ring up, when I have to speak to somebody to confirm some fact for my articles. I was on the Internet of a Dot Com from 6.45 P.M. to 7.45 P.M and answered questions on my life and Priyadarshini Matto murder case. It is the murder of a young lady allegedly by a police officer's son. The case was acquitted, as the Judge gave the benefit of the doubt to the accused. The result is that the CBI has become the accused, and is being tried by the media. The retired life has its own charm. One might retire from government service, but not from life, as long as there is energy left in the body.

The big fight

I had to skip my full morning walk to keep the appointment for the recording of a programme for Star News, called The big fight, to be telecast on 18th of December. There was a direct attack on the CBI from the editor-in-chief of the Indian Express, Shekhar Gupta, who has been in the vanguard of attacking the credibility of the government institutions. Shekhar said that the CBI was feeding the media with wrong information. I put the matters in the proper perspective by saying that the CBI had produced before the Courts whatever evidence it had collected. There was no reason for it to help anybody, as it did not have the culture of helping. Priya Ranjan Das Munshi, a Congress M.P. and Chief Whip, openly admitted about the misuse of the organisation by the politicians. I said that the order of the Supreme Court dated 17th December, 1997, wherein the CBI has been placed under the supervision of the Central Vigilance Commission, should be given a trial. It took more than three hours to complete this engagement. It was followed by an interview to the correspondent of the Vir Arjun, a Hindi and an Urdu paper. The afternoon was taken by another recording of a TV programme for the National Channel of the Doordarshan. Mr. Vijay Goel, M.P. on the panel for the discussion on the TV, invited me for lunch to the Taj Man Singh hotel where the programme was recorded. What looks glamorous on TV, has a lot of hard work and sweat, behind it. The recording of a two minutes bite can take even two hours or more, depending upon the location of the recording studio, make up and the availability of the time slot, even when present in recording studio. One has to be careful of what one says on the television, because there is no retraction and no denying of what the camera catches. In Delhi, most studios are located in Noida. One has to plan at least for 45 minutes, travelling time, either way, plus whatever time may be spent, in the actual recording. More than one interview, on one day can make one stale. But at the same time, I consider it as a part of my duties as a citizen, to enlighten the countrymen on the issues facing the nation.

Bofors, on the scene again

The Bofor papers were received by the Indian Embassy in Berne, on Friday, 17 December 1999. I gave two TV interviews, one on Doordarhsan about the likely outcome of the Bofors case. They were to telecast today. Today again,

Asianet TV and Doordarshan had a recording of the Bofors case. Obviously public interest in this famous case, which led to the defeat of the Congress party in 1989, is running high. It is the first case, which cast a shadow on the proclamations of an elected government about its honest dealing with a foreign arms supplier. My idea is to keep the interest of the public, in the corruption, in high places alive. Unfortunately people have become cynical and have accepted corruption as a way of life. They have come to believe that nothing ever moves, without being moved with the money power. My efforts will be to use this case as a handle, so that a movement against malpractices could be started.

All the newspapers prominently carried my press and TV interview about Quottrochi's (an Italian, who was close to the then late Prime Minister, Rajiv Gandhi and his family) efforts to explore the possibility of making a complete and full confession in the Bofors case. He had received a kick-back of 7.34 million dollars from the manufacturer of the Bofors gun, for having secured them a contract of over Rs. 1400 crores from the Government of India. I kept on answering a number of phone calls, and gave a press interview to a private channel on the same. The story was about somebody approaching me and telling me that he wanted to make a full and true confession and come to India. This had been going on for a long time and I realised that it was time that it was shared with the country. It was a sensitive matter and I did not want to keep it to myself. The gentleman, Quottrochi's friend, used to meet me regularly in Lodi Garden. I had told him that in the event of his co-operating and making a true confession of his involvement, the Court might consider showing him some clemency.

In the evening, I was the Chief Guest at a programme called Freedom Movement to rid the country of the myriad problems and malpractices. A good thing, which is happening now, is the interest of the intellectuals and general public in the various problems, facing the country. Only from discussions, the solutions can emerge. The meeting went on for four hours. Everybody wanted to speak and advise others. Speaking was thought to be a substitute for action. I, in my address, suggested that each one of the persons present is to be permitted to take up the public or personal issues, in writing, at least once a month. This is the only way in which we can improve the country. In the night there was a contributory dinner, hosted by the IPS association, for the serving and retired IPS officers. This annual dinner is held generally to coincide with the annual conference of State Police Chiefs. This is an opportunity to meet old colleagues whom one might not have met for years together. Otherwise, food is the least interesting part of such programmes. With the passage of time, the number of acquaintances and friends in the service is declining considerably. Some colleagues, apart from finishing their tenure with the government, have already finished their tenure on the earth. Every day brings each one of us closer to death, though none knows the precise moment.

Home food best food

Overeating at the last night's dinner upset my stomach. I had to eat 'Churan', to overcome the stomach pain. In truth, dinner hardly suits me. I cannot resist the temptation of good food. I indulge myself. I visited a farmhouse in Mehrauli area to attend a fellow retired batchmate, Yash Kapur's daughter's marriage. In some weddings, I have seen the bride to exceed 100 kgs. I admire the young man taking on such well-built women, with whom the honey moon will be more of a wrestling bout than anything else. May be this is the result of either too much prosperity or eating too rich oily food or may be some hormonal imbalance. As usual, I had a number of people coming and greeting me. They had either read my articles, or seen me on the Television. I used to visit such functions, primarily to meet old friends and acquaintances. Otherwise, in huge crowds, one is totally lost. I did not touch food and straightaway went for the dessert, which was Gajjar Halwa with ice cream. It gave an impression to the host that I had finished my lunch.

Normally the food served by the hoteliers and caterers is full of spices and a generous dose of cooking medium, which is normally the cheapest variety of cooking oil. It is bound to ruin your digestion, if you take such rich food everyday. There are no laws and norms, which insist that only fresh vegetables or food be served. Even if there were such laws, there is no enforcing agency and nobody would take them seriously. It is a common sight to see over-fried and stale food being recycled. Even some five star hotels have been guilty of serving substandard food. After eating fish in a five star hotel in 1982, I did not touch seafood for the next ten years. When all is said and done, the best food is the one cooked at your home and eaten without too much ceremony.

It took two hours of travel by car and one hour at the marriage function. This is the usual time taken in Delhi as the average driving speed including the halts and traffic jams can vary from 8 km an hour to 20 km per hour, depending upon the area, and the timing of the day or night. Missing the lunch did me a lot of good. With a light stomach or not an over-full one, I slept for over one hour during the day.

Preparation is the key

It was again a day where I had to give two TV interviews, one for DD1 (National Channel) and the second for Doordarshan News. With over 30 channels competing, any small news is blown up. Occasionally, the questions asked in the interviews are the ones that lead to the poor exposure of the interviewer. Some of the anchor persons like Mukesh and Ajit who interviewed me today, are simply brilliant. They had done their homework. They could bring out the best out of the person being interviewed or portray him as an ignorant fool. Preparation is the only answer.

When one has to go to the Studio for recording, more time is taken in commuting than in actual recording. I use such time as something gained, either in reading newspapers or in finishing some pending work or making telephone calls. There is an advantage while travelling that you cannot be disturbed unless you want to be. The cellular phone maintains the connectivity but I am very selective in giving this number. Not more than half a dozen people know this number. It is not that I do not wish to talk, or avoid people, but it is because cellular phone calls are expensive. One has to pay for receiving calls. A one-minute call costs Rs 8 and you end up paying Rs 6 per minute, when receiving the call. Thanks to Delhi High Court orders, the call charges have been reduced to less than half. I do return all the phone calls, but at the time which suits me. It is for each one of us to maximise, what we get of the 24 hours at every disposal. I also adopt another trick when people want to meet me. I give all of them the same time, being sure, that some will come, few minutes earlier and some will turn up a few minutes late. Some people do not even turn up. In fact, I ask people to tell me what they want on the telephone itself. I try to dispose them of at that time itself.

Sixty plus and still incorrigible

A friend who came to see me was all praise for the rough and ready justice being disbursed by a local Sub-Divisional Officer, belonging to an All India Service. The official during his checking found a number of people driving their vehicles without the driving license or other documents. Like a teacher punishing the children for mischief, he would ask the defaulters to slap themselves for violating the laws and repeat to themselves 200 times, that they would not commit such a mistake again. It had better effect than any fine or other sentence could ever have. It was a cold day. I like to enjoy the sunshine, rather than overclothe myself in heavy woollens. Entirely opposite to me, Surinder clothes herself very well. I call my wife a moving heater. She righlty goes on advising me to protect myself against the extremely cold weather. But perhaps, there is a streak of incorrigibility in me. I say Yes to everything she tells me, and do exactly as I please. She says that in this respect, I am exactly like my father, who listened to everybody and his wife, but did precisely what he felt like doing. I have to safeguard myself against unexpected visitors. I had a very funny visitor, who before delivering some bank papers to me in my own house, wanted me to establish my identity. I just threw him out and fired him for entering the house without knowing whom he was meeting. It is strange that sometimes people want you to establish your own identity in your own work place or house. How does one do it? They too have a point. It is their responsibility to deliver the papers to the right person. In the night, I left for my periodic visit to Jalalabad by Punjab Mail, by which I must have travelled thousands of times. The only difference is that instead of travelling by the lowest class I travel by the highest, for no other reason that, with age, it is not always possible to take the rough-and-tumble, pushes and pulls. I make it a point, to carry my packed dinner from the house, so that I have a feeling of having a picnic in the train on my own.

Goodness, still prevalent

I reached Jalalabad this morning (22 December 1999) from Delhi by the overnight train from Ferozpore. Om Prakash, my Man Friday received me at Ferozpore railway station at 5.30 A.M. a rather, unearthly hour for me to be up. I spent the day in meeting old friends relations and sleeping. My neighbour and good friend Dr.Tilak Raj Kumar, along with his wife, Susheila, was the first to drop in and enquire whether I needed anything to get the house going. He and his wife are very helpful. His presence saved the life of my father, when he had his first heart attack in 1982. It was at his insistance that he was rushed to the emergency in the Francis Newton Hospital in Ferozpore. The second time, he could not be saved and breathed his last in the hospital on 23rd January, 1996. Dr. Tilak Raj has educated his children well. His one son Ajay Singh, and daughter Anshu are both qualified doctors. Ajay has married a doctor. Though Dr. Tilak Raj does not hold any MBBS degree, but GAMS, he is better and far more competent than many MBBS doctors. He has the knack of making his patients comfortable and quickly and correctly diagnosing their disease. He is honest enough to advise, when any specialised treatment is required. He is the most accessible doctor, having his residence on the top of the clinic. In the days, when the profession of medicine has been totally commercialised, he has never refused to treat a patient, who could not afford to pay.

Another pilgrimage, another condolence

Yesterday was spent in about seven hours of travelling to Hanumangarh, via Mukatsar, Malout and visiting a restaurant called Silver Oak en route. I had thought that going to Hanumangarh, via Mukatsar, would be a shorter route. It will also give me an opportunity to pay homage at the Gurudwara Mukatsar. Mukatsar is associated with Sikh history in a big way. Forty Sikhs, being tired of hunger and deprivation, had written a disclaimer and given to the Guru Gobind Singh. They had renounced their being his disciples, and had returned to their home in Khidrana village, now called Mukatsar. They were put to shame by their women folk for their cowardly conduct. The Sikhs realised their folly and fought valiantly with the Mughal forces. They lost their lives. Guru Gobind Singh was so touched by their devotion that he asked a sole surviving Sikh, his last wish. The Sikh told the Guru to tear off the "Bedawa" or disclaimer and take them back to his fold. The Guru tore off the piece of paper, personally cremated all forty of them, after saying prayers to the Almighty. This is the only instance, in Sikh history, of the 10th Guru saying a prayer, for somebody. I always get rejuvenated, when I visit any holy place associated with Sikh religion. Everybody has a personal and special relationship with God or Guru. My wish was once again to salute the "Father of the Khalsa". The main purpose was to visit the Gurudwara. I had agreed to combine the visit to Mukatsar, with addressing the members and the gentry of Mukatsar, at the instance of my friend Joginder Chabra. My namesake Joginder has been a good host. Later on, another friend and my neighbour Dr.Tilak Raj pointed out that this would mean spending an extra one-hour on the journey. So I decided that I would go straight and not take the circuitous route. Joginder had arranged the function in less than four hours notice. I could not let down a friend as my Man Friday, Om Prakash, had already tied down the details. I reached Mukatsar as if commanded by the Guru and having committed myself to paying homage to him, there was no way I could not go there. It was a divine call, to which no man has the authority to say "No". God creates conditions and circumstances, where one is compelled to follow a particular course of action. Some may call it a rational decision, or the creation of circumstances. But I look upon such incidents as the 'call of the divine'. As usual, Om Parkash had driven Pappu's Esteem with perfect control. Pappu, Inderjit Singh, my cousin, had also agreed to give me company during this one trip. It enabled us to discuss many matters pertaining to the College and Giani Gurbux Singh Trust, headed by me. The road on this 155 kilometre stretch was good in parts. Mostly, it was full of potholes, speed breakers, unpredictable children, women, and buffaloes who would suddenly appear on the road. Even in the best car, the average speed, with all these imponderables coming in the way will be 40 kms. per hour. On the way, we stopped at a tourist spot of Punjab government called Silver Oaks, a few kilometres from the Badal village, of the present Chief Minister of Punjab, Parkash Singh. Probably the visitors coming to see the Chief Minister, would find this good eating place handy. But good food, clean air and canal side location, do not compensate for extremely stinking toilets, which visitors, especially the ladies are compelled to use, in the absence of any covered facilities. That way Harayana tourism fares better. My TV appearances had made me a familiar figure. Many persons remarked in Hanumangarh that I was exactly as I look on the TV. Only politeness prevented me from retorting that I am myself, whether on or off TV. Lunch at the place of a landlord, Mr. Gill, gave me an opportunity to answer a number of queries from the press people. The press and the people wanted to know as to how soon corruption will end in the country. My reply was that it will end the day when one decides not to bribe, whatever be the sacrifices and difficulties. I visited my cousin, brother Babu Ram, to condole the death of his wife. Babu Ram is one of my closest living relations. His mother was the only real sister of my late father. Since my father is no more, I have to discharge some family responsibilities. The priest was taking an inordinately long time in completing the prayer to the bird "Guarrd" to probably take the soul of Sheila, Babu Ram's wife carefully. I could not understand much of what he was saying. Even if I had understood, I would not have cared much. This bird is the nearest to the aeroplane, and is probably the carrier of souls. I made suitable commiseration and left after a bout of tea. One is not expected to stay for more than a decent interval, so that the aggrieved can receive condolences from others too. As everybody shows love by offering something to eat, it leads to overeating and discomfort. A bumpy journey had sufficiently churned and turned the stomach upside down, levelling everything eaten. The taste of the food is only till the taste buds. In stomach, every morsel of food has to be in the shape the stomach can treat to get the best out of it.

Of business and keeping gods happy

I decided to visit the DAV College in Jalalabad, of which I am the Chairman. I informed the Principal as I did not want to be sorely disappointed with its poor functioning. I along with him visited the examination halls and saw three hundred boys and girls taking their test. My handwriting is illegible. Quite often, I myself cannot decipher what I have written. But I was left miles behind by the handwriting of over 98 percent students. There were only two students, who had a reasonably good handwriting. I also noticed the teachers gossiping in the sunshine. I had to tick off the Principal and tell him to ensure that instead of wasting time, the teachers should prepare themselves for the lectures. There were a number of complaints of poor discipline. It was reported that the teachers were spending more time in giving tuitions than in the classes. This fact was confirmed by Sardar Zora Singh Mann, M.P. of the district in a function at Ferozpore, where I was the Chief Guest, for the launch, of a daily evening newspaper. Probably the same story might be going on elsewhere. Dedicated and inspiring teachers are difficult to find. One of the speakers warned the newspaper about indulging in blackmailing for financial gains. It is not uncommon to see small papers extorting money from the corrupt and dishonest by threatening to expose their doings. I knew of a late gentleman, who would give some details of the scandalous conduct of an official of the Department of Food and Civil Supplies or other Department in one issue. The paper would announce that it would give full details in the next issue. In between the two, he would negotiate for an amount depending upon the bribes earned. He would insist on 50 per cent of the ill-gotten money and ultimately slightly lower his demands. The next issue then would forget about the exposure. Every year, he would make two to five lakhs in this way. Afterwards, on the insistence of the organisers, I joined for lunch, but I did not eat anything. I called on the Commissioner of Ferozpore Division, J.C. Sandhu and had a simple plain cup of tea, before leaving for Amritsar. Mr. Sandhu appeared to be a competent officer, who had also studied, in my Alma Mater, Government College, Ludhiana. Manmohan Singh Kamra had fixed the appointment. I normally do not like to trouble government officials. My reasoning is that everybody has his own schedule and I have no favour to seek for anybody. Most government servants might get the wrong impression that I was seeking time to see them for some selfish reasons. It is not the fault of any individual government official. It is a kind of expectation culture, inculcated in the government servants, that anybody coming to see you is a sucker.

On the way to Amritsar, I stopped at Taran Taran to visit the Gurudwara of Guru Arjun Dev. I make it point to pay homage at all religious places, not only of Sikh Gurus, but also of other religions, when I get a chance. It is a kind of mental satisfaction, which is inexplicable. Another place, where there is a kind of mental calm is in Calcutta: Belur Math associated with Paramhans Ramkrishan and Swami Vivekanand. I have discovered Sikhism through English language, as I have just managed to learn reading the Granth Sahib, the holy book of the Sikhs in Gurumukhi script. Arriving in Amritsar in the night, Om drove me straight to Guru Nanak Dev University Guest House, which is located in the University. On the 26th December 1999, I combined my morning walk, with exploring the University. It is located on a five hundred acres area and was set up in 1969, to commemorate the five hundredth birthday of the first Sikh Guru, Guru Nanak. I feel uncomfortable, if I miss my morning walk. The morning walk gives me a feeling of having done my duty in keeping myself fit. It alone is not sufficient, unless it is combined with a balanced diet. I was the Chief Guest at a function of the Swadeshi Jagran Manch, an organisation dedicated to the protection of the domestic industry. The Vice Chancellor of Guru Nanak Dev University, Dr. Harbhajan Singh Soch, while welcoming me as the Chairman of the reception committee, described the CBI as synonymous with me, for my fight against corruption.

I urged the participants to have a two-pronged strategy of making the quality of the Indian goods immeasurably superior, along with protecting our own industry. Mr. K.S. Sudershan, number three man in the RSS hierarchy at that time and now number one and, the Mayor of Amritsar, Subhash Arora along with a number of important dignitaries from all over India appreciated my stand. I purchased a ready made suit, fitting to my measurements, at an incredibly low price of Rs. 1600 as against Rs.2000, which is the cost of stitching a new suit in Delhi. I make it a point to visit the Golden temple whenever I am in Amritsar. The Golden temple is located in a water tank and a marbled path leads to it. The third Guru, Guru Ram Dass, constructed it. I always do a perambulation of the parameter of the holy shrine before entering it. There was a huge rush of humanity, wanting to enter the sanctum sanctorum. There was no chance, of my gaining entry into it, without either help of the office bearer of the SGPC or the local police. I had to remain satisfied by praying from a distance and putting my donations in the nearest receptacle. It was for the first time in my life that I could not enter the sanctum sanctorum. But in the past, I always had somebody receiving me and taking me around. This time, I was on my own. I am sure, God will forgive and will accept my homage from a distance of 100 yards. Obviously, some kind of influence is required even for a quick darshan, especially if you are hard pressed for time. It is true in all popular religious places, including Tirupati. Some places charge special rates for having a look at the presiding deity. Fortunately, Sikhs do not have any rates for entry or special darshans. It is not obligatory for anybody to give any fixed donation. It all depends upon the dedication and devotion of the Sikhs. I was tired at the end of the day and retired early for another day of conference of the Indian Economic Association, which was inaugurated by Dr. Manmohan Singh, Former Finance Minister of India, with the Governor of Punjab, JFR Jacob as the chief guest. Having not been a student of economics, and the modern economics being more of mathematics than economics, I frankly confessed that we should neither be socialisim- or communism- inclined, but should be inclined to Indianism. I urged the economists, including Dr. Manmohan to ensure, that every scheme for which any money is sanctioned, should have, a built-in system of checks to ensure that the money sanctioned has been well used. Lunch with the Governor and Dr. Manmohan was a restricted affair, confined to a select group of invitees. Governor Jacob being a former Commander in the Indian Army is not only hardworking, but has definitely very constructive and useful views in tackling hijacking. Of course, constitutionally, he can only implement his ideas in the Union Territory of Chandigarh of which he is the administrator. But I am confident that Punjab Government will not say no to his suggestion, for being ready to handle any hijacking. He has no interest except the good of the country and the nation.

There is a need for trained commandos

An Indian flight hijacked from Kathmandu landed in Amritsar. The flight was taken to Pakistan and finally to Kandhar by terrorists. Stationed in Amritsar, who can tackle any hijacking. This is the third hijacking landing, so far as Amritsar is concerned. Punjab will always have some problem or the other because of the turbulent nature of the people. Not only Punjab, but all the states having their border with Pakistan like Rajasthan, Gujarat and Kashmir should have their own commandos instead of depending on the central forces. Mr Jacob told me that when he took over as Governor of Goa, hardly anybody was coming to the office. He had to change the culture to one of work culture. Even in Chandigarh, where he is also the administrator apart from being the Governor of Punjab, he attends the office regularly. He has not lost his zeal and enthusiasm, while still remaining within the confines of the constitution.

I left for Ludhiana at about 3 o'clock. My wife Surinder had gone to Beas for some Radhaswami programme. I thought I would see her for a few minutes on my way. I earmarked half an hour for the visit, but it all went waste. Radhaswamis have also copied the government culture with ignorant people at the gates. Nobody could guide me to the exact location of the Hostel number 4, where she was staying. I had to answer umpteen questions for purpose of my visit. I felt it would be a waste of time to make more efforts to enter the fortress. Probably they are right because Radhaswamis were also under tremendous threat during the days of terrorism. In any case it was not correct for me to go anywhere without prior intimation. It saves lots of time and hassle. This is what I apply to myself, and also to others whom I meet. I had violated my own principle, and, in the bargain, realised that I should never try to take others by surprise, because you may be surprised yourself.

I straightaway proceeded to Jalandhar from Beas and from Beas to Ludhiana. I had a brief stop-over at the house of my friend Jatinder Mohan Sahdev for a cup of tea. Jatinder Mohan is an enterprising businessman who has become a multi-millionaire many times over, through his small tools manufacturing business. I have never purchased a screwdriver or hammer, because he keeps gifting me whatever I might need for small household jobs. Not only me, but my servants also, who have stolen many such items, must be grateful to him. Many a time the repairman asks for the tools given to me by Jatinder Mohan Sahdev and simply takes them away. Otherwise I could not have lost at least a dozen sets of screwdrivers or hammers, carpentering tools and gardening tools. I have told Jatinder Mohan that he has earned the goodwill of God by supplying tools to many thieves. It was getting foggy so I decided to leave Jalandhar earlier for Ludhiana. At Ludhiana, I was told to come to Hotel Grewal by my host, Kulbir Singh from Delhi, for a programme on 28th December. I booked a room. I felt that at the worst for my stay on my own, I would pay Rs 1500 for the night. It is a very comfortable two or three Star Hotel with very good food. I had Chinese dinner along with my relative Harbans Singh and dozed off. When I got up at midnight, I could not find the switch to switch off a number of lights in the room. The hotel had a central room-light switching off mechanism. The moment you took out the key of your room from the key slot, all the lights went out. This is a good devise for energy conversation, which is still to be copied in many homes and offices. I had to send for the room waiter to show me the electric switches. The moral is that, when you go to a hotel for stay, make sure that you know all the control switches, instead of realising it in the midnight. Ludhiana is one of the richest towns of Punjab. I had studied for six years in the Government College, Ludhiana. I spent all the six years in the hostel, where I was the assistant prefect and prefect or the student hostel head. The only privilege for the prefect was to have a single room with an attached bath room and fan to himself. The possession of a cycle was a luxury and I had that in my fifth year of stay. For the first four years, I did not think much of six to eight kilometres walk, twice or thrice a day. Instead of spending money on human pulled carrier called rickshaw, I preferred to spend the same on seeing a movie in ten annas or sixty paisa class. There was no television but only a solitary radio in the common room. For the benefit of two hundred students staying in the hostel, the music from radio Ceylon would be beamed through the loud speakers. The nearest entertainment to the television was the live dramas or music competition in the college or the circus, displaying the skill of the animals and the artists. The artists would be attractively dressed and would floor many young potential lovers. It was a question, which Thomas Hardy had raised, when he said in his novel, "Jude the Obscure" "Many a time a man half in love with a dimple, makes the mistake of marrying the whole girl". My class fellow Daljit had expressed his love for every single girl in the circus. He beat a hasty retreat, when he met one of them, in the Trio cafe during the day time. I had an engagement to address a meeting presided over by the Speaker of the Punjab Assembly, Sh.C.S. Athwal. Lunch was at the residence of my class fellow Darshan Arora, who had invited my other friend, Mohan Adya. I finished the lunch and decided to catch up on some sleep in the afternoon, as usual, before the meeting of the Indian Economic Society.

The meeting was a hurried affair. The speaker of the Punjab Assembly wanted to leave on the ground that the Chief Minister has called him. It may or may not be true, as most of us do not like to stay after our part of the programme is over. Speaking is an art. It is difficult to acquire without preparation and practice. I noticed that other speakers had not prepared themselves for the programme. The result was evident in the expression of the spectators and the audience. Most of them appeared to be bored to death and were yawning. It also appeared that some speakers were not interested in what they were saying. It appeared a routine for them to be done with. It is essential that once you accept the engagement you should be ready for it. The speeches were followed by giving awards of excellence by the society. Any award, given to anybody, is welcome like the gift, though the giver of the award may not have scanned the persons receiving the same. I must also give an incident, which happened to me personally about a year back.

I received a communication from a non descript person that I have been conferred their top award. But the bottom line was that I must send them Rs 1000 before I can be called for the function to receive the award. The only strength of the award was that previously the Prime Minister of the country had given the award. I had to write to the Prime Minister that he should not allow his name to be misused like this. I refused to accept the award on the ground that the person giving the award had no standing and that they were cashing in on the personality of the person giving away the award. But in the present case, I had known Kulbir Singh, the Executive Director of the Economic Society. He is a well off person. He does not need any money to live off any function, or any grant. It was a bonafide recognition of the persons who had contributed to the society through work in their respective spheres. With a view of honourable expectations, most Non-Government Organisations, getting grant from the government, including the wives of the senior officers heading the same, believe in one way traffic. The government goes on giving grants only, without any physical verification, of any work done at the ground level. For the next instalment, only a certificate from the Chartered Accountant is required that the previous grant has been spent for the purpose it was sanctioned for and the accounts are in order.

No personal ethics

It is well known in our country that it is not difficult to obtain a certificate of any kind or even a forged certificate. It is not only the criminals but even the former ministers and politicians, facing the prospects of going to jail, manage to get admitted to hospitals, so that they can avoid the rough-and-tumble of jail life, for criminal offences including cheating. I have seen a politician taking a four kilometre walk regularly in Lodi Garden, when he was facing prosecution for his part in the 1984 anti-Sikh riots. But the day the police came to arrest him, he got himself admitted to be hospital with serious heart ailments. He became sick to avoid the nemesis of his sins. Otherwise he was fine and fit. He would play the same trick when faced with a prolonged detention in the jail. There is a deterioration in the values of ethics in every profession. Nobody wants to have trouble with the high powerful and the mighty. As the programme was over in time to catch the superfast train called Swarn Shatabdi, I left for Delhi on the 28th December, 1999 itself at 7P.M. from Ludhiana.

Punjab can be extremely cold in winter but the journey by the air-conditioned Swarn Shatabadi Express from Ludhiana to Delhi at the speed of 100 kilometres per hour protected me and other passengers from all cold, heat and dust. The executive class in the Shatabadi Train is as comfortable as in an aeroplane with the same standard of service and a hostess enquiring about the type of meals passengers would like to have. Despite a distance of about 300 kilometres, the train was almost on the dot. It covered the journey much faster than by the best car. Little things make life comfortable and travelling in one's own car from the station to home ensures that at least one reaches home safe despite zero visibility due to fog. I had the benefit being driven to my home by my private driver.

New Year Eve - nothing unusual

There is a kind of hype about the new year and the new millennium. The new year hype is something, which happens every year. It was the new Millennium added this year, that is the transition from 1999 to 2000. I, somehow do not like to disturb my routine. I stuck to my usual routine even in the last days of the year and the century. In the last two days of the year, hotels and restaurants had become very expensive for the dinner on 31st December. Some of them were charging as much as Rs 13,000 per couple. One dinner at the most expensive hotel would have meant spending my full month's pension. As a country, we are following the tradition of the West, in sending new year greetings cards. I am slightly different. I write personal letters to give a personal touch to the greeting. I must have received more than 400 greeting cards and replied to more than 250 of them. The greeting cards continue to come up to the end of January. One of the biggest reasons why I do not reply to all the cards is that some people do not write legibly and also do not write their names and addresses. This is presuming too much that the person receiving the greeting card would somehow make a guess, as to who had sent the card. Such persons have to remain contented without getting any reply from me. It is for the simple reason that I am not an astrologer or a clairvoyant. I have also noticed that people are reluctant to introduce themselves, presuming that they are so well known and such familiar figures, that every one knows or should know them. This is again an illusion. I do not presume too much and I always reintroduce myself.

No bluffing, but a fact

On 4th January 2000, I went along with my wife to see my friend, Sh. Chatterjee. Another gentleman came there and met me effusively. I introduced my wife to him and his wife, and mumbled names deliberately unintelligibly. But he did not reciprocate and kept quiet. When we were travelling back in the car, my wife asked me who he was, who met me so affectionately. I said, I did not know. She said that the way he had met me, appeared as if he was my life long friend. I said, this happened to me all the time, because of my TV appearances.

Those who have seen me on Television, also confuse between knowing me personally and having seen me on Television.

I have been avoiding sweets and items of fat food but a number of friends drop in with sweets, pastries, cakes and flowers, around new year day. I give away the gifts and pass them on to others. This makes the recipients happy. It makes me doubly happy, because it removes the temptations from me. If I see good food and sweets in front of me, I succumb to the temptations like other mortals. It is the case with all of us including my mother who is over weight like me and would find some excuse to celebrate by eating sweets. This is a common human failing and feeling. It is also a common virtue of liking the good things of life.

It was rather a heavy day. It included addressing a seminar on corruption along with N. Vittal, Central Vigilance Commissioner, KPS Gill, Former Director General, Punjab Police, and Justice Jaspal Singh. It was not exactly a breast-beating seminar, where we lament the present condition in the country. It was a business like approach, wherein we gave practical suggestions. The most important thing is the lack of will on the part of the people and the government to fight the menace. It is lacking, or if present, it is in a diluted form. Later I called on the RSS Chief, Prof. Rajender Singh, Sar Sangh Chalak. The RSS is a socio-cultural organisation dedicated to national-cultural objectives of building a strong India. It has more than one-lakh followers all over the world and in India. Its preachers and office-bearers have no earthly goods. It exercises only moral authority, on the present government. In short, it is a pro-India organisation, without being against any Indian. Prof. Rajendra Singh or Raju Bhaiya as he is called, has devoted his life to the organisation. Despite heavy strain on him, he is carrying on very well. The government has provided some security to the headquarters of the Rashtriya Swayam Sevak Sangh but it is not worth writing about. Believing that nothing will happen, the security people appeared to be lax, and not checking anybody. I expressed my unhappiness to him, over a nuclear power like India, going on bent-knees, to get the passengers of the hijacked IC 814 plane from Kathmandu to Delhi released. I also told him that unless the bureaucracy is controlled and led, the country would remain mired in inefficiency, dishonesty and corruption. In the perception of the people, there has been no difference in the quality of governance, between the present and the past government. He issued a statement later, expressing his unhappiness on "Hindu society" becoming weak, and lacking the spirit of sacrifice.

A season of cultivating (January 5, 2000)

The temperature in Delhi today is below four degrees. One has to sit in front of the heater, and be properly clad to fight the weather. The cold weather has reduced the number of morning walkers in Lodi Garden. Only the hard-core and dedicated walkers like myself are the ones to be seen around. The only way to have a good walk is to cover the extremities, including the hands with gloves. Covering the hands with gloves enables me to brave the cold, during the morning walks, even with lesser woollens. In the afternoon, I attended an Iftaar party hosted by Shri H D Deve Gowda, former Prime Minister of India. It was a mixture of people, which included politicians, ministers, and close associates of Deve Gowda. The Iftaar is a season for hosting parties for Muslim friends, who observe rozas but this has been converted to a vote bank politics device. It was a party attended by politicians from AIDMK, Congress and by various hues of people and politicians, including Sonia Gandhi.

In this party, the serving Prime Minister, Shri Atal Behari Vajpayee was the only minister from the government. Apart from him, the Prime Ministerial hopeful Sonia Gandhi was present. Photographers, TV camera crew, and journalists occupied half the party. A few of us who had worked with Deve Gowda, like my batch mate K Padmanabiah, Meenakshi Sundram, Advisor to the Planning Commission, D R Karthikeyan and R C Sharma were present. Hardly any senior serving bureaucrat could be seen. It is not that people do not want to go, and attend the party hosted by Deve Gowda. But their apprehension is that they may not be misunderstood and become the target of vendetta, by their follow bureaucrats. It is a natural tendency in the bureaucracy to backbite each other, so that they can climb to the top at the cost of others. I also noticed how former ministers in the Deve Gowda Cabinet did not even respond to his invitation. It only re-emphasises a common lesson that unless one is strong politically, socially, and economically, one is left behind. I greeted the present and the past Prime Ministers, with a warm handshake. They were effusive in reciprocating. I indulged in a small chit-chat with Sahib Singh Verma, Former Chief Minister of Delhi. When I asked his cell phone number, he said that there was a theft in his house and the cell phone was stolen. I asked him to lodge a complaint to the Prime Minister himself, who was sitting next to him. I wanted to stay back and taste Biryani - rice cooked with chicken, but I resisted it as I have already put on a lot of weight. In any case, I had to go for another function of NRI Institute, of which I am the Chairman, at Hotel Inter-Continental at Barakhamba Lane. After a decent stay of half an hour, I left Deve Gowda's house. My old colleague, Commandant Sidra of CRP, had taken me out from the SPG protected Deve Gowda's House. As a former Prime Minister, Deve Gowda would have the protection of the Specially Trained Commandos of the Special Protection, for a period of five years after demitting his office. This drill is to guard the SPG Protectees, from threats. Getting to my car took another ten minutes because it was parked far off, along with other five hundred plus vehicles of the invitees. In the night time, like myself my driver lost the way but somehow we could reach the Hotel by a longer route. Nareshwar Dayal, the High Commissioner designated to the United Kingdom arrived, fifteen minutes after I had reached. Mr. L M Singhvi, a distinguished lawyer and Former High Commissioner to the United Kingdom was at his charming best and like always kind to me. During my speech, I had to tell off a thing or two to the High Commissioner Designate, Nareshwar Dayal. I mentioned to him that for a change he must see his office himself by going around. This way he will know, how the public was being received and treated in the High Commission. There is no way to know at first hand, the condition of one's office, except by visiting each employee, and each place of work. The impression that anybody, not in the government, gets from the government offices is that he is the least wanted commodity. Any normal work, which should be routine, is doled out as a favour. I was aware that he would be subjected to a lot of public pressures and expectations. But that is what the High Commissioner is paid for. Nareshwar Dayal assured me that he would be accessible and do his bit to improve the environment. I had invited a number of my batchmates and friends for the dinner, but I found the response was very unsatisfactory. Later on, a friend telephoned after two days, that is 7th of January, and said he had received invitation for the function of 5th January on the 7th of January through special courier. It shows that private sector also is not always the best, and it too has its faults. A mixture, a competition between the government and the private sector, seems to be the only way to improve the conditions.

I remained busy with discussions on Zee News TV channel about the handling of the hijacked Indian Airlines plane IC 814 in Kathmandu and the exchange of hostages by the Indian government by releasing three militants. My stand was that this is nothing but a manifestation of a soft state syndrome.

By the time the reality is told, to the decision-makers the position on the ground has changed. The problem keeps crying for attention, some action and some reaction. But everybody dodges a decision lets there an adverse fall out. The Intelligence agencies came out, with a beautiful explanation and analysis, as to how the hijacking has occurred. One wishes that they had spent some time in getting pinpointed information to prevent such happenings. Such events as well as the activities of our enemies are get bound to get accelerated, because inaction has never been punished. The hijacking of the IC 814, on 25th December, 1999, was the 11th in the series of hijacking of India's planes. I doubt very much whether even one person has been sacked for his action or inaction or poor response.

The political master has tied himself in knots by giving all power to bureaucracy and by his total dependence on it. Governing is a professional job. Somehow, the politicians have come to believe that making bold speeches is a substitute for better governance. Whenever any problem arises, a committee or commission is appointed. It is forgotten till the next incident occurs, to be followed up by another committee to divert the attention of the public.

The classic case is that of a committee set up, in the first week of January 2000, under a retired Home Secretary to look into the police reforms and for toning up the intelligence agencies. When he could not do this job, who was in the chair as a serving Home Secretary, what could the poor fellow do as a retired official is anybody's guess. It can be said in his justification that, like the rest of the government, which does only fire fighting all the time, he might have spent all his time in dealing with the immediate, rather than the long term problems. Even if he submits the best of reports, it will be buried, like hundreds of other reports in the government archives. He himself might have consciously or unconsciously, buried several such reports and committees.

The political master does not understand the game of bureaucracy. This is because he is ignorant of the devious ways of how bureaucracy avoids taking decisions, unless it is a question of increasing their own pays, perks, and pension benefits. Bureaucrats are basically, mercenaries and incidentally nationalists. Moreover they are not accountable, except in a vague sort of way through a non-existing or at best through a moth-eaten system. That is why, even after a civil servant of the eminence of Dharamvira gave his report after four years of labour, his report for reforming the police in the country running into eight volumes is gathering dust since 1977-81. Committees after committees have examined it, and left it untouched. What was the purpose of setting up a commission under Dharam Vira, who was the highest civil servant, at the peak of his career as the cabinet secretary of India and then, the Governor of a number of states? The ultimate sufferer and loser is the common citizen. It is he who stands to benefit from an improved police force. Earlier there used to be some effect, if a newspaper took up a cause but unfortunately, it is a past story now. Even the exposure of a scam does not harm anybody's health and reputation, as from the day one, operation cover-ups start.

Miss and mix up

I had accepted an engagement on a request from Shri Vijay Kumar Chopra, Editor-in-chief, and Punjab Kesri on the 9th of January at Jalandhar. Due to fog, the trains are generally late in December and January. Sometimes the delay in the train can be beneficial. I left by Golden Temple Mail or Frontier Mail two hours later than the scheduled time. This proved very helpful, otherwise I would have reached Jalandhar at 4.30 a.m. in the morning next day. Instead I reached Jalandhar at 6.30 a.m. after adequate sleep. If I do not sleep adequately, then the chances are that I would not be able to put in my best the next day. Accommodation was arranged for me, at Circuit House in Jalandhar as well as in police officers' mess. I preferred to stay at the police mess, primarily because a lot of open space close by would enable me to have my morning walk. There was hardly any time left, after the morning walk and bath, as the function was to start at 10 o'clock. I went over to my friend Jitender Mohan's place, as he was my local host along with Ishwar Chander Sharma, SP and CID. We went together to the place of function at Baba Mohan Dass Ashram. Baba Mohan Dass was chairing the function organised by the largest circulated daily in Hindi, Punjab Kesri. Baba Mohan Dass runs a number of charitable and educational institutions for the benefit of the community. The organisers of Ram Lila and Dussehras from all over the country had been invited to be honoured by Shri Vijay Kumar Chopra, Editor-in-chief, Punjab Kesri. Shri Chopra had brought on one platform leaders of all political parties including the Chief Minister of Punjab, Shri Prakash Singh Badal, Captain Amarnider Singh, President of Pradesh Congress Committee, Punjab and representatives and ministers belonging to BJP and Akalis were also present along with the representatives of CPI, Jalandhar Municipal Council and prominent citizens of Jalandhar.

The crowd was in no mood to listen to any speeches. I found that Shri Prakash Singh Badal was an eloquent speaker in Punjabi. He was logical, coherent and to the point in his speech. I made a faux pas, by referring to Prakash Singh Badal as Prakash Singh Gill. I covered it by saying in my speech that sometimes it is good to make mistakes. A shawl and a piece of cloth with the word 'Ram' repeatedly inscribed on it were presented to me. Mercifully, I left the brass or brass-like substance momento, presented to me at the place of Jatinder Mohan. I have collected so many momentos, that I now like to give them away. My own place is getting cluttered. I have sent most of the momentos to Gaini Gurbux Singh DAV

College at Jalalabad. It's a problem keeping them clean and well dusted.

Having come to Jalandhar I felt I should visit some holy places associated with Sikh religion. Sultanpur Lodi is one such place, situated at a distance of 50 kms from Jalandhar. I excused myself from lunch, and instead preferred to take packed food. This was to save time, so that I could be back in time from Sultanpur Lodi for my next programme to address the thinkers of Jalandhar forum at 4 P.M. It was wrongly estimated that it would take 35 minutes to go and 35 minutes to come back to Jalandhar. Instead it took me two hours of commuting and about forty minutes there.

Guru Nanak is said to have stayed there for over thirteen years. He got his enlightenment there. His two sons Baba Lakhmi Chand and Sri Chand were born there. He worked as a chief store-keeper of the ruler of Sultanpur Lodi. He was also imprisoned there on the alleged ground that he had given away the foodstuff from the king's store, without properly accounting for it. On verification, all these allegations were found to be untrue. Gurudwaras have been constructed at all the places associated with Guru Nanak. I could visit only two, Beri Sahib and Hat Sahib. I was recognised and the President of the local municipality presented me books connected with Sikh religion. Sardar Jaimal Singh, Member SGPC, and President of Municipal Committee insisted that I should have a cup of tea with them. I rushed back for the next function and was late by one hour. I apologised profusely for the delay. The topic of my talk was the scenario in the country and dealing with corruption. It was followed by a very stimulating discussion, with the elite of Jalandhar. The function ended at 7.30 p.m. just giving me enough time to pack up and have my dinner at Jatinder Mohan's place and leave for the station.

Ethics of advertising

The train arrived at about 8 o'clock at Delhi from Jalandhar. There was still some time to complete my morning walk and attend to the phone calls on my answering machine. I had a TV recording, On opinion Today at Jain TV in the evening, which took away almost three hours, leaving no time for any serious writing, or other work. TV appearances are connected with the writings in the national dailies. I found that Jain TV is offering quality programmes. It is a News and Views channel. It has made its appearance again, after five years of closure. Any news channel is bound to run into red initially. I addressed a meeting of Delhi Advertising Club on ethics and the legal position in advertising. It is an interesting study. Advertising features both negative and positive points. The following are possibly the unfair and deceptive practices in advertising, emphasised by me. They can be considered unethical.

The courts have held that these acts constitute unfair or deceptive trade practices and are therefore illegal.

False promises : making an advertising promise that cannot be kept, such as "restore youth" or "prevents cancer."

Incomplete description : stating some, but not all the contents, of a product, such as advertising a "solid oak" desk without mentioning that only the top is of solid oak and that the rest is made of hardwood with an oak veneer.

Misleading comparisons : making meaningless comparisons, such as "as good as a diamond," if the claim cannot be verified.

Bait-and switch offers : advertising an item at an unusually low price to bring people into the store and then "switching" them to a higher priced model, than the one advertised, by stating that the advertised product is "out of stock" or "poorly made."

Visual distortions : making a product look larger than it really is - for example, a TV commercial for a "giant steak" dinner special showing the steak on a miniature plate that makes it appear extra large. Or showing a "deluxe" model that is not the same as the one offered at a "sale" price.

False testimonials : implying that a product has the endorsement of a celebrity or an authority, who is not a bona fide user of the product.

False comparisons : demonstrating one product as superior to another, without giving the "inferior" item a chance or by comparing it with the least competitive product available, such as comparing the road performance of a steel belted radial tyre with that of an average "economy" tyre.

Partial disclosures : stating what a product can do, but not what it cannot do, such as claiming that an electrically powered automobile will go "60 miles per hour - without gasoline" and not mentioning that it needs an eight-hour battery recharge every 100 miles.

Small-print qualifications : making a statement in large print ("any new suit in stock - Rs. 500 off!") only to qualify or retract it in smaller type elsewhere in the ad ("with the purchase of a suit at a regular price").

Social accusations have been directed at advertising in such pungent, imaginative and descriptive terms that they appear to emanate from talents as creative as those within the advertising community. Advertising is said to destroy the finer things of life. It is described by some as vulgar, idiotic, degrading, shrill, noisy, blatant and aggressive. It is said to exalt lower values glorify mediocrity and good taste.

A number of humanities and social science scholars view advertising as intrusive and environmental, and its effects as inescapable and profound. They see it as reinforcing materialism, cynicism, irrationality, selfishness, anxiety, social competitiveness, sexual preoccupation, powerlessness and loss of self-respect. These are strong indictments. They imply that advertising is a powerful force. However, the history of advertising is replete with failures of advertising campaigns, difficulties in proving advertising effectiveness, and indications that only a small percentage of advertising is actually noticed.

Socially, the defenders of advertising note that it has a beneficial effect on several basic areas:

Information: advertising aids in the education of the general public, facilitates the exercise of free choice and free will, and subsidises mass communication providing essential services to the public.

Values and life styles: advertising contributes to improvement in the standard of living, contributes to the sharing of opulence among the masses, and represents an essential factor in the economies of abundance.

However, some observers declare that advertising may contain misinformation and be excessively persuasive, that the values and life-styles, promoted through advertising, are unacceptable, and that the new and interesting experiences are often objectionable. While none of the critics tend to argue that advertising alone is responsible for these conditions, it is appropriate for researchers to take assertions, about the unintended consequences of advertising seriously, and examine these issues. Such an inquiry does not require researchers to believe that advertising will be absolved of all charges, as much as it requires having faith, that the institutions of advertising have a potential for self-correction.

Advertising can perform a socially useful function by educating the public about product qualities so that consumers can exercise their free choice and free will in the market place.

Moreover, retail advertising, catalogue advertising and much industrial advertising provide a substantial amount of information. Even television advertising is perceived as informative by substantial groups of people. There is a lot of consumer ignorance prevailing in industries, that don't use, advertising and suggests that this prevents the shopping public from intelligently comparing the attributes of competing brands or even from recognising as identical the same brand on sale in different outlets. Critics concede that because of brand advertising, there is a wide assortment of goods, in performance, or quality grade, although some critics assert that this variety is excessive.

Advertising and free choice

Critics declare that the information provided in advertising may manipulate people to buy things they don't really need. They point to the example of the Listerine Company in the USA which took the word "halitosis" and through intensive repetition in widespread advertising infected Americans with the fear of bad breath - making up to $20,000,000 in the process. Critics also declared that the old Lifebuoy ads shouting "Body Odour," caused the psychologically insecure and inadequate to become uncomfortable and apprehensive so that if "they detected nothing else, they did smell their own primitive fears, guilt feelings and insecurities..."

It is claimed that motivational researchers have studied man's unconscious needs and then put a dangerous manipulative tool in the hands of advertisers. Messages may be sent below our threshold of consciousness and still affect us. We are being brainwashed by hidden persuasion.

There is some justification in the idea of effective persuasion through advertising. In fact, much advertising is designed to the persuasive. Persuasive advertising is used primarily as a type of propaganda. The essence of propaganda is that it conditions people to act in a way that is favourable toward the product being advertised. There is no doubt that we have, largely on the basis of improved knowledge in the various disciplines of psychology, sociology and anthropology, developed increasingly refined and effective means of persuasion. However, just as the persuaders become more sophisticated, so do those who are to be persuaded.

Does advertising persuade people to buy things they do not need?

Advertising is said to create excessive demand, sometimes for unnecessary goods. According to John Kenneth Galbraith,

... Along with bringing demand under substantial control, ... (the management of demand) provides in the aggregate, a relentless propaganda on behalf of goods in general. From early morning until late at night, people are informed of the services rendered by goods - of their profound indispensability. Every feature and facet of every product having been studied for selling points, these are then described with talent, gravity and an aspect of profound concern, as the sources of health, happiness, social achievement, or improved community standing. Even minor qualities of unimportant commodities are enlarged upon with a solemnity which would not be unbecoming in an announcement of the combined return of Christ and all the apostles. More important services, such as the advantages of white laundry, are treated with proportionately greater gravity".

While advertising is designed to accelerate changes in tastes, swings in fashion and minor product differentiation, it can only be effective, if it is noticed and needed. Consumers are not passive, but selective they are exploratory and receptive to new ideas. My presentation was widely appreciated and it invoked a lot of questions. Basically advertisement has to exist, both for the consumer and the producer.

Unequal in market, unequal in life

In the afternoon, I went over to Delhi Race Club. The Chief of the Army Staff, Gen. V P Malik, was the Chief Guest for giving away the Army Cup. Despite the best efforts of the club and the stewards, it is not possible to stop malpractices. It is impossible to prove that money has changed hands, in either making a horse win or lose. In the meeting, we fine a number of trainers and jockeys for deliberately not doing their best in making their horses win. Detecting malpractices in races is a technical job and the stipendiary steward Mr. Sodhi has a very keen and sharp eye. The Delhi Race Club offered the High Tea to the Chief of the Army Staff, Gen. V P Malik and his wife. The menu consisted of pastries, fried stuff like patties, pakaras, samosas, and chips, which hardly was eaten by the Chief Guest or by the member of the Managing Committee. The tea served to the stewards, particularly the sandwiches, are very good during the meeting after the races. I help myself generously to the same. The result is that I have no place left for dinner.

Videography helps a lot in the identification of the lapses during the race. Conservatively about Rs.40 to 50 lakh business is conducted on every race day. All over the country more than five lakh people including the horse breeders, trainers, veterinary doctors, supporting staff cyces, and bookies must be subsisting on the horse racing. In the evening, I along with my wife went over to Kotla, a lower middle class locality for shopping. The prices there are 100 percent less than one ends up paying in Khan Market. We used to visit Kotla thirty years ago. But since 1988, perhaps this was the first visit after twelve years. Peas being sold for Rs. 12 per kg. are available there for Rs. 6 per kg. Gachak, a snack made of Gur and groundnut, cost Rs.32 per kg, as against Rs.60 per kg in Khan Market, close to my house. Khan Market is the market for the rich, the famous and the diplomats. Shopkeepers there, do not like, the customers, who inquire about the prices, of various products. Infact, they are indifferent to such clients, and prefer not to sell them anything.

Three decades plus four of married life (19 January 2000)

Last week was a hectic one. Yesterday, I presided over the function of the Non-Resident Indian Institute at Hotel Meridian. The British High Commissioner to India, Sir Rob Young, was the Chief Guest. It was a well attended function, with a number of former Indian Ambassadors to the USA: Abid Hussain, Hamid Ansari to Saudi Arabia, BM Oza to South Korea, and Gajendar Singh to Turkey were present. The function was over within one and half-hours including the lunch. The brevity was the best part of the function. Nobody has the patience to listen to dull, long and boring speeches. In any case, most of us love to listen to our own voices. The voices of others do not have attraction for long dissertations. I like to confine myself only up to the time I notice interest in other people's eyes. There is a kind of clear indication, clear to the perceptible eyes, when something unpalatable is happening around any one of us.

Today is my 34th wedding anniversary. Except for my second daughter, Choosie, nobody else remembered it. I wished my wife and she wished me. I took her out for a quiet dinner cum snack to the Ambassador Hotel's South Indian Restaurant Dasa Prakash. The restaurant serves good South Indian preparations like idli, wadas, dosas and uppama. We had idlis and uppama as our private celebration. For lunch, my friend Prof. N.K. Singh and B.K. Goswami at the India International Centre had invited me. I had a Chinese lunch, as it is comparatively fat free. I ran into a number of friends I had not met for a long time there. Those were the kind of friends one likes to say 'Hello' to and be in touch with once in while. Nothing very personal or intimate but just a neutral relationship. Most of us bear that kind of relationship with acquaintances. Everybody in the India International Centre is not only a social and political climber, but also believes that he could become the Prime Minister, following an unfortunate example of a hoax, who, by pretending to be an honest intellectual, got a prominent position in the country. The food rates are reasonable and are within affordable limits. I am not a club type and not a member of the Centre. I took belatedly membership of the India Habitat Centre. I visit the place, once in a while, with a guest or two, mostly for lunch. It is spacious, has a better decor and more variety of food. My eldest daughter Randeep, remembered belatedly, that it was our wedding anniversary and wished us. Gagandeep had already wished us and the third Harveen did not remember it at all. Obviously, after sometime, your special days are significant to you alone.

A taste of food poisoning

I had a plethora of visitors and plenty of aimless phone calls. One worthwhile phone call generates at least two calls. Telephone, as an instrument, is the greatest distance and time saver. In the past, finding out the availability of a person or an appointment, could be sought, either by writing a letter or sending a messenger. Now, all it takes is dialling a few roman numbers and all the information is available in a jiffy. I left for Jalalabad by train with my mother to observe the 4th death anniversary of my late father Mahant Kartar Singh on the 23rd of January. Somehow, I have an apprehension that I would be hungry in the night. So on a train journey, I make it a point to take my food, and eat it when the train is moving. It is a kind of a picnic for me. I ate Papaya, which was slightly unripe, in the afternoon. The stale cheese preparations caused food poisoning. I could not sleep for the night. I make it a point not to bother my mother, with any of my ailments. It is to save her the stress, and to me the exaggeration of my ailments to the visitors. Om Parkash was there at Ferozpore to receive me at 5 A.M. on the arrival of the Punjab Mail on the 21st of January. He had brought the esteem car of my cousin, Inderjit Singh. I remained on liquid diet for the whole day and the night. Only then could I overcome the result of food poisoning. Liquids helped me to throw out the poisonous substance from my system. I just went to the College at 12 P.M. for the starting of the recitation of the Holy Granth Sahib (Sikh scriptures). I stayed there for an hour or so. The Principal had asked me whether he should make it compulsory for everybody to attend the start of the Granth Sahib recitation. I told him that it would not be fair to interrupt the classes and affect the studies. It is purely a voluntary function, and there should be no compulsion. I have no moral right to do something, which I do not want others to do. Moreover, in these matters, apart from its being a personal choice, it is also a question of whether one would like to divert the time of the students and the teachers for a purely family function. My reason for holding it in the college is that my father was the founder of this college. He perhaps would have been happy to be associated with it even after he is no more.

In Jalalabad of India, not of Afghanistan

My wife, Surinder, my daughter, Gagandeep and her husband Gunveer Singh along with Harveen, my youngest daughter arrived from Delhi. Om Parkash had gone to receive them at Ferozpore. Two cars had been arranged to fetch seven members of the close family. The recitation of the Holy Granth was to continue till mid-day. I had arranged for everybody to reach there, so that apart from visiting the college, they could also have lunch there. I had fixed the holding of a meeting of the Local Management Committee there, followed by a lunch hosted by me for the staff, members of the Management Committee and my own family. It was a simple affair, consisting of two vegetables, chapatis and rice.

I went to the college, as the principal has proposed to build six rooms, adjoining each other so that it could be used as an auditorium for functions. The construction of an auditorium is very much required. Somehow, the entire town is neither satisfied nor happy with the principal and staff of the college. It is due to the poor results and performance. The MP of the area Sardar Zora Singh Man had also mentioned it to me last month. I had accordingly brought his complaint to the notice of the Management Committee. At the instance of the principal, Hansraj Josan had remonstrated to me. I had told him that I couldn't ignore anything brought to my notice. I had also mentioned to him that the principal did not have control over the staff or even on the affairs of the college. In fact, even for the death anniversary of my late father, who was the founder of the college, I had told the principal not to make attendance compulsory. I had left it to the individuals concerned. Unfortunately or fortunately, despite the poor results, the college is charging the students Rs. 6000 per year. The subject of increase in the college fees was never brought to the notice of the Local Management Committee. The principal on his own did it. In fact, the budget never got approved from the LMC. I have changed this practice. I feel that transparency is essential. Another interesting feature was that all the income of the college was used only for paying higher grades, and salaries to the regular staff.

Functions and celebrations

I had stayed an extra day in Jalalabad, on 24th Janaury, 2000, after observing the death anniversary of my late father. The trouble with staying in Jalalabad, longer than essential, is that all kinds of people approach with disparate requests ranging from getting government jobs to recommending the judges and district officials for a favourable verdict. I on the advice of Om have agreed to listen to everybody. But I do not believe in advising others on how to do their job. On the way to Delhi, I dropped in to see the Deputy Commissioner of the District Mr. Sidhu at 9 P.M. I was meeting him for the first time. I received an effusive welcome. We discussed the District administration. He said that in the modern days the Deputy Commissioner was no longer a free agent. He had to spend a lot of time, in the transfers of the junior officials, who always managed to bring in recommendations, or call them commands, from the elected representatives. Even the Chief Minister despite a keen desire on his part for good governance had to compromise. On 25th of January, I chaired a session on the Investment opportunities and obstacles in a seminar organised by the Non-Resident Indian Welfare Society, in Delhi. It took away my whole day. I told the people of Indian origin that they always had a home in India, despite their being away from the mother country. I outlined as to how the country had progressed from quota permit Raj to the present day liberalisation. It was time that they extended their hand in the development of the nation. One gentleman from Thailand complained of complicated and frustrating procedures, for getting any sanction. He was blunt in saying that the claim of cheap labour in India was not correct as the productivity of the labour was low and infra structure in the form of roads and power was far from encouraging. It is vain to deny the difficulties on the ground. I said that the government is sincere about improving the situation and things are bound to improve. There was a message on my answering machine from Rashtriya Sahara, English Magazine. I called them and was told that I had an invitation to visit the programmes organised by the Rashtriya Sahara Group on any day from 26th January 2000 to 31st January. I opted to visit Luknow today along with my daughter Harveen and nephew and nieces, Bikram, Golu and

Jasneet. A special charter flight took us from Delhi at 5.30 P.M. and brought us back by 5 A.M. to Delhi. The atmosphere both at the Airport, in the flight and in the Sahara India Complex was that of an arival. I had never travelled by Sahara Airlines and was rather sceptical about the planes and the quality of service. Mr. Parveez Damania, Director of the Airline, was not only there at the Airport, but also accompanied the flight to ensure that it was totally hassle free. Such personalised attention and care probably impressed everybody on the flight. The snacks served were excellent, better than one gets in the five star hotels. I enjoyed the chicken Tangdi Kabab and chicken patty, as those items appeared to be freshly prepared. Mr. Subroto Roy Sahara met me at the complex, where crackers to celebrate the Republic Day were being lighted. The sparkling crackers were a delight, and the show lasted about five minutes. A programme of entertainment, in probably the biggest auditorium of Uttar Pradesh, followed it. The auditorium was so large and seats so plushy that giant TV screens had been put up to give a close up of the artists. I understand that, as a non-banking financial company, Sahara Group has a very good reputation. It is also into the media business, housing, air transport, and newspaper. It celebrates only 15th August, the Independence Day and 26th January, the Republic Day. Sobrity, gaiety and a right mix of seriousness mark its celebrations. The return flight to Delhi was at 5 AM in the morning, so the day was spent on catching up on the sleep and lazing. Time really flies, unless one is careful in using it. I try to strike a balance by keeping myself reasonably busy and reasonably rested.

On Sunday, the 30th January 2000 my batch mate Mr. R.K. Puri invited me for lunch at Gymkhana Club. It is supposed to be one of the poshest clubs. The food preparation was very poor and full of oil. I had to leave half the food in between. The food was so heavy that I did not feel the necessity of having snacks in the evening, dinner and even breakfast next day. Mr. Puri's affection compensated for everything else. Other guests invited by Mr. Puri was Mr. Gajendra Singh who did not turn up. In the morning, I attended the last rites and cremation of late, Mr.T. R. Tuli, the President of DAV Management Committee, at Lodi Road crematorium. In a place like Delhi, people have no time to individually inform everybody, except perhaps the closest relations. The advertisement/intimation in the Newspapers with the photograph of the person concerned is considered sufficient intimation and people do reach. At least five hundred people had reached for the cremation, which punctually started at 10.30 A.M. and was over by 11 A.M.

The chase of Jain hawala case

The Trial Court has acquitted a number of officials and politicians in the case known as the Jain hawala case, in which Rs. 65 crores had been paid to the high officials and politicians to win their favours. The case was based on a well-documented diary maintained by the accused. But as the court wanted corroborating evidence which was not forthcoming, they were acquitted. In the cases, where kick-backs are paid, there is a very remote possibility of the accused persons giving any receipt to the bribe givers, so that it could be used as an evidence. As such, transactions are done on one-to-one basis. No witness can either be planted or produced to confirm about the payments made under the table. Moreover, as both the bribe-giver and bribe-taker stand to benefit, nobody else will be in a position to tell as to what transpired between the two. The Star News Channel interviewed me and I repeated the above points. But only a small part in which I had said about the inevitability of the political interference was telecast. It is not obligatory for any TV Channel to telecast the full text. They will telecast only that much portion which supports the angle they want to present. In the night, I went for dinner to the Indo-Tibetan Border Police, where the Home Minister LK Advani was the Chief Guest. Advani is the de facto and de jure number two man in the Cabinet and is a very clear thinker. He has ideas about improving the system, particularly the judicial and administrative system. But his limitation is that of anybody in the coalition governments, with partners, having disparate or no thinking. He agreed with me and said that it was more important to have judicial and administrative reforms, than constitutional reforms. I also told him not to dilute his security, as he can be a soft target for others. An individual called Lal Krishan Advani, was not important. It was the Home Minister of India, an office held by Lal Krishan Advani, who was to be protected. Any mishap to the Home Minister would give a lot of mileage to the enemies of India. I also told him that the bureaucracy was having an upper hand. It needed both to be controlled and tamed. Procedure and rules had become so lengthy that it was impossible for the system to deliver.

Mr. Advani also jokingly said that he was used to dealing with the disciplined party. But the entire approach had to be changed, due to the formation of the coalition. In a democracy, people are to be carried with you. Everybody's views have to be considered and given due weightage. The problem of governance is complicated due to the different background of the people, different perceptions and different approaches. Another good thing about democracy is that nobody has any divine right to wisdom. The ITBP dinner was another occasion to meet old friends and retired associates. As people live so far off in Delhi, it is difficult even for the best of friends to meet regularly. Your best friend is always your neighbour.

It was a very heavy day for me next day. At 9.15 A.M. in the morning, there was a programme of TV recording by Nalini Singh on the putting up of the list of the senior officials of the government, involved in various cases by the Central Vigilance

Commission on the Internet. Mr. N Vittal, Central Vigilance Commissioner, was also participating and was rather hard put to defend it. Other participants included Mr. Prabhu Chawla of India Today, KPS Gill - Former Director General of Punjab Police, myself, Ajit Jogi, former MP and Congress Spokesman and Amod Kanth a serving IPS officer. The CVC was under attack, for doing either too little, or too much. I said that all the names on the web site were well known, and had appeared in the newspapers for several acts of omission and commission from time to time. It is a strange world, where if you do anything, even if constructive, you are criticised. If you do not do anything, you are criticised for not doing anything. In the afternoon at 3.30 P.M. there was a programme of obituary, ritual rites and homages to the late Chairman of the DAV Management Committee, Shri. T R Tuli in Vasant Vihar. It was attended by more than 2000 people indicating the respect he commanded in the Aryan community. Shri T R Tuli was a thorough gentleman and was one of the cleanest bankers and a fine human being. At 5.30 P.M. I had to rush to the programme recording at Noida for Subha Savere for the Tele-casting on the morning on the Doodarshan National channel on 2nd February. The focus was on the Jain Hawala Case, of kickbacks and bribery by the officials and politicians and its acquittal. I had to explain that it was not open to the CBI to convict an individual. It was something where every section of the society had to co-operate for exposing the guilty before the courts. The final word lies with the courts. I came back from Noida after 80 minutes of driving to proceed to the reception held by the British High Commissioner in honour of Keith Vaz, Minister of State for Foreign Affairs in the UK. Keith is a British citizen of Indian origin. George Fernandes, the then Indian Defence Minister, was also present at the reception. I have known George for the last ten years. He is not only upright but has a professional approach to any job he does. After spending 15 minutes with the British High Commissioner, I drove back again to Noida to Zee News studio. Zee TV has launched a one-hour programme of news. It is not only reading the news, but also interpreting it, with visuals and with the help of analysts and experts. I had with me Chandan Mitra, Editor, The Pioneer Newspaper, for the News Hour, which is telecast live, with no scope of editing.

Attending to TV programmes and reception in the evening, was at the cost of two dinner invitations, one from Vaartha Group of Newspaper and an other from my friend, Harbhajan Singh. It was a pretty tiring day with myself turning into the bed at 11.30 P.M. in the night. One can do manage at this pace of activity for 2 or 3 days, but beyond that, it is just not possible.

Today (03 February 2000) my secretary was absent by intimation. I worked for sometime on the computer to correct my book on self-improvement with the usual interruptions of the telephones and two visitors. I do not allow anybody to waste my time and keep on working in spite of his or her presence. It was a signal for them to disappear, which they caught belatedly. Most people take time to realise that they have overstayed. In such cases, I tell them that I have to go for lunch, if they are around lunchtime. The excuse of dinner holds good in driving away unwanted people around that time. I like to spend time on the things which matter to me and which are on my priority list for the day. The afternoon was taken by a live TV recording, and appearance on Doordarshan News, on the subject of corruption in the government and publicising the names of the corrupt on the web site of the Central Vigilance Commission.

Lunches, dinners and outings

Last week was full of dinners and lunches, which were unavoidable. One such dinner was in a Five Star Hotel Taj. It had rained during the day, leading to a crawling and jammed hotel road, as everybody was keen to avoid getting wet. As usual, I stayed in the hotel for half an hour and left discreetly after registering my presence there. The temptation of five star food does not hold me down, as the food is both oily and greasy. Being a virtual stranger there further compounded matters. I was a stranger in the sense that I did not know anybody personally, though most people knew me and were keen to shake hands and get photographed with me. The week had packed in a TV appearance for me on the Malyalam Channel, Asianet and the Good Morning India on Star Plus channel. The final product shown on pre-recorded programmes is sometimes not even one fourth of what I would have said. In the live programmes, like Good Morning India on Star TV, there is no scope for anybody to cut or edit. On Saturday, visit to the market, bank, and a programme for improving public services under the banner of freedom movement, tied me up for the whole day. A young enthusiastic small time businessman Rajiv Kumar is the moving spirit behind organising groups of people for public causes. He has been spending his own money on the booking of the hall, sending intimations, inviting speakers and on coffee, tea and snacks for the participants. A city, like Delhi, makes you self-centred, and ego- centric. Still in this vast place, one can find a lot of unselfish people, who want to see a better India. I was feeling hungry in the evening, and wanted to have some idlis and dosas. I along with my wife Surinder had fixed up earlier to see my second daughter, Gagandeep, her husband, Gunveer and her father-in-law Prof. Balwant Singh Ansu, who had come, on a visit from Batala. While going to their house, I took whatever I wanted to eat, plus the items of their likely choice, consisting of Pizzas. It was a kind of a picnic at their place in Vasant Vihar, where Gunveer Singh has got the official big three bed room flat. Gunveer is a financial genius, having Chartered Accountancy as his background. I had the food of my choice. So did everybody else.

Carrying everybody along...

Today, Saturday, 12 February 2000, I spent all the daytime working on the Apple Macintosh computer. It appeared to be a waste of time, as it refused to give the print-out of the articles I wrote for the newspapers. My other laptop IBM had got annoyed with me and spent three days with its doctor, the computer engineer. I feel lost when I cannot do my day's writing. Yesterday, I attended a function organised by the RSS weekly paper, Panchjanay to honour the nationalist-minded writers in various Indian languages as well as English. Prime Minister, Vajpayee, Home Minister, LK Advani and other Ministers attended the function. I was struck by the Statesman-like approach of Vajpayee, when one of the speakers lamented the delay in making Hindi as the only official language of India, on the same lines as Kamal Ataturk had done by making Turkish as the official language overnight. Vajpayee quoted an incident, wherein, to a reply to the question put in Hindi, the Minister concerned replied in English. The questioner, a Hindi lover, M.P. objected to the reply in a foreign language. The Minister replied that for him Hindi was a foreign language. This stunned Vajpayee. It was the Prime Minister's way of saying that, in a country of the size of India, it was only fair to carry everybody along, rather than ram anything in to the throat of a segment of the population. Compulsion never works in life.

On the 10th February, I had a late night appearance on the Zee News about the investigation of cases, particularly the Jain hawala case. One of the officials who had been shifted by Vijay Ram Rao, my predecessor, as Director CBI, was the subject of his attack. I defended him by saying that it is not necessary for the seniors to accept whatever is put up to them by the juniors. The top man has inputs, from more than one source, and he is the best judge to take an overall view. The rain and the traffic chaos had made the twenty minutes journey of 15 kilometres to a fifty-two minutes crawl by the company car. The problem of prosperity is too many vehicles and the same old congested roads with no parking place with limited land: The only solution, which ultimately may have to be resorted to by the authorities, is underground and overground parking. No such project seems to be in sight. We seem to be resigned to the worsening of the situation.

The weather is playing truant. It is cool today. It has been a busy day with hardly any time left for self. The morning was taken by a press reporter doing a story on the modernisation of the police forces in the country and the afternoon by another pressman wanting to know my reaction to the possible setting up of a Federal Bureau of Investigation office in India. My reply was that we should enhance co-operation between the the USA and India. In any case the drug officers from USA and other countries are already working in India. I also addressed the BMA and BBB students of Indian Finance Institute at Ashok Vihar at the invitation of its Chairman and Director Mr.J.D. Aggarwal, on the subject of cost of corruption to the Country. The students were quite inquisitive. They asked probing and searching questions. The crawling traffic and lecture took four hours of the best part of the afternoon and evening.

Yesterday, that is 13th of February, 2000 was spent socialising on the occasion of the wedding of the daughter of OP Sharma, Governor of Nagaland. The wedding was at Surajkund in Haryana. Sharma was one of the low profile dedicated IPS officers (1962) of U.P. cadre, who served in Punjab during the heydays of terrorism. His contribution to the raising of the morale of the Punjab Police, as IG, and later on, as Addl. Director General of Police and Director General of Police, first as in-charge of the intelligence and later on, the State Police, was no less than that of other high profile DG's of the State. Being a thorough gentleman can sometimes be disadvantageous and he suffered on account of the lapses of others. But ultimately, he stood vindicated, when in recognition of his services, he was given the gubernatorial job. However, it is a fact that IPS officers are generally given those jobs, which nobody else wants and which are almost considered punishment postings as Governors. As on today, the Governors of Kashmir, Nagaland and Arunachal Pradesh are former IPS officers. IAS retired officials are occupying Raj Bhavans in Orissa, Bihar, Maharashtra, Delhi and the Andaman Nicobar Islands. Others from the Army, Judiciary and other services are Governors in Kerala, Karnantaka, Andhra Pradesh, Rajasthan and the rest are ex-Politicians rewarded for being faithful to the party, or whom the party dumps in Rajbhavans, to get them out of the way to make room for juniors.

In fact, the policy of giving post-retirement jobs is one temptation to bureaucracy to perform both legal and illegal actions at the bidding of the politicians. It is strange that, while taking a pledge to uphold the laws, precisely the opposite is done. There are two sets of laws, one for the person with approach and the other for the person with no godfather and no approach. Fortunately, even in this climate the constitution has insulated and ensured independence to the Judiciary, Union Public Service Commission, and the Election Commission. Only one reform which is needed is that nobody holding any constitutional office should be given any job under the government. This itself will ensure reasonably independent functioning. New Delhi is a city of class. Its roads are broader, electricity and water supply is assured to some extent. Delhi, though the capital of India, is not India. It rudely reminded me so while travelling on awfully bad roads full of potholes from Delhi to Badarpur. The road I was travelling was National

Highway (Mathura Road). Every vehicle was trying to bypass the others creating total chaos. I stayed for the wedding reception only for one hour till about 3 o'clock. The return journey took only 26 minutes as I took a different route at a non-peak hour's time. In the bargain, I missed my lunch, which perhaps was good in a way.

Delhi Police is not up to the mark

Today, 16th February 2000, is the Raising day of Delhi Police. I attended the ceremonial parade, at which the Union Home Minister Shri L K Advani took the salute. Most of these functions are self-back patting ones, with each organisation praising itself. The perception of the common man is to avoid the police, as long as, and as far as, possible. At such occasion, very glossy brochures are brought out incurring huge costs. These brochures contain mostly photographs and messages. They are thrown away after a glance. The following is a message in the brochure from the Chief Minister of Delhi:

"I have no doubt in my mind that without resorting to confidence-building measures among the masses, the Delhi Police cannot fulfil its role of maintaining a social and public order with a reasonable crime rate. Co-operation of people in prevention, detection and investigation of crimes is a must. It is, in this context that such events assume importance. Of late, it appears that the communication gap between the police and the public has been increasing. The common men shudder to approach police functionaries, even when facing grim situations because of the negative perception of the police which they carry. It will be rewarding for the police if this negative perception is changed by reorienting and sensitising the Force particularly at the lower levels, so far as their dealing with the common people are concerned. It will need continuous organisational efforts. I am sure Delhi Police will strive for achieving this, for the Delhi Police week is nothing but a manifestation of this desire only".

Earlier, I used to drive myself or ask my driver to take me to all functions. But I noticed that at any function of the uniformed service, a civilian driver has no place or recognition. He has to answer a number of questions while entering a security-sensitised area. I never used to consent for any departmental vehicle picking me up for the functions for which I was invited. Considering the inconvenience to which I was exposed and the fact that every invitee was going in the police vehicle, getting a free run of the way, I agreed to use the vehicle, which was sent to me. In my own vehicle, it used to take ages to cover the distance. It was covered in minutes because police drivers, while going for a police function, are never questioned by their fellow policemen. On principle, I do not go to any function unless invited. The person inviting, in all fairness, does not expect a retired officer to make his own arrangements for commuting. So for the first time, I used the vehicle sent by the Delhi Police. The result was that I could use the time for reading my newspapers and making phone calls on my cellular phone. It was one hour well utilised. I felt happy as I had not wasted any time. I was happy to know from the distributor of my book “Inside CBI”, Shri O P Arora of Variety Books, that there is still a demand for my book, "Inside CBI" and my books are doing well with a steady demand.

The modernisation and modern gadgets always need some kind of attention and maintenance. The Apple Macintosh computer, which my daughter uses, again became intransigent. I had punched an article on this machine. The computer refused to give the print-out. It is resting in peace, at the repair shop. A computer engineer spent two hours on it, coaxing it to work but to no effect. One has to learn to live with these problems. There is nothing much anybody can do about it. The Computer is a machine, where you cannot take out the spare parts and tinker with them. It is something, which is rectified by giving some commands. It is amazing that this machine can repair itself provided it gets the right commands. Once in a while, some virus enters, and the whole set of files get corrupt. Even engineers have a hit and trial approach. They are better than me, as they have some basic knowledge. But, by and large, they also work on guesswork. It's for the reason that the instruction manual of the computer in the computer itself is lengthy, bulky and too difficult to absorb. I do not think any computer user would have gone through the entire computer manual.

In the evening, I met Mr. Ashok Singhal, President of Vishwa Hindu Parishad, at his invitation. Vishwa Hindu Parishad members are not militant Hindus. There is a mistaken impression about them. They are only trying to protect the interests of the Hindu community, without harming others. It is strange but true that except for the Hindu and Sikh religion, all other religions are trying to make followers from other faiths by conversion. Proselytisation is an article of faith with the Christians. They want maximum people to join their flock. Muslims also believe that non-believers in one God are infidels. Muslims do not believe even in their Prophet Mohammed Sahib as God. In fact, Mohammed Sahib was looked upon as a guide and messenger of God. Christians believe that Lord Christ was the Son of God. Salvation is only possible through the Son, that is Lord Christ. It is a moot point as to which religion is good, or is the best. In my view that religion is best, which suits an individual and voluntarily invites him to believe and preaches in the language people can understand. I must make a confession that I have learnt about my own religion, only through the English language. The one book which has stuck me having the maximum living inspiration is the Gita.

Though Hindu religion has been most tolerant, yet its own followers in many countries are not allowed to practise their faith. I was told that in Saudi Arabia no religious book, except the one pertaining to Islam, is allowed entry. Even the photographs of other Gods are not allowed. A Foreign Service Officer told me that once an Indian diplomat, landing in Saudi Arabia, on a posting there, was arrested on the ground that he had a Hindu religious book with him. His mistake was that he called the Gita and the Ramayan as holy books. He was put in jail, and with great difficulty, the Indian Government succeeded in getting him released. He was not allowed to serve in Saudi Arabia. He had to be posted out. The Vishwa Hindu Parishad is trying to stem the conversions from Hindu religion to other religions, by enlightenment, preaching and providing facilities in backward areas.

While returning after meeting Mr. Ashok Singhal, I was tempted by South Indian food, which is my favourite. I brought home some dosas and idlis, at 1/3rd the price one pays in Five Star Hotels. The quality was better than that of Starred Hotels. My wife Surinder and I shared it. As a result of my service in Karnataka, I have come to relish South Indian Food. It was a hard task earlier to eat South Indian Food. Now if I have a choice I eat only South Indian Food.

Some mundane affairs/A fairy-tale wedding

The last few weeks have been hectic on some days. It has suited me as I can attend to my writing work on other days. Television is a great temptation. It is especially so in the night, when the blockbuster pictures and shows are shown. I have been elected Vice President of the DAV Management Committee. The Committee ably headed by a distinguished educationist Sh. G.P. Chopra, a Padma Shree awardee, is moving with the times. It has got a fully computerised extension counter of a bank, opened in its premises. It has the double advantage of providing service and getting deposits. I attended a pre-wedding reception of the son of a rich businessman, who is a co-morning walker with me. He falls in the category of the super rich who really does not know what to do with the pile of wealth accumulated every day. The reception was held in his farmhouse near the Delhi International Airport. His farmhouse, with just three acres of land, had a boundary wall of ten feet, with a palace built on stilts. It had a swimming pool, and its own electricity generation arrangements. The entire area was decorated with glittering lights of different colours. Each tree had a contrasting set of blinking bulbs, hanging like grapes.

The snacks served had a variety of South Indian, Chinese, Continental and Indian vegetarian and Tandooris. Choice of fruits included even non-seasonal fruits like mangoes and imported Kiwis, apart from the fruits of the season like bananas, apples, oranges, pomegranates and different types of water-melons. For those wanting to eat Chat, all kinds of spicy, or pungent or non-pungent items were there. I doubted if anybody could eat any dinner, after stuffing himself with the choicest offerings there. For those who wanted to imbibe drinks, there was enough variety to drown themselves. By a conservative estimate, he must have spent well over a million rupees apart from what was spent on the petrol by hundreds of visitors on their cars. The bride, decked with gold and diamond jewellery on every visible part of her body, came for the ceremony in a six-horse-driven buggy. Crackers were exploded and six brass band played to welcome her. With so much jewellery, it was difficult to assess whether she was a film star or an ordinary girl. I stayed there hardly for one hour. It is difficult to go on smiling with strangers and make small chat. The jaws start aching and even the teeth resent too much grinning. In big parties, especially those where one has only sporadic connections, one may be only a lone ranger. I am used to making friends everywhere, despite the above handicaps. I suppose this is the price of socialisation one has to pay. It used to happen during my foreign visits also, as in India.

Taking for a ride

My daughter Gagandeep was not well and was admitted to Sita Ram Bhartiya Research Institute. Most of the organisations have taken land from the government in the name of some research or teaching institutions and have commercialised prime property. An institute teaching MBA course was making more money by renting out a part of its space than from its main activities. There is no machinery with the concerned authorities to check the misuse. After some time, the misuse not only becomes *fait accompli*, but is institutionalised and taken on a face value. With the passage of time nobody remembers the purpose for which any government facility was given. We blame the government for bureaucratisation. But private firms or institutes have become carbon copies of over-bureaucratisation. Since the population of the country is large, most of us put up with humiliations, delays and tantrums by the underlings of such institutions, as there is no other alternative. This is despite the fact that one is paying exorbitant rates for every service. Of course, nobody is under compulsion to go to such places. But as medical or educational facilities matching world class are available at only a few places, most of us want the best or at least what is told to us, as the best. I had to wait for half an hour before the clerk at the reception desk permitted me to see her. The delay was because the entry pass was with my daughter, who was advised not to move about. She was all alone and till some gate keeper brought the pass, I had no right of access to her. Only when I asked for permission to speak to the Chief, I was allowed entry. Of course, hospital rules and regulations have to be followed. Like in the government sector, there is a need to implement them with a human touch. Gagandeep, affectionately called "Choosie" is my second daughter. She is a very persistent and determined lady. Slim, trim and smart, she can get around anybody with her winning and charming manners. I call her

"Dale Carnegie" incarnate. Dale Carnegie is the famous American consultant on developing human relations and the author of many "How to do Books". I personally have learnt a lot from him.

Dr. Khairiwal, an orthopaedist, from near Jalalabad joined me for lunch. He had looked after my late father Mahant Kartar Singh, when he was alive. These days he is working in a Saudi Arabian government hospital on a fat salary. To save time, if somebody wants to see me, I invite him either for lunch or tea so that I do not have to allocate exclusive time. He told me that strict accountability is enforced in Saudi Arabia, even on the doctors. Doctors have to take real care of the patients there. They can even be jailed. Public execution of the criminals or the amputation of the body parts is common. On the day of such punishments, which are done in public places, there is a carnival type of atmosphere and people come to witness the same in large numbers. The result is that you can leave a house full of gold and go away. Nobody will dare to touch it. There is capital punishment for importing drugs. In one month, there were as many as 40 executions in Saudi Arabia mostly of Pakistanis. As the number was too large, the executions were spread all over Saudi Arabia. Prosperity has its own hazards. It is quite common to see men and women weighing between 100 to 140 kilograms there. The result is the wide spread of diseases of heart and arthritis. I make sure that any guest who comes for lunch does not eat into my siesta, apart from lunch. I use various ploys like the next engagement being at 2 P.M. and throw indirect hints. Most people understand and take the hint. Those who do not are told clearly that I have to get ready for the next engagement. This does the trick. I rest in the afternoon so that my efficiency and alertness extends the to afternoon and the evening.

I went to the races in the afternoon, as a part of my duty of being a steward. While going for the meeting, I passed behind a horse in the Race Course and narrowly escaped being kicked by him. The horse tried to give me a fatal kick. But I side-stepped. I had forgotten the old adage that one must never cross the back of a horse and never come in the way of a senior officer or minister. I was luckier with the horse, whose aim misfired. A strong kick from a well-cared for and well-tended racehorse at a delicate spot of the body could have been fatal. This was a near brush with the end. I believe that unless you have finished your job and tenure on earth as ordained, no power on earth can kill you. Next day was the celebration of International Women's Day. I was the principal speaker at Teen Murti auditorium. An assortment of politicians was there on the dais. Everybody viewed the women's problem from his angle and forgot till the next celebration of International Women's Day. Mr. Shiv Raj Patil, a former speaker and a few other M.P's and Ex.M.P's were on the dais. The fact remains that any noise made does have some effect and focuses on the problem.

Upside down

A change in weather, in the sleeping time, a change of beds, the hardness or softness of a pillow-all has an effect on the sleep cycle. I got up at 2 A.M. and kept on tossing and turning in the bed; I could not sleep. I did the next best thing and sat working on my book. I finished editing the Police book. After working for two hours, I felt sleepy. Work is a better sleeping pill. I caught up on my sleep from 5 A.M. to 8 A.M. There was a meeting of the Board of Directors of The Pioneer, the best presented, leading English daily of Delhi. Due to the initiative and enterprise shown by the Editor and Managing Director, Chandan Mitra, the paper has turned a corner. It was making losses of nearly Rs. 18 crores per year before Chandan Mitra decided to salvage it from the Thapars. With staff, cut by half and with a drive to earn more and more revenue, the paper is comfortably placed. Chandan himself is a passionate writer and he writes with feeling. I dropped in to look up my morning walk friend, KK Bajaj, who has volunteered to publish my articles in his monthly magazine. Bajajs have been handling my investment portfolio, which is not much. Having been a bureaucrat all my life, I have always believed in playing safe and investing my money only in government securities. My articles have been appearing regularly in the English daily, Newstime, published from Hyderabad, at least once or twice a month. I get a number of complimentary magazines. One writer in an article in a Punjabi magazine proposed that I should be the next Chief Minister of Punjab. It is gracious of the writer to think highly of me. But I am just not available for the tumble, rumble and underhand dealings one has to do, to survive in politics. There is compromise at every step of life. The transfers and postings have been so much politicised that nobody thinks less than approaching the Chief Minister for any work. The legislators in many states call the shots. The result is good-bye to good governance, if you have to survive in politics. One former member of parliament told me that he had stopped speaking to his best friend, the then Chief Minister of his native State, when he refused to accept his recommendations for suspending a highly honest officer to settle his score with him. The Chief Minister came to his house uninvited for his daughter's wedding, touched his feet and begged forgiveness for not carrying out his wishes. Only then he forgave him. But he still remembers the incident as a grouse against a fellow politician. It is difficult for a bureaucrat to compromise his conscience, and sacrifice good administration for the sake of a political office, to such a great degree. Of course, it has been happening all the time. Officials with a view to survive have been compromising, at the behest of political masters. It appears that a vast majority of people have lost their backbone in standing up and doing what is right.

Ceremonies and ceremonial presence

I had briefly headed the Central Industrial Security Force in 1995, as an additional charge to my substantive job of being the Director General of the Indo-Tibetan Border Police Force. Normally all organisations have been inviting its former and retired Chiefs for the annual day function. But the invitations stopped coming, when a former CISF Chief was subjected to a CBI inquiry. I had nothing to do with the inquiry as it started after I had left the CBI. But, the then Chief, had approached me to bail out a senior officer from a CBI case. I politely declined making it clear that if the person recommended by him was not involved in any wrong doing, he need not have any apprehensions. In my career, I have never countenanced wrongdoing or tolerated other's interference. I refused to entertain any calls from this officer. The result was that all CISF functions were out of bound for me. I did not bother when for a couple of years, I was not invited. But I did mention to Mr. T.N.Misra, the then Director General. This led to the CISF re-including me in its invitee's list. It is not that one is looking for any invitation for any function. It is because when one has been a policeman all one's life, and no one continues to have some interest in the latest goings on. In fact, anybody going for any function, involving a travelling time of 90 minutes both ways and two hours of parade and tea, is doing a favour to the organisation. But it is time well spent as one becomes abreast of the latest developments and progress in the organisation. The Central Industrial Security was created to guard the Central Government Industries. It is much more expensive than any private security, as all the officials have to be paid, as per the pay scale applicable to the other central forces. The result is that cost is such a deterring factor that a vast majority of public sector undertakings are not in a position to pay the charges. One job of the CISF officers, posted in such units, is to collect the arrears of charges due on their account. It would have been simpler, if the Home Ministry accountant keeping accounts could raise a debit for the services rendered by the CISF, to the respective ministry. Now the Commandant or his Deputy or even Inspectors spend most of their time running after the management to pay the dues they owe for utilising their services. There is no end to the simplification, if it is required to be done. All the money is going from the government or government-sponsored or government-owned companies. A budget provision could have been made in the Home Ministry to meet the extra expenditure and a corresponding reduction in the budget of the ministry or ministries, for which the CISF is deployed. The Director General mentioned that the traditional top heavy approach needs to be given up. What public sectors want are the small CISF units, headed by an Assistant or Deputy Commandants. Very few units can afford the high salary required to be paid to the DIG/Commandants. Fortunately, the decision of the Airport Authority to hand over the security of some Airports to the CISF has come handy in utilising the force. The standard of the parade was excellent. Home Minister, L.K. Advani, was the Chief Guest and he took the salute. It was a two hours function, which included the parade, presentation of medals, a dog show and a demonstration for handling fires. Advani is a soft spoken National Leader, who believes in creating minimum friction. All para military forces, including the Central Reserve Police Force, Border Security Force and Indo-Tibetan Border Police Force have a brick-and-mortar fort wall in the background. Even the style of parade and the post parade programme is almost the same. It is like the TV Channels, copying each other's best features. I chatted briefly with the then Director of the CBI, Mr. Raghavan, an officer of 1963 Batch. Soft spoken, Raghvan has conducted himself very creditably in the hot seat, which I occupied for eleven months before Gujral, who occupied the Prime Ministerial office, by a fluke of circumstances, got annoyed with me for not carrying out his bidding in the fodder scam case, moved me to an idle parking slot in the Home Ministry. After the parade, there was an assault on the refreshment tables. It appeared that most people were more interested in the refreshments than in the main function. I used the return journey for going through the day's papers.

Condolence, mere pretence

I visited Saharanpur on Tuesday, 14 March 2000 for the condolence Bhog of Mohinder Singh, elder brother of my brother-in-law Tarlok Singh. My younger sister Sarla married Tarlok Singh in 1963. Tarlok Singh has inherited the cloth business and his two sons, nicknamed Titu and Situ, are helping him out. The entire family was present in Saharanpur. Mohinder Singh was a very cheerful, hospitable and affectionate person. Everybody appeared to be decently remorsful about the death, for the sake of the occasion. Many whispered that it was a great relief for the deceased, who had undergone extreme hardship, with cancer, affecting his vital part, in the last stages of life. His son Inderjit is called Bitu. The result of nicknames is that most often we cannot identify our closest relations except by their nicknames.

Programme with more than objectives

I left for Punjab on return from Saharanpur. The train arrived in time at Ferozpore. As usual, Om drove me to Jalalabad. My mother has been staying there for the last two months in our family house with her maid servant. She feels happy, contented and usefully occupied. The house there runs to her convenience. She attends to all phone calls herself, though she hardly understands anything. My visits every month are only to ensure that she is comfortable. I try to stay at least for three to five days in a month with her. I avoid all politics in the college or in any other local matters.

I left Jalalabad on 21st March 2000, en route to Batala, via Sultanpur Lodi. Whenever I get a chance I try to mix pilgrimage with my visits. While working as IG, CRPF in Kashmir, I had also visited the Hazratbal Shrine, reported to be the repository of a hair of the Muslim prophet Mohammed Sahib. As Hinduism, Sikhism, Jainism and Buddhism were born in India, naturally there are more places associated with them, rather than those belonging to Christianity or Islam. In any case, neither Christ nor Mohammad Sahib ever visited India. Most of the places belonging to Christianity and Islam are associated with the holy leaders and followers of those religions. Such places are generally the birth places of those religions. Sultanpur Lodhi is one place where Guru Nanak, the founder of Sikh religion, spent over 13 years. His two sons, Lakhmi Chand and Siri Chand, were born there. The house he stayed in is now a gurudwara called Guru Ka Bagh. It commemorates his stay there. His married sister Nanki used to live in Sultanpur Lodi with her family. There is a gurudwara to commemorate her memory as Bibi Nanki's gurudwara. There is also a gurudwara called Hat Sahib, where Guru Nanak was in charge of the shop or stores of Sultan of Lodi. He was accused of misappropriation and imprisoned. But as the charge was false, he was freed. Another Gurudwara Ber Sahib is the place of meditation and enlightenment of Guru Nanak. Sultanpur is the holiest Sikh city, more holy than Amritsar, as the founder of Sikhism had blessed this place with his stay of over 13 years. Unfortunately, the roads leading to this place of Saint Nanak are in a discreditable condition. It has a lot of unexploited potential of being the Capital of Sikh religion. It is one of those towns which still has to attract the attention of the Sikhs. The town is as humble as was Guru Nanak. At Goindwal Sahib, I visited the birth place of Guru Arjun, the place of meditation of the third Guru Amardas, and the place where he and 4th Guru Ram Das passed away. Khadur Sahib is the place where

Amar Dass was anointed as Guru and the place of penance and meditation and formation of Punjabi. At Baba Bakala, the discovery of the 9th Guru Tegh Bahadur was made by a trader, who had promised to make an offering of 500 gold coins or Mohurs to the incarnation of Guru Nanak, in the event of his safe arrival from the sea journey in the turbulent weather. He could not find the true successor of Guru Nanak. He searched for the true Guru every where. Eventually he was told that the true Guru was living in Baba Bakala. He came to the town and found a multitude of persons claiming to be the true Gurus. He offered two gold coins or Mohurs to every claimant. All of them blessed him. He was disappointed that nobody had divined that he had come to offer 500 gold coins to the true Guru. When his search was almost over, he inquired whether there was any more Guru in Baba Bakala. He was told that there was one more person, called Tega. He was rather eccentric and recluse. He was busy with prayers and meditation. He rarely met anybody. However, on his insistence, the trader Makhan Shah Lubana was allowed to meet him. He offered two gold Mohurs to Teg Bahadur, who reminded him that his commitment was to pay 500 gold coins. He was getting away by offering two gold coins. At this, he realised that he was the true Guru. He climbed on the roof top and proclaimed in a loud voice that he had found the true Guru. There is a Gurudwara to commemorate the event. In the same place, Guru Teg Bahadur was shot at by the supporters of his rivals. Batala, my next place of visit, was the place of his in-laws. Guru Nanak had married a girl there. Guru Nanak had sat, under an unsafe wall, as a bride groom. When advised to move away, he replied that this wall will be remembered through ages. I attended a function of ABVP on the necessity to amend the constitution and explained that there is no harm in having a look at the constitution. I met Prof BS Ansu and his wife. He is the father-in-law of my daughter Gagandeep and father of Gunveer. I do not like to prolong my stay unless it is necessary. After the function, Om left me in Amritsar in time to catch the evening train Golden Temple Express for Delhi, when I arrived next morning.

Forgotten heroes

Friday, 24 March 2000 was spent in two functions to pay homage to Martyrs, Shaheed Bhagat Singh, Sukhdev and Rajguru, who had been hanged on 23rd March, 1930. It is surprising that, except for one or two functions, nobody remembers the contribution of those martyrs. A film star of yester years, Manoj Kumar, in a rather inebriated condition was the star attraction. But he spoke very well. He had played the role of Bhagat Singh in a film made on that great Martyr. He embraced and appreciated my frankness, in speaking about men and matters, especially about corruption. The new generation has its own heroes. I have a feeling that they hardly know or care about the sacrifices made by the giants like Bhagat Singh in the past.

Weddings of the rich

I visited DLF Enclave, Gurgaon for a wedding of relations of my son-in-law Gunveer Singh. The wedding party was late, as is usual, in Delhi. You have the choice of either waiting or suffering in silence or chit-chatting. As at all weddings of the rich, one meets fat and bulging men and indifferent guests. There are equally hefty ladies with traces of old body and charm. Some are in delapidated conditions, due to the ravages of time and food. Only their ruins tell that once upon a time there was a magnificient building. After some time, one runs out of topics of conversations with total or near strangers, except the weather, food, common friends or the general get-up of the place. The charges for some weddings can be as high as Rs. 1000 to 3000 per guest, depending upon the quality and brand of the liquor served. The money spent on one wedding, sometimes, is more than earmarked for one year's development in one district. The difference between the too rich and too poor is as vast as between two countries separated by an ocean. Many a time, it becomes a matter of competition between the neighbours or fellow business men as to who spends more. The rich, who have spent all their lives in metropolitan cities, cannot comprehend the conditions of the poor parts of India. In fact, all the goodies of life, whether medical treatment or public school education, or creature comforts are available only in the big towns and the capital of the country. It is for this reason that people migrate from rural to urban areas. The best educational institutions, the best hospitals, the best road are in the central or state capitals. Delhi has the highest car population, with an average of one motor vehicle for four citizens. I too, would have remained ignorant, but for my periodical visits to my village and lands. It is money, which generates money. Earlier in the day, I addressed Indian Economic Society in India Habitat Centre. I put the onus on Indians to develop India. I said that it is better, if we forget our favourite blame game, and concentrate on doing our own job well. Bhisham Narain Singh, a former Governor, said that contracts are given for winning elections in Bihar. The amount can be as much as Rs. 25-30 lakhs for driving away voters and booth capturing.

I also attended the re-launch of Life positive magazine, by Dr. Karan Singh, MP. Mostly all such programmes are self-praising and self-patting sessions. Most people only want a reconfirmation of their stand, and view. Like Karan Singh, I stayed for enough time to register my presence, and left for Delhi as the function was held in a hotel near Faridabad.

Late nights, not for me

There was a book release function at the PM's house on 28 March 2000. As the book by Ms. Anita Arya, MP had been brought out by my publisher, who had persistently requested me to attend the function, I agreed to do so. I normally do not like to get involved in political matters or politicians. I was doubtful whether the PM would recognise me. It was proved wrong when Sh. Vajpayee told me that he was glad that I came for the function. I thanked him for his kind words and presented my book "Outside the CBI" to him. I showed him the paragraph, wherein I had mentioned my previous meeting with him, when I had presented him my book, "Inside CBI". Jagmohan, the then Minister for Works and Housing, was also present at the function. He is a go-getter and is clear in his thinking, apart from being a man of high integrity. I told him that his reputation was that of a man, who needs only a steno for his working. The Prime Minister said in his speech that there is no dearth of laws to ensure that things move properly as conceived by the constitution makers. It was the need of the hour that outdated practices which had outlived their utility were given up. Education is the agent of change. Without reservations, there is likely to be no progress in the status and life of women. He said that he did not want to go into the percentages. But the women excelled in whatever jobs they had done. Political parties selected the candidates on the basis of their winability and the women were perceived to be non winners. In the evening at Ashoka Hotel, I attended a party hosted by Amar Singh, MP. His dinner arrangements are like the ones one sees in films with beautiful girls decked nicely, like the brides at the steps to welcome you. The dinner was hosted in honour of Kerry Packer, an Australian Tycoon, who was welcome by caparisoned elephants, horses and a musical band. Film Star Amitabh Bachan was also introduced to me. He has grown a white beard, only on a part of the face. His public image is still of the angry young-man of the eighties and nineties. After usual helloing and registering my presence with the host, I was back at home by 10.30 PM. A number of film stars and actresses were present. But I am not very good at remembering the faces of thinny and skinny girls, as they all look alike. I feel that my connection with any film star is over after I have paid for seeing the particular film.

Today a friend Jasweer Singh (name changed) dropped into share his tale of woe. He visited a Gurudwara and was given a big doze of lecture that he must have a long undyed flowing beard. The person delivering the lecture was a small shop keeper. Jasweer Singh told me that he let him have it with compound interest. He said; "I told him that for some of you religion consists in external appearances and formalism. Do not tell me, what Sikh religion is. It preaches practice of certain basic values, which most people do not do. Never give any unsolicited advice. There is no co-relation of the intensity of your being highly religious either with the colour or length of the hair grown either on the head or on the face". I told him that there was no need to be abrasive and he could have ignored the advice. He fired me by saying; " You are exactly like me. Why did you not protest, whenever any such advice was tendered? Only if you had done, none of the self-appointed custodians of the religion would have the guts to give lectures. Sikh religion is one of the best religions. But I do not accept everything told to me as gospel truth, because the appearance of the narrator indicates that he is a priest or priestly looking. Most of these people are illiterate and do not understand the meaning of religion. Religion is a life style, a way of approach and not a way of looking. It is this narrow-minded approach which has prevented the spread of Sikh religion. Let the illiterate Sikhs not make the size of the beard as a criterion of being a Sikh, and you will see this religion, overtaking all other religions put together. Being the youngest of the religions, it contains all the best which has been thought and written about by the Sikh Gurus and other saints. I do not visit any Sikh Gurudwara to please any priest. It is a question of my own equation with my Master. Let the middlemen stop meddling with me and my God. In any case, it is doubtful whether such people are self-appointed guardians or appointed by God". I told him: "Please do not fight with anybody over the religion. Fighting with the people, especially those preaching orthodoxy would never lead to your winning. Fundamentalists in every religion have a louder say. Nobody fights them for his own piece of mind. Though most people dislike and oppose any return the to middle ages, where those who did not fall in line were burnt at the stake, yet the same people are quiet. Fundamentalists themselves do not lead any unalloyed life. They have their own weak spots, which they cover up, by theology or lectures or by looking grave or by their appearance of being portly and learned".

The mercury has been soaring. Sometimes, even the air conditioners literally give up, when the temperature exceeds 46 degrees centigrade. My acquaintance with air conditioners date back to 1970, when I did not know that a hill station like atmosphere could be created in a room. I went to see a friend, Dr. R.K. Jain on Mathura Road, beyond Apollo Hospital. It took me twenty minutes to reach and 45 minutes to find out the location of his office. The numbering system in Delhi is so bad that you can get lost in a maze of wrong numbers and wrong turns. It is strange that a simple thing like proper numbering is not there, in most of the towns, what to talk of villages.

System seems to have overtaken

A friend who claims to know the Prime Minister well told me that even the PM feels that the system of governance has become so lethargic and unresponsive that nobody can do anything to improve the situation. I do not know how much truth there is, in the alleged information. But the fact remains that there are too many people doing too little. The result is that the letter of the rule has become more important than the spirit behind it. I have two telephones in my residence. One is the official telephone of my wife. The other is my private telephone. I went for my private telephone well before my retirement. It was to save my wife from any possible allegations that her husband is using her official phone for his personal work. It is a fact, that even a retired person would need to use a telephone. My wife, Surinder, who has headed the Publication Division now heading the DAVP of the Government of India, is very meticulous in paying her telephone bill for the private calls made. In fact I did not even tell her telephone number to any of my contacts and batchmates. I make it a point to make an advance voluntary deposit of my telephone, so that my telephone is not disconnected. I am normally surplus by about Rs. 5000 with the telephone department. I sent my secretary to pay Rs. 5000 by cheque in Jor Bagh post office. The clerk there refused to accept the advance payment on the ground that no bill was pending against my name. When told that it was a voluntary advance deposit, as permitted by the rules, he replied that he was not aware of any such rule. Next day, when my driver went to deposit the cheque, he was advised to go for depositing it at Janpath. When my driver went to deposit the cheque, an objection was raised that the form had not been filled. This is the hassle one goes through in depositing money, in the government account. Nobody takes the government work seriously, because a government job is there for life whether one works or not. It is for this reason that the spirit of working for the public is totally absent from the government work. Nobody has ever lost his job, for not being responsive to public needs or for not taking care of the government interests. The public just gives up in despair saying that there is no relief from the bottlenecks and harassment. There is no will either in the senior officers or in the political masters to rectify the situation. Their only activity is to issue circulars or make speeches. That is why, even after more than half a century of independence, there is no perceptible relief for the common man. The day there is a political will, to turn a corner for the betterment of the country, things will start moving.

Animals too like air-conditioned comfort

Somehow, we human beings feel that only we need comforts and not lesser creatures like animals, dogs or cows. This impression was dispelled today, when I went to Star News Channel for a TV recording regarding the allegations made, for cricket match fixing made by a player, Manoj Prabhakar, against the former Cricket captain Kapil Dev. I appeared in a Television programme of questions and answers on Star TV News Channel from 7.30 P.M. to 8 P.M. It was about the cricket match fixing and the videotapes released by one of the cricketers, alleging the role of fellow cricketers, in match fixing, for alleged bribes. A television appearance has a snow balling effect. In the next few days, I appeared on the Jain Television/Metro Channel and News Channel of the Door Darshan, to give my views on the evidence of the tapes, for match fixing. The Indian cricketers were a cohesive lot. But every relationship goes through various phases. If the exposure of match fixing does some good to the game of cricket, it would have been worth it, in spite of the inter-personal relationships, external circumstances and emotions involved. Wisdom lies in doing the correct thing, so that the dark clouds of uncertainty are blown away. I told the viewers that whatever may be the perception of others, there is no legal evidence at present which can sustain the charge that the loss of the match or its winning was a contrived affair.

I noticed a huge dog sleeping blissfully right in the middle of the air-conditioned staircase. Nobody wanted to throw out the dog for fear of being bitten. People let him sleep undisturbed, in the air conditioned comfort, rather than incur its ire. Most of the time, most of us believe in letting sleeping dogs lie. If any proof was needed for this, it was here in the form of the huge canine, who by looks and the sound sleep, gave an impression that disturbing him would produce the most disastrous consequence. A vast majority of the population believes that letting sleeping dogs sleep is the only reliable mode of survival. It is for this reason that bullies carry on merrily, and civil servants toe the line, of meeting even the most illegal and unreasonable demands of the people enjoying political power. A sour neighbour is like a canine about whom you can do nothing. He is going to stay where he is. Interfere with him and you create hell for yourself.

I travelled from Delhi to Coimbatore by the Indian Airlines flight on 3rd June 2000. One thing which struck all passengers was that Indian Airlines had put grandmothers on duty to serve as airhostesses. Many hesitated to ask them even for the basic services like serving of water. The Airline presents a fagged-out, old woman's face, by putting old women, as its show pieces. The passengers judge an Air-Line by the visage or frontage it puts up. No wonder that its rating has gone down in the travelling public. Perhaps I am being over charitable. Some of them appeared to be the grand mothers of grandmothers. Lack of accountability in a government organisation and its non-enforcement is the undoing of the government and its organisations. Everybody wants to play safe and not wake up sleeping dogs or raise controversies. Commercial activities and the government are not exactly the best of partners. The flight going to Coimbatore was bashed up by a negligent tow vehicle driver at Bombay. It delayed 140 passengers for three hours and caused tremendous inconvenience to those who had to board it from Coimbatore and Kozikhode on the way to Doha and Baharein. I learnt that the negligent personnel was suspended but reinstated within three hours as all his colleagues went on a lightning strike in

Bombay airport. The weak-kneed and over-bloated management just bowed. An official in the airline told me that there is a kickback in every functioning and every deal in the airlines.

Death in Ooty

I have been in Ootacomund, generally called Ooty, since the 3rd of June for a programme organised by Delhi Productivity Council headed by amiable KS Maheshwari and his efficient assistant, Programme Officer, Rajiv Mehta. Rajiv Mehta is the man Friday of the Delhi Productivity Council. From the time of arrival at Ooty at 7.30 P.M. till my departure it has been constantly raining. Initially it was a great relief to come from a temperature of 43 degrees C at Delhi to 12 degrees. But the rain has tied me in the room for the last five days in this hill station at a height of 7600 feet. It is all right to enjoy weather for a few days while in the room itself. But after sometime one feels like a prisoner. The only activity has been delivering lectures, meeting the participants, the same faculty members and eating something or the other all the time. Sometimes it becomes so cold that even two blankets and the room heaters are inadequate. Thanks to my computer, I have not felt bored. Even the fallen TV aerials have knocked off the TV transmission due to strong gale and rains. The only contact with the outside world is the telephone and the newspapers, which are received in the afternoon. The Hotel Monarch, the venue of the programme, has tried to make our stay very comfortable, despite the fact that power supply has snapped due to strong winds. The hotel has been generating its own electricity. The atmosphere outside is full of thunder and rain. For two days, I had my walk and exercise indoor in the hotel lobby. I was told that in 1988 there was no electricity in Ooty for eight days. It does not make much difference to the residents in the hotel, as there is a full back up generator lighting the place. The only snag is that the lift does not work. One of the faculty members died in the hospital due to a cardiac problem. But it did not upset anybody's schedule, as others conducted his classes. Since I had to catch the morning flight to Delhi on 8th June, I was advised to be ready to leave at 6 A.M. This was to give a margin for any possible blockade of the road.

Heavy rains spoil the day

I had a few hours of sleep and got up at 5 A.M. My faithful alarm clock woke me up and I finished my ablutions and bath in 25 minutes before even the hotel tea arrived. I had done my packing the previous evening. I am bad at packing, at a short notice. I did not want to get delayed, because of packing. In the rarest of the rare cases, I was ready before 6 A.M. However the driver came afterwards and we started our journey in the Cielo car of Mithun Chakarvarthy. Mithun has been very nice and considerate to me. I spoke to him last night and thanked him for the efficient hospitality extended to me. Mithun's driver brought me to the airport from Ooty non-stop in a flat 2 hours 15 minutes. I was feeling drowsy on the way. A few sips of water and a drought of fresh air kept me awake. I arrived at the airport two hours before the flight departure timing. The flight left in time. But it could not land at Bombay, due to heavy rains and was diverted to Nagpur. The executive class in IC658 was totally vacant except, for some pilots and crewmembers returning to Bombay. After a waiting period of one hour, the plane was taken back to Bombay. It took one hour to reach Bombay and one hour more of waiting there. Ultimately I landed up in Delhi at 7 P.M., four hours after the scheduled arrival. The lunch was served to us at about 5 P.M. en route from Bombay to Delhi. A delayed lunch, not only upset my stomach but also caused food poisoning in the night. Obviously the food had been stale. It necessitated a visit to the doctor who put me on Norflox and Nimulid the next day. The heavy antibiotics coupled with loose motion left me weak. So I missed my morning walk the next day, that is 9th of June. I could hardly get up from bed and had to decline an invitation for lunch from my friend Prof. N.K. Singh. I just had enough energy after taking the medicine to go for a funeral of an IPS officer, RS Sahaye, who had passed away in the early morning. Earlier I had visited his house to pay my last respects to Sahaye, who was also related to my brother-in-law Tarlok Singh. I literally forced myself to have an evening walk in the Lodi Garden to get the happenings of the day out of my system. One of the best ways to forget and put behind any unpleasant happening is to vigorously exercise. It is a kind of universal therapy. The modern medicine is able to take care of both minor and major ailments. The entire weekend was spent in recovering from food poisoning. The TV has more advertisement than the contents of the programme. I am back to listening to the radio, which does not require any turning or twisting your head to ensure that one is not missing something worthwhile. Except for one visit to Connaught Place, I, by choice, have been staying in the house and spending most of the time in writing and the other set routine of walking, sleeping and eating, at pre-determined times. Occasionally, I feel hungry at the mid- or late-night, leading to keeping myself awake. Only after I have eaten something, I can get back to my sleep. Also alternately, there is a craving to eat sweets and salty stuff. I go on eating something or the other during my entire waking hours.

To London

At the invitation of office bearers and the Secretary General, Jagmohan Singh, I had agreed to head an organisation called Non-Resident Indian Institute based in Delhi. Its main function is to bring the Non-Resident Indians and those in India together with a view to promote foreign investment in India.

One of its main activities is to honour a Non-Resident Indian, who has made it good in life almost by starting from scratch. This year, the function is slated on the 7th of July 2000 in London. I travelled from Delhi in the British Airways Jumbo 700-400. It is a massive plane and can seat 409 passengers. It has the capacity, power and fuel to travel up to 7,178 miles or 11,555 kilometres non-stop at a cruising speed of 575 miles per hour or 925 kilometres at a height of 35000 feet. The length of the plane is 70.1 metres or 231 feet and wing span is 83 feet or 25.5 metres. The most comfortable class for travelling is first class. The fare is nearly two lakhs for a journey, of nine hours and twenty minutes on the forward leg of Delhi to London. The return journey takes forty minutes less, that is eight hours and forty minutes. This is due to head winds against the plane, which blow at a speed ranging from 60 to 100 kilometres. Outside the plane, which flies at a height of 35000 feet, higher than the highest mountain in the world, that is Mount Everest, the temperature is -40 degree centigrade. The technology has progressed so much, that every minute the private TV screen in front of your seat displays the speed at which you are flying, the time from the starting point and how long it will take to reach the proposed destination. It constantly displays the estimated time of arrival at the destination, local time at the destination, local time at the starting place. There is a facility of audio and video to every club and first class passenger. There is a choice of English or Hindi movie. The movie prints are excellent. If you do not like movies, you can listen to your favourite Hindi or English music on the private headsets given to you. On the inter continental flights, like the one I travelled in, the seats have been designed for maximum comfort. You lift the seat headrest to the required height or you can raise the leg rest for stretching or vary the cushion length. For lumbar rest you can inflate your seat or can have a tilting recline. The airlines give attractive names to the seats calling them cradle seat as the most comfortable seat in the air. The flight left at 12.10 AM on the 5th of July and arrived at Heathrow, London, twenty minutes ahead of schedule at 4.30 A.M. There is hardly any custom clearance for the passengers. The immigration officer took hardly one minute to allow me entry as I already had a five years visa for England. My friend Manohar along with his wife Krishna was there to receive me at the airport at 5.10 A.M. I was expecting that I would go straight to the hotel booked for me. But it appeared that no room was available for me till 6th of July. Manohar had kindly volunteered not only to put me up but also gave me his bedroom. During the day, Manohar and I travelled to Oxford Street and had lunch with the Secretary General of the NRI institute, Jagmohan Singh at Gaylord, an Indian Restaurant. Jagmohan had invited the Press Trust of India Bureau Chief, H.S. Rao and the Hindustan Times Bureau Chief, Vijay Dutt for lunch at the Indian Restaurant called Gaylord. It is interesting to chat with the press people, because they are mostly the repositories of all-local information and gossips. One of them told me that a former Civil Aviation minister had accepted Rs. 4 crores in a deal in the recent past. Another interesting thing that emerged was that, though Air India had stopped operating its flights to Frankfurt in Germany, it was still maintaining a twenty-member office there, for the last one and a half years. It was naturally costing crores of rupees to maintain an idle establishment there. When the Government of India talks about cutting losses, it forgets to see that right under its nose, crores are being wasted. One German working for Air India had told a London-based Indian Pressman that obviously some high-ups in the organisation or Government of India must have accepted huge kickbacks to leave the field free for Lufthansa. One of the depressing features of foreign visits is a feeling of loneliness and being in wilderness. But when one is amongst known faces or friends or talking in the same language over the meals one is used to, such a feeling disappears. I did not feel a stranger at all in London on this account. Unlike other countries, where there is a language difficulty, I feel at home in the United Kingdom. I am certain that if I get lost, I can always ask somebody the way back and be sure that I would be understood. This is not so in France, because every Frenchman insists on speaking only in French even if he knows English. London has a number of tourist attractions which require many days to be thoroughly seen. Madam Tusaud's is one of the ultimate accolades of fame; currently it has over 400 stunningly life-like figures. It also has the eerie Chambers of Horror, "Spirit of London and time travel ride". The Tower of London is a medieval fortress, where crown jewels are kept. It is a monument about the bloody and dark deeds of more than 900 years of royal history. Another place of horror is The London Dungeon. It is guaranteed to give a chilling experience. The London Museum has a fascinating history and you can see items from pre-historic times. The tourist industry is well organised and nobody cheats, like back at home. However nothing is free, and you have to pay anything between 4 to 15 pounds for each visit to different places.

After lunch Manohar took me on a train tour of Canary Island. The skyline of London is full of skyscrapers. Residential and commercial areas look alike. But the system of numbering, and directions is excellent. By following the signs and printed guides, you can reach almost anywhere in London. Nobody breaks the queues and the obedience to the traffic laws is universal and unquestioned. There are about 900 TV channels available in the United Kingdom. There is no delivery of newspapers at home in England as in India. Newspapers are available only at stands. Unlike in India, newspapers or magazines are just discarded after reading. There is no market for 'Raddi' or junk. You have to pay for removing the outlived material or junk or newspapers. England would be a delight for a 'Kabadi' or a junk dealer. Normal shopping hours are from 9 A.M. to 5 P.M. However, some flexibility is there, in some areas and places. By the time we came back, it was 8 P.M. There is a time difference of four and a half hours these days between India and England. The body system does not easily accept the time change, though the local clock shows that it is 8 A.M. which means 12.30 P.M. Next day, I shifted to the Hotel Gallery where my reservation was there from 5th to 10th of July. While the hosts do their best to make one comfortable in their own home, yet there is no substitute for independent stay. One can plan one's own rest and work timings. In my case I am used to drinking at least half a dozen cups of tea. Naturally one cannot ask the host to go on giving pots after pots of tea. I carry my own tea making kit with me, while on tour, in and out of India. The Universal adapter purchased in Germany in 1981 is still going strong. With tea bags and powdered milk, I can enjoy my tea anywhere. In place of sugar, I used an artificial low calorie sweetener, to keep my weight under check. In the hotel room, there was a tea-making kit with plenty of coffee and tea bags. The first thing I do, when I go to any hotel is to find out what facilities are available and where are the control switches. All this information is available in brochures and hotel information folder kept in the room drawers. I make it a point, to familiarise myself if necessary by asking the hotel staff even the basic information. Manohar dropped me in his car to the hotel. He could not find a parking place within ten miles of the hotel. He went back to his house and left his car there. He came back in the evening by train to join me for the dinner of International Punjabi Society. In the evening, I along with the Secretary General of the NRI Institute met Sharad Pawar, former Defence Minister of India and now a member of the Lok Sabha to invite him for the NRI function. Every country has its own methods of functioning and systems. It is not like back home, where influences and pressures can adjust the rules, regulations and practices in favour of the high and mighty. Mr. Joginder Sangar, Chairman of the Hotel Washington, Mayfair located at 5, Curzon Street (TF. 0044 0207-499-7000) London W1Y 8DT told me that his mother-in-law had passed away during sleep in London on a Tuesday. It is mandatory to have an inquest done. Her body was shifted to the Coroner for post mortem. There is a waiting list, even of the post mortems, which in her case was done on the Friday, that is, three days after her death, to rule out any foul play. Then the next problem was to get the cremation preparation done, from a funeral director. By making a special request and by agreeing to pay 1000 Pounds (equivalent of Rs. 70000), the cremation was done on a Saturday. The payment of overtime is generally avoided for funerals on Saturdays or Sundays as in any case it would make no difference to the dead, for another two days. There is just no possibility of cremation the same day. For the dead poor, whose relations cannot afford the high cost of Rs. 21000 or 300 Pounds, the local council or the voluntary organisations take care of the cost. The cremation is done, as per the standards laid down. The body is kept in a wooden box. The quality depends upon the capacity upon the heirs of the body pay of casket. Even the carriers of the dead body come from the funeral house. Only they can officially seal the box of the body, before its cremation or burial, which is also cremated. Mr. Sangar made his millions, by working in double shifts, as a labourer and then as an assistant foreman. Even the well-to-do prefer to travel by tube or buses, to avoid wasting time in finding parking places. I visited a Casino in London, the Casino's slot machine gobbled up my five pounds. Mr. Nirula who was honoured, was the host for the Casino visit. Mr. H.S. Nirula started his life with Rs.5000 given by his father in 1972. By dint of hardwork, his group is over a 800 million $ group. He has believed in keeping a low profile. His theory is that to be considered successful you must be a millionaire, by the time you are 40. People in London have big cars; plenty of convenience and a comfortable existence, except one If and one But. This If and But is that at any given time, half of London, is busy finding a parking place for their cars, while the other half, either prefers to stay at home, or travels in underground trains to their place of work or for shopping. This is the problem of prosperity. It is almost unheard of to have a driver of your own to drive you around. Very few people have the luxury of a private servant or a private driver. The minimum wages are 8 Pounds or Rs. 560 per hour or Rs. 4460 per day. It is wrong to be taken in by the high wages, in terms of Indian rupees. A one day combined rail and bus ticket costs you 4.10 Pounds or nearly Rs 300. When people earn in pounds, they also have to spend in Pounds. A loaf of bread can cost Rs.70 or one Pound.

There is no place like home-land

After the function was over, I returned from London by the British Airways flight, which left at 9.55 P.M. on the 10th of July and arrived in Delhi at 11 A.M. on the 11th of July. In London all the time was spent in seeing big departmental stores or meeting a few friends, who made the lonely existence in foreign lands bearable. I was invited for being honoured with a Siropa or a robe in the Gurudwara at Hunslow on the 9th of July, 2000. I told the President of the Gurudwara Mr. Gurcharan Singh Chatwal that I was grateful for the proposed honour and would be delighted to come. But they would have to make arrangements to transport me there. It is a fact that the biggest hassle is in getting around to any place whether in India or abroad. It is more difficult abroad. This is more so because in a place like London, one has to have a combination of taxis trains and buses. Most often it is by tube, which itself is expensive. With the limited foreign exchange one has bought and not the government per diem, one has to be careful in spending. The use of taxis is out of the question. In fact, the foreign visit on a shoestring budget, as I was on, would always be better avoided. The infrastructure of the use of embassy facilities of vehicle, or somebody to take care of you is not there. But I am capable of adjusting everywhere and do not mind mixing and meeting people. I have a capacity to befriend people and the result is that I get along with people anywhere. People are generally helpful. So Mr. Chatwal picked me up in his Mercedes vehicle. The atmosphere in the Gurudwara was more of a carnival and ceremonial rather than solemn. The constraint of space has led to the construction of the two-storeyed Gurudwara, with arrangements for office, toilets and Langar place on the ground floor. The first floor is reserved for the holy book and the congregation. The Ragis or the persons reciting the hymns, are mostly visitors on the sponsorship of the managing committee. Each of them returns with enough pounds, equal to about Rs. 5 to 6 lakhs in the six months stay in the United Kingdom. This time, the stay in London was only for five days. Even this period appeared too long for me. Doing the same things every day, which included taking a walk on the Oxford Street or visiting some departmental store or the other was very boring. I felt relieved, when I could get my reservation by the British Airways flight leaving for Delhi at 10 P.M on 10th July, 2000. It was a touch-and-go affair, as the reservation, even for the club class, was confirmed only on the same day. The average traffic speed, even by the best cars in London, works out to be 16 kilometres per hour. I was happy to be leaving for home by the flight which brought me ten minutes earlier than the schedule. As there is a time gap of four and a half hours between the U.K and India, I left London at 2.30 AM as per Indian time and arrived in Delhi at 11 A.M. Whenever there is a change of time zones or vast time difference, I make it a point to take a sleeping pill. The next two days were spent in adjusting to the local time and getting the body cycle and food habits adjusted to the local timing and weather. In fact, the weather in London was just like that of India. Choosie and Bibban had a common birthday celebrations on 12-7-2001, as both sisters were born on 12th July in 1972 and 1977 respectively. This is a kind of a hat trick and must be rare in any family. Not that we planned it. It just happened.

Next day, I left Delhi by Swaran Shatabdi or the superfast train for Ludhiana en route to Phagwara for inaugurating a computer training institute started and sponsored by a TV Channel. The Punjab Higher Education Minister Pundit Mohan Lal was the guest of honour, whereas I was the Chief Guest. I was requested to inaugurate the centre. It was a brief function and was over by 2.30 P.M. My intention was to leave for Jalalabad as early as I could. I wanted to visit the historic Gurudwaras of Sultanpur Lodi, as it was on the way. Guru Nanak had spent over thirteen years in Sultanpur Lodi. For Sikhs, it is a place of pilgrimage. Somehow we missed the way and decided to skip the visit to the Gurudwaras at Sultanpur Lodi. Perhaps one cannot visit such places whenever one desires. One has to be summoned, to pay homage to the holy people. My cousin Pappu, Inderjit Singh Madan of Kissan Solvent, had also come for the function with his business partner Pramod from Ferozpore. Kissan company has done extremely well both in terms of money and reputation. Sardar Jagir Singh, Pappu's father, started from scratch.

Amongst the super rich

My son-in-law Abbassi with my daughter Randeep and grandson Danish arrived from Assam in the last week of July. The whole house revolved around two years old Danish, who was tired as a result of the long flight. He was bitten by an insect and cried a lot, While playing with other children, he tore off their kite. We compensated the boys with money, for his damaging their kites. It was a rare occasion that the lights went off due to power shedding. A fabulous dinner party was hosted by a former MP Subrami Reddy at a five star hotel. I had been requested at least a month in advance to join for the dinner. It was a collection of the country's big wigs and top political leaders to greet and congratulate the best Parliamentarians of the year. Pranab Mukerjee and Jai Pal Reddy had this honour for the current year. At hotel Taj Man Singh, a number of 'who's who' of the country were present. Some of the politicians were the clients of the CBI. They had either faced inquiries or were being prosecuted by the CBI. I carefully avoided all of them. Though retired, I still try to keep myself off and away from unsavoury and doubtful people. Very few politicians from the ruling party were present. Even the social functions tend to get divided on party lines. Every alternative day, I ring up my mother to inquire about her health. She is in Jalalabad and this is the only way to be in touch with her. She cannot hear properly. But it assures me that she is all right.

Honouring the media

I arrived in Indore on 11th November by a private airline. It was on time, which was a pleasant change from the usual Indian Airlines flight. The young, energetic and immensely popular Mayor of Indore, Sh. Kailash Vijayvargiya, was present at the airport. Apart from being the Mayor, he is the third time elected MLA without having lost an election. It is a rare feat in political life. It was a genuine affectionate welcome. Almost straight from the airport, I drove to the function for honouring the Press men of Indore for excellence in work. The only break, I took, was to change into a suit at the government circuit house called Residency. The awards have been instituted in memory of late Rajender Mathur, Editor of Nav Bharat Times for the Print Media. Rajender Mathur was a brilliant news analyst in Hindi language. For electronics, the awards are given in memory of Surender Pratap Singh, the anchor person of Aj ki Baat on Doordarshan Metro. Sh. S.P. Singh would make even the dullest news sound like a fairy tale. The function went on till 11 P.M. including the dinner. The city corporation had spent about five lakhs in awards and cash rewards. The government circuit house is also the lung space of Indore. I stayed in the same room where the Chief Minister of Maharashtra was lodged the previous evening. The single room where I stayed was bigger than all the two bed rooms and study in the present government accommodation allotted to my wife in Delhi. The dressing room was bigger than the drawing room. The bath room was bigger than all the four bath rooms put together in our present accommodation. But the glorious part ends here. The blankets on the bed were rough and needed to be washed. I like to read before going to sleep. The table lamp was mercifully there. But the bulb was of low power and of no use for reading. Whatever be the condition of the bed, it is just not possible to sleep comfortably anywhere except in your own bed. Next morning, despite my constantly ringing the call bell, there was no response from any attendant. I always carry my own tea making kit, which is an electric kettle, some powdered milk and tea bags. In place of sugar, I use an artificial sweetener to equalise my rich and generous consumption of sweets. I have a hankering, as well as a craving for sweets. After I had made tea, one indifferent attendant turned up to inquire whether I needed any tea. I gave him a piece of mind for his indifference. He explained that the bell was not working. I managed to squeeze in about half an hour for my morning walk before being hurried through the day's programme. I was ready at 8.25 A.M. which is rather unusual for me. The Mayor, Kailash Vijayvargiya arrived at 8.45 and we left for the Gurudwara Imli Sahib, which commemorates the visit of the first Sikh Guru Nanak to Indore. I, like most other Sikhs, who have no relations, or friends in Madhy Pradesh, was unaware of this fact. The Gurudwara is located on a busy road in Indore. It must have been the outskirts of Indore during the Guru's visit, when the population of Indore, like the rest of India, might have been, hardly one per cent of the present population. My own visits, to all religious places of all religions, are an uplifting experience. The Sikh religion was a mission to educate and make the community to realise its basic duty of devotion to God and fair play and justice to other human beings, by the great Master. I always say that I have reasonably good relations, with God and his messengers. Probably, I am always on His right side and, as far as possible, I do not annoy Him and His beloved ones, irrespective of what religion they might have founded. I feel, equally at home, in a gurudwara or a church or a mosque or a temple. Later on, I was taken to Ranjit Singh College, founded in the memory of the only Sikh Emperor, who ruled over parts of Punjab, that is the present Pakistan and Afghanistan. There are about 50,000 Sikhs, in and around Indore. There are two colleges set up by the community, as well as a public school. The only way any community can excel is by ensuring excellence in education. Unfortunately, the present copying culture strikes at the very root of doing your best. I also visited the office of a popular Hindi daily, Dainak Bhaskar, and met the Editor Sh. Shravan Garg and the dedicated staff there. This paper has crossed a readership of over one crore in the country. A newspaper never sleeps. In search of news, the press people are ubiquitous. For excellence, the papers have to make sure that they are ahead of others. I get all the published papers of Delhi. I notice that almost all of them vie with each other for getting the attention of readers. Indore has also started a project of tree plantation in a big way. This is a brain wave of the active and intelligent Mayor, Kailash Vijayvargiya. Anybody can plant a tree in the name of his loved ones by paying a fee of Rs.251. Indore Corporation will look after it. I was also taken to plant a tree, which I did in memory of my late father, Mahant Kartar Singh. The painter painting the name board asked me whether he should write swargiaya or in heaven in front of the name. I replied that my father had passed away on 23rd, January 1996. I am not sure, where he is. It looks that heaven is rather overcrowded. I still have to see anybody saying that his relation has gone to hell. I told the painter that he was free to write whatever he wanted, because I have no information where he would be. He was an excellent human being, who spread love and sunshine everywhere. So I presumed that he might have been suitably placed by God Almighty. Everybody present had a good laugh at me, taking a dig at my own family. The painter asked me about my mother, whether he should write her name and whether she was also swargiaya or had gone to heaven. I replied that till I left yesterday, she was alive. I do not know whether she has gone to heaven today. This provoked another laughter. A lunch had been arranged in my honour to meet the leading members of the Sikh community and the top gentry of Indore. As it happens, the host tried to linger on and delay the lunch so that I could spend some more time. I had the next engagement at 3 P.M. I also wanted to snatch some twenty minutes for the post-lunch siesta. I told the host that I was hungry and he better serve the lunch quickly. It was true that I had no time for the morning breakfast. After lunch, there was only time to pack my clothes and leave for the next programme of addressing a seminar on the subject of introduction of Commissioner of Police System in Indore. My view is that it is time to trust the elected representatives. The Corporation needs police for demolition work, for dealing with stray cattle, for proper advice on city planning and road planning. It should have a dedicated police station under it. Just after finishing the function, I met members of the local branch of Bharat Vikas Parishad, who have done excellent work in the field of social services. After encouraging them, I left for the airport in the company of my host and by this time, now a good friend, Mayor and MLA, Kailash Vijayvargiya. A hurried visit packed with engagements from the time of my arrival to departure at 7 P.M. had just ended on a happy note. After two hours of flight, I landed at Delhi at 9. P.M. The food served was not tasty. Perhaps, it could also be due to the fact that I had overfilled myself with the food. The press in Madhya Pradesh is both vocal and independent; this is my impression.

On the 22nd September 2000, I had gone to address the senior officials of the Customs Department about efficient and honest working. My friend Sh. S.P. Srivastav, the then Chief Commissioner of Customs, had invited me to address them. I urged them to be innovative and face the challenges boldly to root out corruption and inefficiency. On 23rd September, I flew to Bombay to attend a seminar on terrorism and intelligence agencies of Pakistan's Intelligence Agencies and activities in India. The organisers had sent an official to receive me at the airport. I have lost count of the visits to Bombay. In the initial stages, the very thought of visits to Bombay used to be exciting. It was reported to be a city of mystique and beauty. On the contrary, slums greeted you, on arrival from the aircraft, as well as on the roadside. Bombay is a city of opportunities. But unlike other metropolitans cities, it lacks space. People have to live in cubby-holes with hardly any privacy. Even the middle class, rich and super rich will just have place for their own living. Rarely is there a place for a guest to be put up. I have always preferred to stay in a guest house or a hotel, rather than with anybody else. It enables me, to live as I wish to live. Occasionally, I have stayed with friends, when they have insisted. The trouble with staying with anybody is that you bind him to your living and you are bound at least informally to follow the rules of the house. You are expected to join them for breakfast, lunch or dinner and observe their timing. The organisers of the function on the activities of terrorism and foreign agents had told me that they had arranged to put me up with a Punjabi family. I declined it outright, that I possibly could not stay with somebody whom I had never known in life. Anticipating this contingency, I had made arrangements for my stay in a guest house through a friend. The plane was late by one hour. By the time I reached the guest house, it was already past 2 P.M. I had a quick lunch and met friends from 4.30 P.M. onwards. I took a quick round of the Fort area and a quiet dinner, at the place of a Bombay Industrialist, Sh. Ishar Singh Chawla. My friend Darshan Singh had taken me there. Darshan Singh is in the hoteliering business and has done well in life. Due to a rich life style, his eyesight has been affected by diabetes. He offered his chauffeur-driven vehicle for my use. I told him that I had no plans to go anywhere next day, except for the morning walk on Marine drive, which was not even 100 metres away. The only engagement of the day was attending a seminar and for going back to the airport, for which arrangements already existed. The former Deputy Chief Minister of Maharashtra Gopi Nath Munde inaugurated the programme, for which I was indicated earlier to be the Chief Guest. At the time of function, it was announced that I was also the principal speaker. I received thunderous applause, both during and at the end, of my presentation, which was extensively covered. A number of TV channels interviewed me for their programme after my speech. I had already packed my baggage and brought it in the car, so that I could straightaway drive to the Airport. The average speed of traffic in Bombay is slower than in Delhi. Sometimes, one can walk faster than driving in the vehicle. I reached the Airport in 55 minutes. It was a reasonably fast speed to cover about 24 kilometres. Like in Delhi, in Bombay there is also a separate terminal for departure of private airlines. I felt relieved to leave Bombay in time and reached Delhi at 10 PM.

Publishers take writers for a ride

I generally relax in three instalments. One is after the breakfast, which lasts for 30 to 45 minutes. The second instalment is after the lunch for 50 minutes to one Hour. The third is in the night. I find that periodical rest between work and other activities gives me enough energy to carry on with a lot of efficiency. For writing, one has to do a lot of reading. I must be spending at least three to four hours on reading. The net result, even after this much labour, is hardly 400 to 500 words. In the evening I went for a function for the release of a book of poems and to cheer Dr. Neelam Saraff, daughter of a senior Supreme Court Advocate, Mr. Saraff. It was a valiant effort for an Indian to write poetry in English. The maiden attempt of the young maiden, has come out well. She told me that her publisher has cheated her and has not distributed the books. The fact remains that exploitation of new authors is very common in our country. The same thing happens to the young heroes and heroines in the film industry. In all functions, the essential ingredient is meeting people and saying the right things all the time. In any case, it is against all etiquette to express disapproval of anything as a guest. The person arranging the function does his best to show his or her best side. The function went off well.

2nd October was again a day which kept me busy with socialisation and meeting people. The first visit was to Lajpat Nagar to the house of my uncle, Balwant Singh to say good bye to my cousin and his son Dr.Gurcharnajeet Singh, who has settled in the USA. He has become an American citizen. He had come to Delhi posthaste on hearing that his mother was not well, and had to undergo endoscopy for extraction of gall bladder stones. We affectionately call him Channa. He is the mainstay of his family, whom he supports generously with dollars. He has set up his elder brother and sister in the USA in business. Conservatively, he must have spent at least a million dollars on his family. His son is finishing his medicine and his daughter will pass out as a lawyer. He told us that on the last birthday of his wife, he presented her a BMW Mercedes costing nearly seven lakh dollars or about Rs.35 lakhs. The rich and super rich, always give gifts to themselves or their family members. The net result is that all gifts remain in the house. Afterwards, my wife and I went to the farm house of a friend Ashok Sawhney where he was celebrating the Mundan or shaving off ceremony of his first grandson. Money can create a heaven in a jungle. It was a grand party, in an area, which is full of farm houses. The Chatttarpur Road is a religious mall. There are a number of religious establishments and abodes of godmen on the ten kilometre stretch. The traffic was extremely slow moving. The roads are cluttered with a variety of vehicles, both man driven and petrol driven. A single breakdown will bring the traffic to less than a crawling pace. The average speed, does not exceed 20 kilometres per hour. Modernisation, urbanisation and the abundance of wealth has its own problems. Like America, in the rich families every member of the family has a car for his or her use. There is not enough space, even for parking the vehicles, which are mostly on the road side. In the night, there was a dinner hosted by Sh. Vinod Sethi of Capital Foundation Society, in honour of the young minister, Arun Jaitley. Jaitley is not only handsome, but very articulate and thorough in his job. He has done an excellent job as a Minister for Disinvestment and Information and Broadcasting. Now he has moved to the Law Ministry as a Minister for Law. He is one of the few very clear-headed and honest ministers. Others who were in the dinner were Former Chief Justice of India, Justice Ahamadi and Justice Krishna Iyer and a number of other educationists.

More about TV

I had gone to the Punjabi TV Channel Tara for recording on current issues facing the country. The discussion included the conviction of the former Prime Minister in JMM bribery case and the delay in the disposal of the cases. All media interaction, whether it is the TV or print media, is a battle of wits and I could answer all the questions to the satisfaction of the anchor and the audience. I have been using the air conditioner till today. Whenever I have to meet visitors, I make it a point to be properly attired. It was again a very busy day. I had a TV recording of Karan Thapar Show with Advocates, Kapil Sibbal, R.K. Anand and Sh. P.N. Lekhi to discuss the sentence of former Prime Minister PV Narsimha Rao. Sibbal, a good friend, was forthright, in condemning corruption, irrespective of the parties involved. It is refreshing to find politicians of his breed in the country. Lekhi, a soft spoken crusader, has carried on the fight, against the corrupt politicians in the country. Truly speaking, he has been on the same side as the CBI for dealing with the crooks. But for his crusade, the case would not have seen fruition. The only difference is, that the CBI has also to take into account the visible and invisible pressure, from the government, the media and other unspecified authorities. The power of investigation and bringing the case to the Court is only with the Police. The Police not only acts dishonestly at times, but also has ulterior motives. Such cases are reported in the press almost everyday. It is not the failure of the system, but the failure of supervision and political interference, which quite frequently determines the fate of a case. In the evening there was a second interview on the CNBC channel on Bofors and the involvement of the Hinduja brothers. The Hinduja's are supposed to be the richest Indians, who have become British citizens. My stand, which is the normal practice of the CBI, is to verify everything, was that it would be better to verify the stand taken by them, so that if there is a case, it is fool proof. If there is no case, it would be better to examine the issue from all sides before taking any other action and let them off.

Yesterday, the evening was spent in social functions. More than seven hours were spent in meeting people. It is also a part of one's existence. It also gives a feeling, that one is still wanted and contributing something worthwhile to society. A long outing takes all the time for writing. I try to balance socialising with my work so that, at the end of the day, I have the self satisfaction of having attempted and accomplished something. I have reached an age and stage, where my own satisfaction is more important to me than the approval of others. These days, there is a surfeit of freebies. All kinds of temptations are thrown to make you part with your money. The newspapers carry advertisements, that if you buy a fridge, you can get a high segmented priced car for free, with a number of second prizes as small cars, or TV's or music systems or computers. If you subscribe to certain magazines, for five or ten years, the prize item is almost equal to the money paid in the open market. Many friends subscribe for the sake of the free items, and not for the sake of the principal object. I get a lot of mail of this nature, which ends up in the four waste paper baskets in the house. It costs a lot of money to put a two rupees stamps on thousands of printed envelopes, attractive leaflets, mailed or even telephone calls. If there was nothing but only loss, in such ventures, nobody would have attempted. Obviously, the suckers succeed in beguiling the innocent and the gullible.

The charge sheeting of the Hinduja brothers in Bofors and the conviction of a former Prime Minister, in the Jharkhand Mukti Morcha bribery case, is the hot news today. I have been invited to a number of TV channels for giving my views. My views are very clear that all such cases, though true are difficult to prove. Most of the witnesses, are liable to be brought under pressure and temptations. I went to Sahara TV for my views on the quantum sentence which should be awarded to the convicted Prime Minister. I feel that VIP's go for the highest in every aspect of life. The highest sentence should be theirs as a matter of right, in line with their demands and expectations in other spheres of life. Mahesh Prasad, my friend and a retired colleague, had the following incidents to mention about corruption in public life. He told me that a former Governor (during the President's rule) of an important State called the then Chief Secretary of the State and demanded Rs. 40 crores for passing it on to the political masters, who had appointed him. The Chief Secretary, a fairly honest person, took it as a joke and ignored it. After one week, the then Governor called him and asked him as to what he had done about the money. The Chief Secretary told the Governor that he had no experience of collecting any money. He would send half a dozen officers with vicious reputation of vast experience in that direction. He suggested that His Excellency could discuss whatever he wanted with them and do whatever he pleased. The Governor, a retired civil servant, collected Rs. 60 crores, enough for him for his next three generations. But unfortunately he did not live long enough to enjoy the ill-gotten cash. Another political Governor beat all the past records in collecting money. The appointment of the Governors in the country used to be a matter of prestige and only well known, proved and tried people were appointed. Now, one has to make an effort to find the name of the governors, not in the Who's Who list but Who. The remedy for remedying the situation lies in the hands of people, enjoying political power. No bureaucrat, who is appointed by the government, has the power to rectify the situation. Mahesh Prasad also told me about the human side of the late Prime Minister, Indira Gandhi, whom he had accompanied on a tour to Lakshadweep, as a Joint Secretary in the Home Ministry in December, 1976. He told me that Mrs.

Gandhi was a light eater and she never had a second helping. She liked coconut water, which she consumed in place of lunch. Like ordinary human beings, she enjoyed collecting shells on the beach. Mahesh Prasad had to lend her his handkerchief, for packing shells, which she returned later on. It is important for the people in top position to have the right people around her or him. It is they who convey the correct impression about the leader or the person they were around with.

On 12-10-2000, I completed 61 years of my existence on earth. I have still fresh memories of my late grand father, Mahant Natha Singh, who died in 1972/73. He was always affectionate to me. His generation had long ago disappeared. My father, Mahant Kartar Singh, died at the age of 82 in 1996, January, 23rd. He was a kind and an affectionate father about whom we can say "he was a man". I do not do anything extraordinary on my birth day. I complete a Path on this day, as I do for my wife, and daughters, on their birth day. My daughter Gagandeep, and her husband Gunveer Singh also attended the Path. As everybody including my wife, Surinder, daughter Harveen, daughter Gagandeep and her husband are working, I have to finish it well before 10 A.M. For me, also it was a busy day. Immediately, I left for the TV recording for Cafe Academy. It was a discussion on the CBI. I traditionally lunch or dine out on my birth day with the members of my family. Today, my two daughters and wife joined me for lunch at the India Habitat Centre. I went for the buffet lunch, whereas others went for South Indian Thali. There is a good spread of food items. One invariably tends to overeat, when there is a vast choice. Consciously or unconsciously, one likes to have a go at all the items, thinking that one untasted would be better than the previous one. The result is that I have put on at least eight kilograms of excess weight. The most difficult is the battle of the bulge, and to keep the bulge under check. Just after lunch and a brief nap, I went to Noida for the recording of a programme of "Subbe Saveray" to be telecast on 14th of October, 2000 at 7.30 A.M. Again at 6.30 P.M. I had a TV interview on CBNC channel on the conviction of the former Prime Minister, to three years of imprisonment for bribery in buying MP's votes in the No Confidence Vote motion against the government on 28th July, 1993. Three Television appearances on one day and one yesterday is a kind of a record. I was hardly in the house. There are days when I am extremely busy. It was one of those action packed days. But with adequate periods of short rest, I did not feel hassled or tired.

I also chaired a session of Confederation of Indian Industry, on Counterfeiting and Duplication of goods including motor parts and pharmaceuticals. I said that unless the gap between the high prices of the genuine and spurious is spelled out as well as dangers, the problem will remain. At the same time, the industry has to treat this problem as a whole and not leave it to everybody to fight his battles.

It has been a full day of meeting the pressmen, my publisher and friends. The socialisation part is almost over in the morning, with helloing and greeting friends and acquaintances in the Lodhi Garden. It is a curious feature of morning walkers, that though we greet each other, we hardly know each other personally. Only last Sunday, one of the well-off morning walkers, Parveen Gupta, had hosted a lunch to know each other better. It is a good way to interact better with each other. But as there is hardly any commonality of interests, or living in the same locality, the position remains the same. The hotel food served is full of excessive cooking medium. It was the same position for the last Sunday lunch. It is difficult to resist the temptation of fried food. I give way to temptations, and the result is excess kgs of flab. I weigh between 78 to 80 kilograms, as against the ideal weight of 70 kgs. It is a constant struggle to resist tempting and rich food. I suppose this is a problem faced by most persons. Some are lucky that, despite eating rich food, they remain slim and trim. Perhaps, it is not really so, as really slim people eat very slimly. The weight does not come from the air. It comes from excessive eating. After putting on excessive weight, we tend to blame either our constitution, or body structure, for the tyres around the belly. We ourselves are the real culprits who exercise no self-control.

Cheerful Sunday

It has been a fairly cheerful Sunday. PC Sharma, Special Director, CBI is one of the fastest walkers and I could keep pace with him in Lodi Garden. It was possible to cover four kilometres in less than 37 minutes. I have rarely achieved this speed. As usual, I rested for about 30 minutes. Post breakfast rest period, till lunch, leaves me fresh. This is worth trying, as it gives a fresh start. I used to do this, when in government service also, before leaving for the office. I adjusted my timings, in such a way that I was never late for the office. Even after retirement, I continue to swear by punctuality. I keep on working on the computer, off and on, between the period of watching TV and writing. Of course, this is not the ideal way to work, which should be done with full concentration. If the TV or Radio is on, it gives an impression that somebody is with you in the room and you are not alone. There are over 70 channels given by the cable operator at a cost of Rs. 225 per month. There is so much of choice that it hardly leaves any room for choice. Of course, the government channels have the minimum viewership, in large places. It is not so, it is claimed in small towns, where either there are small cable operators, or no cable operators. The government channels called Doordarshan are said to be free to the air and are just available. Both in revenue and presentation of the programme, they lag behind private channels. Moreover, generally speaking the economy and the government working, are generally poles apart. It is for this reason that government has proved to be a failure, as a businessman, or an entrepreneur.

Vasant Sathe, an ignored hero

One engagement outside the house was presiding over a function, of the release of a monthly magazine, on encouraging the use of natural products in life. The formal release of the Magazine was done, by Sh. Vasant Sathe, former Minister of Information and Broadcasting. Vasant Sathe is one of the cleanest politicians in the country. In fact, it was due to him that colour TV transmission was introduced in 1982, at the time of Asian games. He was criticised very bitterly at that time. Now there are no buyers for black and white television. Nobody remembers his contribution. I spoke about the need to add value to our own life and the life of others we come in contact with. Improvement in our own life and the lives of people we come in contact with, is an on-going exercise, with no final destination.

Meeting an Old, Young Turk (22-10-2000)

Yesterday I presented my book, "Be The Best" to the Vice President of India, Sh. Krishan Kant. Sh. Krishan Kant was the fire brand called as one of the young Turks during the regime of Late Prime Minister, Indira Gandhi. It was very gracious of the Vice President of India to receive me along with my family, that is my wife, Surinder, daughters Harveen and Gagandeep and my son-in-law, Gunveer Singh, husband of Gagandeep. He offered us high tea and spent forty minutes with us. The conversation centred on the present position in the country and was in Punjabi. The Vice President is a Punjabi from Jullundur. After Gaini Zail Singh, he is the only Punjabi to have reached the second highest political office of the country. Sh. Krishan Kant has one of the cleanest and impeccable reputation in the country. He has kept himself fine and fit and in a trim condition. Polite, courteous to the extreme, he exudes affection. Earlier, in the morning, I had received my mother, Lajwanti, at the railway station at 5 A.M. I had got up at 3.15 A.M. It always happens that when I am to go early anywhere, I wake up automatically. Perhaps, it is the apprehension of missing the flight or not being able to reach in time, which subconsciously controls such self remembered engagements. I normally never receive any body, either at the airport or railway station. I never did it even for my late father, when he came to Delhi. They always came on their own in the vehicle sent by me. But, I made an exception this time as my mother needed a wheel chair to come near the car. But without my going, all such arrangements would not have been possible. Later on at 7 A.M. on 21-10-2000 I visited the Railway Protection Force's Parade at Daya Basti to join my old organisation for paying homage to nearly 1300 policemen killed in the line of duty. In the night, I was invited by the Zee TV, at the Prime Time, to discuss cricket match fixing and the report of the CBI. It is strange but true that a report, not officially published, becomes the subject matter of discussion. One is mostly guessing and then talking in the air.

I also went for a Bhog of the mother-in-law of my nephew in the Green Park Gurudwara, which is under construction. Later on I called on the Education Minister, Sh.Murli Manohar Joshi to present him my book, "Be the Best". He liked the book tremendously. Later I visited the Perfect Health Mela and won a crore of health points.

Long queues, longer wait

In the evening I along with Surinder went to the residence of Delhi Lt. Governor to attend the reception of his daughter's wedding. Vijay Kapoor, the host and the Governor of Delhi is also my batchmate, as both of us joined service the same day on 1-6-1961. The Government of India started a system, of combined training, for top class, one services, in 1960 in Mussoorie. The idea was to bring about an integrated and well-knit administration, in which people belonging to the Police, Foreign Service, Accounts, Administration, Income Tax, Customs, Railways and other allied services joining in a particular year, would know each other, on a personal level. Vijay Kapoor joined the Indian Administrative Service whereas I joined the Indian Police Service on the same day in the National Academy of Administration. He, after retirement from service, joined the Bahratiya Janta Party and was inducted to its National Council. His experience and rapport in the party catapulted him to the present job. There was a serpentine queue of more than 200 persons, wanting to wish the young couple, a happy married life. I never stand in any queue. But my friend B.K. Goswami remonstrated, and said that once in a while, I should respect the other's discipline. I agreed and the result was that I had to spend one hour chatting with others, till the queue, almost disappeared. I ran into India's Home Minister, Sports Minister and a number of other senior officials and a few Governors. I lost my wife in the big crowd and found her near the dinner service area. I skipped my dinner. After wishing the newly married young lady, whose husband was not there, and probably gone to the bath room by the time my turn to wish them came. May be, after three hours of standing, the young husband, an American, might have gone to the fresher himself.

The Pride of India, Indo Tibetan Border Police

The Indo-Tibetan Border Police, which is an armed force of the Union of India, was raised on this day (24 october, 2000) in 1962 after the Chinese had attacked India. It started with two battalions and now the strength is nearly 35000. I had commanded this force as the Director General from 31st January, 1995 to 10th April, 1996. I had come to this job from my earlier job of Director General, Narcotics Control Bureau on my promotion to the higher scale. I was drawing the salary of the Additional Secretary in the then pay scale of Rs. 7300-7600 (now 22,000 to Rs 24,500). I had been promoted to the pay scale of Rs. 7600-8000 (Present Rs. 24,500-26,000). There was a difference of Rs. 200 in my salary. I had told the then Home Secretary to let me continue, in the same job, and not shift me for Rs. 200, so that there could be continuity and I could complete the projects I had initiated. But such are the ways of the superior bureaucracy that they would dangle some promotion carrot in front of you. Nobody likes to refuse promotion, for the sake of government work, which is rather impersonal. If anybody is foolish enough to refuse, then he is left behind in the rat race. There are no rewards for doing your job well. Most bureaucrats adopt the trick of doing that much, which is sufficient for them, to keep their jobs. The general approach is that "self before service". Self interests come before the country's interests. The result is every promotion which gave me a financial benefit of rupees two hundred minus income tax of about 66 rupees led to change in my next job. In the last four years of my service, from 17th September, 1993 to 10th April,1996 I changed three jobs. I was Director General of Narcotics Control Bureau from September, 1993 to 31st. January, 1995. I was the Director General of Indo-Tibetan Border Police Force from 31st January, 1995 to 10th April, 1996. I moved to the Railways Protection Force from 10th April, 1996 to 31st July, 1996 in the full Secretary's pays scale of Rs. 26,000 per month. I took over as Director, CBI on 31st July, 1996 in the same pay scale. I was shifted to Home Ministry as a punishment as a Special Secretary on 30th June, 1997. It was a non-descript job, though the then Prime Minister, Gujral, a freak of accident of Indian politics, claimed that it was a promotion. I promptly contradicted it, by saying that it was a demotion, though the pay scale remained the same. In terms of protocol, for the first time, I was reduced from number one to number three. I am generally cheerful. So I took this change in the stride and held on to this job from 1st August, 1997 to 31st October, 1997, that is my last day in the government service before retirement.

On 24/10/2000, I attended a reception given by the Director General of Indo-Tibetan Border Police Force. Almost the same people who had attended the morning parade were present. A number of other officials from the offices close by were also present, as, it is more convenient, to attend any function, in the Central Government Offices Complex at Lodi Road, than in Tigri which takes, more than one hour of commuting time, both ways. In fact, the annual functions of all Central Police Organisations are held, at least one hour, away from Delhi. The Border Security Force celebrates its raising day on 1st December at Chawla, which is near Palam Air Port. The Central Reserve Force celebrates its anniversary at Jharoda Kalan, which takes 55 minutes from Delhi. The Central Industrial Security Force has similar celebrations near Ghaziabad, a good forty minutes drive. Except those who are required to be present on obligatory basis, these parades are rather a closed affair. For retired officials, vehicles are sent to pick them up, and drop them back. Very few retired officials keep drivers to drive them around. The result is that they find it both difficult and expensive to go for any function or even to the market. I have my private driver. But I always insist on an official vehicle to pick me up and drop me. It is for the simple reason that my driver does not know all the ways. Being a civilian, he would find it difficult to gain entry to the venues and he would have to explain that his passenger was the former Police Chief. Moreover, my drivers keep on leaving their jobs, within six months to one year, for higher salary and the new person has to start afresh. Since my retirement, there has hardly been a day, when I did not have a private driver. It keeps me mobile and is of great convenience.

Writing undisturbed

For the last three days, I have been able to write to my heart's content. Even if there is an engagement and it is avoidable, I try to cut it out, so that I have ample time to work. Even on Diwali day, that is 26th of October, except for meeting my daughter, Gagandeep, her husband Gunveer and her father-in-law, Prof. Ansu, I did not go any where. I treated the day, just like any other day. The only difference was that people kept on burning their money by exploding crackers and fire works. There was a lot of noise and pollution in the air. The morning walk in the Lodi Garden is one event I look forward to. It is a walking cum socialisation. I was told that many persons come from far-off places, like Karol Bagh and Noida, so that they could greet and meet celebrities in the Lodi Garden. It is one place where one runs into all kinds of people. We greet each other, without knowing each other. I wanted to go to the former Prime Minister, Mr. Devegowda, to greet him on the occasion of Diwali. But nobody picked up his telephone. It is best not to go to anybody without an appointment. This makes the other person ready to receive you. It also mentally prepares you to express yourself and convey your point of view.

On 29/10/2000, I travelled to Chandigarh to attend a meeting of a Committee to debate about the reforms to be brought about to make the administration more responsive to the people. It was chaired by Punjab Excise and Taxation Minister, Dickshan Sood. My trip was almost off, as I found that my seat had been booked by ordinary AC chair car. I like to work on my computer and the ordinary chair car does not give me the space to work . I had almost decided to cancel my visit. But fortunately for me, I took a chance and occupied a seat in the Executive Class, which was full to the last seat. A railway official whose seat I had occupied told me that he needed only one seat and I could continue sitting there. This way, totally unexpectedly as I was accommodated in a seat reserved, but not occupied. It appeared that it was pre-planned. A small incident like this reveals that it is the destiny, which rules our ends. God gives a small room for manoeuvring. It is for us to take advantage of it. The return journey was equally unpredictable. Mr. Grover, Chief Engineer, Northern Railways, had agreed to give me a lift by road from Chandigarh to Ambala to enable me to catch the super fast train called Swaran Shatabdi of Amritsar at 8.21 P.M. We left Chandigarh at 6.45 P.M. with an ample margin to cover 45 kilometres distance within an hour and fifteen minutes. There was a tremendous traffic jam near Chandigarh which took 55 minutes to clear. The reason was that everybody wanted to overtake everybody else, and different types of vehicles including scooters, cars and trucks, appeared to be in a terrible hurry. Nobody was willing to show consideration to others. Nobody bothered about his lane, or the right of the others. There is no way in a traffic chaos like this. The Police cannot do anything. It has to be a combination of punishment and voluntary compliance. Fortunately, by the skin of the teeth, we made to Ambala at 8.18 P.M. with three minutes to spare for the arrival of the train only to be told that the train was 25 minutes late. I had a full day in Chandigarh, as the meeting lasted for nearly three hours. In between the meeting, I was able to give interview to a press reporter of Dainak Bhaskar, a Hindi daily, and meet a friend General Himmat Singh and visit the house of my cousin, Chinda, who was with me right from the Railway Station on arrival at Chandigarh till my departure. Film producers, Mr. Kanwal and Mr. Nirula met me and decided to make a film based on my autobiography, 'Outside CBI'. I signed the necessary papers, as required by them. The delayed departure of the train had a cascading effect and the arrival in Delhi led to a further delay of 45 minutes. The worst affected was my driver, who reached his house at 1 A.M. I dropped him near his house. I have a sense of guilt, if I keep anybody waiting even if it is due to unavoidable reasons. However, a driver's job is to wait, after driving his employer or boss. One does not hire drivers only to keep on moving in the vehicle all the time.

However, the last four days have kept me busy with TV interviews on Jain TV, Doordarshan Metro, Doordarshan National Channel and Star News. Apart from other papers, my articles appeared on the centre or editorial page of The Pioneer and The Tribune of Chandigarh on 30th and 31st October, 2000. I highlighted the neglect of the farmers in The Tribune, out of a genuine conviction and not for any other reason. Between running from one TV studio to another and from one meeting to another, there has hardly been any time for writing. The observance of Vigilance Week has tied me to address the officials of National Thermal Power Corporation, Central Public Works Department, Engineer India, and Central Electricity Authority between 1st and 6th November, 2000. It has meant travelling from one office to another in my own vehicle. Only one organisation paid for the conveyance and others conveniently forgot. I am reluctant to ask anybody for any payment even when it is due to me. But the credit must be given to the fact that the Vigilance Commission has aroused interest in uprightness and public service.

I walk into a wrong wedding

During one morning walk, I ran into my friend Mehmud Ur Rehamn, who was earlier Vice Chancellor of Aligarh Muslim University. He has been posted as Secretary, Parliamentary Affairs, from the present job of special representative of the Government of Jammu and Kashmir. He was not exactly happy or pleased with his posting. I told him to be happy if the government chooses to pay him the same salary with less or no work. He was earlier Additional Chief Secretary, Jammu and Kashmir Government, when I was posted in Srinagar as Inspector General of Police, Central Reserve Police Force. We have enjoyed each other's hospitality quite often. I told him that if the services, whether IAS or IPS or others want better prospectuses, then the jobs would necessarily have to be split and diluted, leading to reduction in their area of responsibility and importance. Recently, a Secretary to the Government of India sought pre-mature retirement, a few months before his normal retirement, at the age of sixty, on the ground that he was being transferred from one job to the other. Many senior officials believe that they have a divine right to some posts and they should not either be questioned about their performance or transferred. Such people play safe by first putting in the requisite years of service, so that they do not lose the benefit of pension. I was invited for two weddings. Even assuming that one spends just half an hour at one function, the time to dress up and commuting takes easily another two hours, as the average traffic speed in Delhi is not more than 14 to 20 kilometres per hour. So the entire evening is almost written off. By mistake I went to a wedding to which I was not invited. This mistake occurred, because the venues of two weddings were the same. Having gone and presented my gift, I discovered my mistake. It was too late to ask the bride and bride groom to return the gift presented to them. I wished them well and walked off to the next wedding. I just borrowed an envelope and put Rs. 150 in lieu of the gift. I told the host at the scene wedding about the howler I had committed and just laughed off. It was a repeat story of a different kind, where for a wedding of a friend's son, I mistook the date and went one day earlier to find that the wedding was next day. I went again for the wedding next day and told the host, Dr. Dada that it was my second visit to the venue. It was an open admission of something, which should not have happened. I do not claim not to have made howlers and mistakes in my life. Life would be dull, if everything went on smoothly.

Life itself is a game of jugglery

I arrived in Jalalabad yesterday (10 November 2000) early morning from Delhi by the only overnight train Punjab Mail. The train starts from Bombay and Ferozpore and takes nearly three nights to cover the journey. The arrival time at Ferozpore is at 5 A.M., departure at 9 P.M. from Delhi. The timing is inconvenient for those, who have to go to places other than the district headquarters, Ferozpore. I have raised this issue many times with the Railway Minister and other senior officials in the Railway Board, that it would be more sensible and suitable for every body, if the train could arrive by 7 A.M. The important thing in life is not to tell what you want to the Minister or even the Highest Official, but to the clerk preparing the time table, as he has to do a lot of jugglery to keep the numerous trains, running on the single railway line. The result has been no change in the situation. After some times we all get used to the present and carry on, reconciled to the problem. The complacency is forced by the circumstances. It leads to the generation of an attitude that nothing is going to change in our country and no amount of pleadings will have an effect on an immovable administration. Another reason is that instead of dogged determination, we make efforts to change things by fits and starts. The real truth is that the truly non-priority items remain pending.

The major item of the day was to preside over a meeting of the Local Management Committee of DAV College, and to review the result of the students. In a way, it is a review of the performance of the teachers, their the dedication and the hard work they had put in to get better results. After the meeting, I went around to Mahant Kartar Singh Memorial Library, where

I made a silent salutation to the statue of my late father, in whose memory the Library is named. The meeting was over and I had lunch with Pappu, Tony, Des Raj and Mahant Harbhajan Singh, my uncle at about 2 P.M. A number of people look after me during my visit to Jalalabad. I invite them over for a lunch, which is, normally, one gravy chicken with tandoori roti from across a hotel, of Gopal Dass. The lunch is supplemented by whatever is prepared in the house. Since I come to Jalalabad after 45 to 60 days, I have to manage with the help of others. Today, that is 09 November 2000, Sheila, the former nurse cum companion of my mother, came to the house. She prepared the lunch on 9th as well as my breakfast on 10th of November. Sheila, a young mid-wife, left her job when she got married in 1999. The ultimate aim of any girl, as well as her parents, is to get her married. As she had done nursing, it was of a tremendous help to my mother to get her blood pressure checked and take the medicines regularly. Most of us need the help of others to meander through life.

During the morning walk, a scooter trolley carrying children, being driven at a rash speed had almost run over me. It was not exactly a tractor. It was vehicle made out of a used of a water pulling engine, placed on a plank and fixed to a platform, with sides to prevent people from falling. The local police took action. The driver came to apologise. It was not a personal grudge against anybody. I told the driver about my genuine concern that if the contraption had met with an accident, at least 15 to 20 children would have been badly injured. Nobody is serious about the law enforcement, as both the accused, accuser, the investigators and prosecutors, know each other well. Personal equation plays a much greater role, in our day to day life. Whenever I travel, I always carry my personal medicine kit with me. It includes a few medicines of common use, like pain killers, fever medicines, heart medicines, emergency medicines and a few tubes like Burnol or some ointment or Vicks Vaporub and some throat lozenges. I put them in a drawer of my room so that access and spotting them is easier. I have noticed all kinds of rats in my house in Jalalabad. Today, a rat got into the medicine drawer and had a taste of all medicines. When I opened the drawer, I found it drowsy and hardly in any a position to move about. I took it out and let it escape at a very slow pace. Obviously, the different medicines tasted by it had a multiple effect. But later on people working with me instead of catching the rats adopted a short cut. They killed four of them. One big rat, escaped though he or she was the main culprit. It is exactly, like in the real life, where small fries are caught and the big fishes escape.

I was feeling drowsy after the breakfast of a cauliflower pratha. I do not blame anybody except myself for overeating. Like other Punjabis, I am fond of good food and I relish it. I do not miss eating what I like, though, it adds to my weight. I feel that I should live life, as I want to live, as all men should. I have been lionised and praised for my contribution. I have not felt any change in me and I still hold fast to the belief that I am just like millions of my countrymen, an ordinary person, who does nothing more than what is expected of him and who has done just that much. Troubles arise, when every body expects me to be on first name terms, from the Prime Minister of the Country to the juniormost officials, with whom people approaching me would have some work. Most people do not believe when I honestly and genuinely plead my ignorance, and say that I have never believed in recommendations culture and would not violate my tradition or way of working and living for anybody or begging for favour.

I am a film star (Sunday, 12 November 2000)

Yesterday, as planned, the producer, Mr.Kanwal along with Mr. Nirula, of a tele documentary on my life and serial based on my book turned up at 3 P.M. and we went straight for film shooting. It continued till 10 P.M. This project continued even on the 12th of November. In the process, the house was turned topsy turvey. The best part of the stay was getting tandoori rotis, made from the hotel of Gopal, along with chicken preparations. Pappu extended me an invitation to have dinner with Mr. Kharbanda, SDM Ferozpore on my way to Delhi on 12th of November. I travelled with him and his brother Tony. It was a good gathering, Divisional Railway Manager, Mr. Marwaha, General Manager, Telephones, Mr. GS Julka were there along with DSP Ferozpore Rachpal Singh. There was a fire in Ferozpore Town and I advised the SDM, Mr. Kharbanda, to visit the spot, lest he face any criticism of neglecting his duty. He went out and came back in half an hour. He thanked me for the advice. I left ten minutes before the departure of the train and reached Delhi at 5 A.M.

No non-government servant is guilty of corruption

I had a TV recording along with Kirti Azad, MP and a famous cricketer in his right, and Tej Pal of Tehlka Dot.Com which had exposed match fixing, after an intense investigation, by the amateur journalists. The subject was cricket match fixing. The thrust of the discussion was to find fault with the CBI, and not with the people, who had not spoken and spilled all the beans. A report is based on the total assessment and the evidence tendered was my stand. In the evening I went to Doordarshan for National News both in Hindi and English at 8 P.M. on match fixing. I explained that under the law, only public servants can be guilty of corruption and bribery. No private person who has made money, by malpractices, is guilty of corruption. However, every penny has to be explained and tax paid on it. It looks very strange, but this is a fact, that no private person can be guilty of making money directly, as the cricketers have done from private persons. They did not play cricket, in the discharge of their duties. However, middlemen, touting for getting the official work done in offices, can be hauled up under the law, for abetting the crime and influencing the official for doing or forbearing to do, any official task. 15th November was another busy day with first visit to Noida to address the Managers of the Power Management Institute headed by Executive Director, Mr. Nair. I spoke on the subject "How to excel in life". It did not present any difficulty, because, just a week back, my book "Be the best" has hit the market. I urged that the Managers have to learn, and train for managing their time, and paying attention to the smallest details. I also told them that the old theories of fear do not yield results in life and they will havc to devise new solutions to new problems. Every day, each one of us is on trial to prove to the world that he can deliver the goods. In the afternoon, there was a meeting of the Board of Directors of The Pioneer and share holders. The paper, on the death row, has been salvaged by the Editor and Chairman of the Board of Directors, Sh. Chandan Mitra. It stands proved in life again and again that it is the top man, who can make or mar the organisation. The evening was spent in recording a programme for All India Radio on the release of kidnapped Kannada Film Star, Raj Kumar by the brigand Veerappan. The newspapers have confirmed the apprehensions that Rs.30 crores was collected and ten crores paid to Veerappan to release Raj Kumar. Of course, it goes without saying that all such money does not come from the bank accounts. It is black money and unaccounted anywhere.

All cricket show

I spent the forenoon meeting visitors including a senior Editor, Binoo K. John from a magazine called "Cricket Talk". I was told that this is the only magazine, exclusively devoted to Cricket. Mr. John had specifically flown from Bombay to interview me on the "CBI report on match fixing" and the future of the cricket as a sports. He took a lot of photographs and recorded every word I said. It is to play safe as many people deny what they had said when in hot water. I told him that public memory is short. Match fixing is a universal phenomenon, and cannot be wished away. It would be simpler and better to legalise betting. Match fixing in a bigger or a smaller degree prevails, wherever money can be made with impunity.

I caught up with the pending correspondence of requests to attend functions between 25th of November to 2nd of December, 2000. I have already accepted the request of Delhi Productivity Council to conduct a vigilance and a security course in Nepal and then to be in Hyderabad for addressing the valedictory programme on vigilance in Hyderabad National Police Academy. Trying to offer regrets or accepting invitations on telephone does not make for clear-cut understanding. I do not waste my time on routine work, which is done by my Private Secretary. I only write and correct the drafts. All the work relating to taking the print-out of the articles, letters, sending faxes and making envelopes is done by my Secretary. It leaves me time for reading and writing. One has lived life the same way for over six decades. Reading gives me a new perspective, on new aspects of life everyday. It is discovering a new world everyday. One always finds and discovers something new every time one opens a book. Life is an adventure. The only proviso is to spot it. The world of the printed world opens new vistas of knowledge. In fact, I have come to accept that I prefer the company of books to that of people.

Dot.Com a new media

I was invited by Indya.Dot.Com for a chat for an hour from 5.30 P.M. to 6.30 P.M. I left one hour in advance by the Cielo car sent by them. This was to give enough time to beat the traffic blockades, caused by various pressure groups, to get their demands conceded. One group is protesting against the Supreme Court decision to relocate polluting industries outside Delhi. A sensible decision, which should have been implemented, in the over-all interest of the Nation, has been politicised. The only way people show protest is by holding the community to ransom, and by upsetting the even tenor of life. This kind of civil disobedience does not invite any punishment or official disapproval. In fact, it is an accepted feature in Delhi that, in the name of public causes, you can get support from a number of sundry and motley groups, who stand to gain publicity. With about a dozen full time TV News Channels, who are constantly on the look-out for news and programmes, you could be sure of coverage on the small screen, even for an anti-public interest cause. All this is done, in the name of freedom of the press and media. Silly causes are exploited for personal publicity. But this is all that democracy is about. It is a safety valve to let out your steam. The chat on the dot.Com is by asking questions on the Monitor screen to which the reply is typed. There was an overwhelming response to my visit. Most questions were related to match fixing and the punishment, which should be awarded to the cricketers, who under-performed. For me, it was a repetition of the answers given in a TV interview and a repetition of the answers recorded on 13th of November on SAB TV. With literally no count of channels, each channel is interested in presenting exclusive features. But truly speaking, the same personalities and stories are repeated on each channel.

Delhi bureaucrat's evergreen paradise

Sometimes, it is nice to have a ring side view of whatever goes on in the world. It is as good a feeling as participating in the events. I am one of the Judges of Delhi Race Club. The Club periodically invites the VIP's and names trophies and cups after them. This week, the Governor of Delhi, affable Sh. Vijay Kapur, had come to give the award of Governor's Cup. He is one of the most level-headed batchmates of mine. A bit serious, but he has enjoyed the reputation of being a thorough gentleman and an upright person. Before his appointment as the Lt.Governor, he was staying in his own house which he has now locked and shifted to his official residence. He is one of those persons, who would avoid giving room for any kind of controversy. It goes without saying that he has led a totally unblemished life and done sensitive jobs like that of the Chief Secretaries to the Governments of Jammu and Kashmir and Delhi. He retired as Secretary, Defence Production and immediately joined Bhartiya Janta Party or BJP. The job of Delhi's Governor is partly ceremonial and mostly executive. Normally, only experienced administrators have been appointed for this job as they have to control bureaucrats and some of them are positively wily. I had taken an instant liking for him in 1961 when we joined our respective services together in the National Academy of Administration, Mussoorie. Our friendship continues. I do not go and impose myself on any friend for the simple reason that nobody should misunderstand me or slight me for wasting his time. This is the only way to nurture relationships. I always treat him publicly, as a VIP. There is intimacy and informality but no vulgar familiarity. I believe that in all relationships, we should show due respect.

Time a valueless commodity

I missed the RPF investiture parade as somebody had forgotten to escort me to the venue of the parade. My personal driver did not know the way to the venue. I had to be content with attending the dinner hosted by the Director General, RPF, Mr. H.D. Rao and apologised for the goof-up. I met the young Railway Minister, Mr.Digvijay Singh of Samta Party there. I had known him earlier. But it is always a joy to meet an ever smiling person, like myself. He had a dig at me, for the so-called leakage to the press. It is a curious world, where people want you to be transparent. But if you are, you are accused. I take all criticism and value judgements on me, with a tolerant, if not exactly a contemptuous, smile. The dinner timing was 7.30 P.M. I arrived at 8.30 P.M. I was feeling guilty as I was late by one hour. When I reached, I noticed that not only was I well in time, but before time. The Minister arrived half an hour after my arrival. Most VIP dependent programmes in Delhi start late, at least by a few minutes to few hours. Sometimes, the so-called VIP's, neither turn up nor send any message, for not coming, and neither are they apologetic about keeping others waiting.

In the land of Lord Shiva

I had accepted an engagement in Kathmandu for a vigilance and a security programme organised by the Delhi Productivity Council. I had invited my batchmates, Sh.SVM Tripathi and Sh. Talukdar to be the faculty. I had been asked to be course Director. I requested my friend Tripathi to accept the responsibility to which he agreed. I told the Chief Commissioner Customs, Sh. S.P Srivastav for courtesies by the Custom officials for a smooth and hassle free boarding at the time of check in, but the protocol officer failed to escort me to the aircraft, through the security check-up. The plane left in time. But there was total chaos at Kathmandu airport. There were not even enough trolleys for carting out the baggage. An immigration form was filled up. But I got the impression that the person accepting the form was illiterate. Luggage took 54 minutes to arrive. My friend and publisher, Sanjay Jha, with great difficulty, got a trolley for my use. When I was talking to Talukdar, somebody just took it away. I was so engrossed that I did not notice it. Sanjay Jha did the exercise again and was unhappy with me for not being attentive when my cart was being taken away. Thank God, I had not put my IBM lap top computer and my brief case on the trolley. Otherwise, I would have been minus that too. All my papers are generally in my briefcase and all books and lectures for the programme are in the computer. Of course, I have kept the back-up, so that my labour of years does not go down the drain. Fortunately, everything turned out well, and after one and half hours of landing, I was in the Hotel Hararti, comfortably cocooned in my suite. I slept for one hour and was ready in time to start the Vigilance and the Security Programme at 5 P.M. The programme went on till 7.30 P.M. SVM Tripathi and Talukdar shared the burden of the faculty and continued to do so for the next three days.

It was a full day programme as planned. The classes started at 8 A.M. and went on till 2 P.M. with a tea break in between. The participants, thirteen in number against the nominations of twenty, were a lively lot and showed keen interest. The same problem was approached, solved and dealt differently by different organisations despite there being a single set of instructions. It only highlights that there is no single method of doing the same thing. In the afternoon, Mr. Pawan Aggarwal, a relation of Seth Madan Lal Aggarwal, a good friend of mine, took us to the shopping area of Kathmandu. Chinese goods were not only dirt cheap, but also left us wondering as to how anybody could make a profit by selling a table clock for Rupees thirty. Sanjay Jha was with me all through. I was on my feet for two hours. I also visited the holy temple of Lord Shiva, Pashupati Nath. The miracle of miracles was that I did not have to wait for paying homage and seek his blessings. There was no crowd. It appeared that Lord Shiva knew that I was impatient, and did not like to stand in queue. He had taken care of that. It was the second visit, since I had also visited it in 1998 for a similar Delhi Productivity Council Programme. In the evening, I dropped in for dinner at the residence of Mr. Manoj Kumar Bharti IFS, First Secretary in Indian Embassy, who turned out to be the son-in-law of my late friend and batchmate Maiku Ram of Bihar cadre. It was an excellent dinner in an equally excellent company.

Evening at the Casino

By mistake or deliberately, I had kept the heating on, in the room. The result was that I was uncomfortable the whole night, till I opened the windows and let some fresh air of six degree C in. It was a disturbed night, though my friend Talukdar had warned not to keep the heating on. I, normally, am in bunyan and pyjama, when not attending any formal function. This is contrary to everybody in my family who properly clads, himself or herself. Two dinners, one at the hotel and the other at the house of Manoj Bharti, of Indian Embassy had also contributed to my discomfort. The fault was mine, for having overstuffed myself, in sheer politeness, instead of saying no to one dinner. During the day, after the programme, there was a formal launch of my book 'Inside CBI' for Nepal. The local Nepali Press has covered it well. In the evening, I went again to the crowded market selling Chinese goods and bought a few trinkets, as give-away souvenirs to those friends and relations, who expect something from me, every time I go out of India. I ended the evening, with a visit to a Casino. As a matter of rule, set by myself, for myself I gamble for the sake of fun. The limit is either winning or losing of rupees two hundred. When either of these happens, I leave. But I did not do so. Mr. Pawan Aggarwal got the coupons. Instead of money in the Casinos all over the world, you have to play, with coupons or tokens, and convert your winnings into cash at the paying counter. In half an hour, I had doubled his winning and gave him all the money, Rs.10,000 as he was the one, who had put in the Capital. The day was over by 10 P.M. These days, I am reading the inimitable PG Wodehouse. He is a delightful author, who keeps the reader amused. I keep smiling when reading his books. He is worth reading again and again. I always carry a Woodhouse novel with me.

Security checks in Kathmandu are slower than snails' pace

On the last day of the programme, the participants were busy exchanging pleasantries and addresses with each other. It happens in every course. But the addresses and contacts made, remain only confined to the diaries. The forced coming together of vigilance and security officers at least enables them to stay together and exchange notes about the methods they think best or worst in their organisations. What happens outside the class room is more important than what happens inside. In Nepal, there is only the government channel. But the Indian government TV, DD national is clearly available courtesy the cable operators. BBC, Zee TV, Star and Sony are also available. One does not feel out of sort in Nepal because the atmosphere is just like that of India. Hindi is very well understood. Eighty percent of the business in Nepal is in the hands of Marwaris from Rajasthan, Gujarat, Bihar, Haryana and UP. Under Nepali laws, Indians cannot own any property or business in Kathmandu. The prosperity of outsiders will always arouse jealousy of the natives. Despite acquiring citizenship of a country, a foreigner will always remain a foreigner. They have partnership with local citizens, like it is in Dubai for engaging in business. Tax rates are the same as in India. In fact, Nepal sees Indian budget, and then prepares its own budget. Due to the hijacking of an Indian Airlines flight on 31st December, 1999, there was extra security check for the passengers, travelling to India. It was slow, suspicious and time consuming and took over two hours. The result was two hours delay. Instead of arriving at 3 P.M. at Delhi the plane arrived at four and the luggage took ages to arrive. I had given timing to Channel 4 of the United Kingdom for an interview on Bofors case. The team, which had flown in from London and Bangkok, came on the dot. I delayed the recording, by over half an hour as I had to go for necessary natural requirements of visiting the bathroom. The recording took over one and a half hours. There was just no time to prolong the interview, as I had to go for a dinner hosted by my friend, Chandan Mitra, Editor of The Pioneer for a collaboration, with an IT firm. But for the efforts of Chandan, the Pioneer would have folded up, three years ago. The party had a galaxy of VIPs and ministers, including Mr.Venkiah Naidu, Minister for Rural Development, Sushma Swaraj, Minister for Information and Broadcasting, Shanmugam, Minister for Coal, Chief Minister of Delhi, Sheila Dixit, Former Defence Minister, Mulayam Singh Yadav, and a number of Members of Parliament including, Amar Singh. I spent just the right amount of time, and reached home by 11 PM. I repacked my bag for proceeding to Hyderabad in the early hours of 30th November, 2000. There was no time even to talk to my wife and daughter. It was really a full day and half a night.

A day's visit to my service alma mater

I got up without the help of any alarm clock at 4 A.M. on 30/11/2000. One is subconsciously aware of the day's programme and the system responds to the needs. The morning exercise had to be missed, as I left my house at 5.30 A.M., to catch the flight to Hyderabad at 6.30 A.M. The purpose of the visit to Hyderabad was to address the valedictory function of the Vigilance course organised by the National Police Academy for senior officers of the government and public sectors. The flight arrived in time. Before proceeding to the Academy, I met Mr. K.Vijay Ram Rao, my predecessor Director of the CBI. Ram Rao, plunged into politics and won the last assembly election on Telegu Desam ticket against the leader of the Congress party in the State Assembly. Being a giant killer, with an excellent track record, he was inducted in to the Chander Babu Naidu's Cabinet as the Minister for Public Works. He is staying in his own house, rather than in any ministerial bungalow. I presented him my book, "Be The Best".

I requested him to give me his feed-back on the book. I had no other engagement, except addressing the course participants at 3.30 P.M. Before that, I was interviewed by Enadu Television, on the cricket match fixing, as the captain of the Indian Cricket Team Azarhuddin hails from Hyderabad. When I wanted to use my IBM laptop for half an hour in the Academy, I found that it would not start. Even the efforts of the local computer expert of the academy failed. The result was that I could not work on it. I had to spend my time in reading only. The academy Director Mr.Rajgopal happened to be away due to a bereavement in his family. Mr. M. Mahendar Reddy, the course Director had done an excellent job. I walked to the room of each faculty member of the academy, including the Deputy Directors Sh.G.Naik and Ashok Dohare and all other officers. This was one way of calling on all officers, and saying hello to them in their own rooms. Their rooms were well furnished and clean. It is, in stark contrast, to what prevailed in Mt. Abu, where I was trained in 1961. The National Police Academy was located there, since 1948, before it shifted to Hyderabad in the 1970's. It is training ground for all the IPS officers of the country and is the Alma Mater of all members of the directly recruited IPS officers in the country. In fact, it is a great cementer of the country, because after the initial training the officers move off to the states allotted as their cadre. These bonds are life-long and stronger than any official orders. In due course of time, each batch gets a chance to provide top cops to the country as the State Police Chiefs, Heads of Central Organisations, like the CBI, CRP, BSF, CISF, IB and RAW. The scare of hijacking has led to the tightening of avoidable inconvenience of too many security checks at too many points. The Central Industrial Security Force has taken up the security of Hyderabad airport in place of the local police. The staff were alert and courteous and not needlessly offensive. The Indian Airlines flight left on time and arrived at Delhi on time.

Dinner was served in the evening flight, whereas I had my airborne breakfast in the morning flight. The air travel had reduced the 2000 kilometres journey just to two hours either way. I spent four hours in the air and another ten hours on the ground during the day.

Magnetic appeal of good food

I have a big incision on my chest, as a result of the bypass surgery. The wound has been healed, and my life is normal. The only problem is that the growth of hair around the incision causes constant irritation and itching. I shaved the hair off, and felt a lot of relief. The same problem has been faced by all those who have undergone bypass surgery. One has to live with some inconveniences in life.

A lot of time was spent on socialisation yesterday. The forenoon was utilised in attending the wedding of the son of late R.S. Sahay, a service colleague and a relation of my brother-in-law Tarlok Singh. My sister, Sarla, was there at the wedding, held on the lawns of Talkatora Gardens. I had to eat lunch there. There was no way I could avoid young Jyoti, niece of late Rajinder Singh, and her husband on the job to ensure that I ate everything. In India, we show love only through food. I had to eat dinner at the residence of Sardar Jagmohan Singh, the Secretary General of the Non-Resident Indian Institute. The dinner had been hosted to meet NRI's, Mr. H.S.Nirula from London and Mr. Ranjit Singh from Bangkok. Two rich meals outside are tempting. But they add to your weight. Like most people, I have a weakness for good food. I did justice to my craving and stomach.

Should life always be such?

Gorging on hotel food has been going on for the last one week. I visited Ghaziabad on 4th December, 2000 to visit a paper factory of Mr. Parveen Jain, a fellow morning walker. He had called a number of industrialists for the luncheon meeting and my visit to see the production of paper. The industrialists felt that the present laws made it impossible to throw out unwilling and unfit workers. The moment any worker is made permanent, his productivity and output drops. Industrial and Inspector's black mail is something they are to live with. It is for this reason that they are not able to compete with China and other nations producing cheap and quality goods. A number of industries are generating their own power from their captive units, as the UP State is not able to meet their demands. One's own generation of power, in many cases, works out cheaper than the government supply. The state, instead of being a welfare state for all citizens, appears to have degenerated into a captive state which is spending all its resources on paying a huge and unaffordable salary bill to its employees. Most employees, especially at the cutting edge level, treat their jobs as a means to make fast bucks. In the evening I had to go for the reception dinner hosted by the Laos Ambassador, to celebrate his country's national day at hotel Taj Palace. Taj Palace is a five star hotel. But the food served in all hotels whether five star or four or three or starless dhabas or road side restaurants, is the same. The cooks seem to vie with each other in putting a lot of condiments, and oil in the preparation, or in offering fried stuff. It is a paradox that those who should be medically not eating the stuff in such places eat it whereas the poor do not have even two square meals. The same story of over eating was repeated on 6th December. My wife and I breakfasted with Vijay Goel, M.P. now a minister, at his 5 Mahadev Road bungalow and I went for two dinners in the evening. Mr. Goel, the young ebullient M.P. is a perfect host. He overfed us with tempting parathas, which is the weakness of most Punjabis. Of course, if you are resolute, no power can make you go against you will. But here was a case of ourselves, being tempted and succumbing to the temptation. His wife, Preeti, played a perfect hostess. Vijay is enthusiastic about his job as a Member of Parliament and is full of ideas. In the night, my first dinner was at the residence of Mr. Suresh Thakur, at his Vasant Kunj residence. His house is only 14 kilometres from my place. It took 45 minutes to cover this distance due to poor lighting, traffic lights and pocky roads. Vasant Kunj locality has a power cut of four hours everyday. The President of the Resident's Welfare Association told me that they are surprised on the days when there is no power cut. They are reconciled to electricity-less existence in the National Capital and are used to it. But the bigger problem is the lack of water supply. They are not allowed to put hand pumps, as it is against the laws to tap ground water. Here it is a strange case. The government cannot supply you all the water. Yet, it does not allow you to make your own arrangements. It only adds to the corruption, at the lower level. The lower level officers can threaten the citizens with prosecution, and extract their cut, for conniving at the alleged violations of the rules. There can be no better instance of the government working at cross purposes. My second destination in the opposite direction was Hotel Inter-Continental to attend an IT award function, where I gave away the award to one of the recipients for doing well in the Information Technology field. I stayed back for a second dinner to give company to Mr. Vittal, Central Vigilance Commissioner and Mr. Rajan K.V., the then Secretary East in the Ministry of External Affairs. I had met Mr. Rajan first in London, when he was the Deputy High Commissioner and then later on in Kathmandu in 1998, when he was posted there as our Ambassador. He is staying in hostel on Curzon Road. Government of India had built a hostel for the delegates to the UNCTAD or United Nations Conference on Commerce and

Trade in 1956. The External Affairs Ministry had taken a block of flats to be used as a transit accommodation for its officers moving between one posting to another. There were no takers, for these furnished flats in the 1960's. Now there are not enough flats. This is because the general population, as well as the population of bureaucracy, has out-stripped the supply. Moreover, we all want to be choosy in deciding about the place we want to live in. A senior official can afford to be choosy and get whatever he wants. But a vast majority has to live with what befalls their way. The only difference is that the rich can bribe, and still get whatever they want.

The next day was no better. I had five programmes for the day. One was a book rclease function, two marriages, one meeting of the Institute of Directors, of which I am one of the office bearers and one anniversary of the magazine, called Day After, all between 7 P.M. to 10 P.M. I attended all the functions by making use of my now famous stop watch. The trick was to wish the chief host all the best, and move off to the next function. Though all programmes had dinner as the main item, I avoided them by saying that I had to move on to the next programme, which was absolutely true. I find that the truth still provides the best and honest solution for any problem. I have to balance my time between social requirements and my routine of writing. The biggest problem is how to prevent others from wasting your time. There has to be a combination of diplomacy and firmness in tackling this problem. I make up my mind to spend a fixed amount of time for every activity and then start my stop watch. I use this time of spending at functions actually in meeting and making my presence effectively felt to the host. I make it a point to talk to all the guests and then apologise for leaving early, for the next commitment and then leave. I noticed that hosts appreciate this kind of frankness. On Sunday, there was a Lodi Road morning walkers lunch hosted by Subhash Malhotra of the UNI. It was a good way of renewing acquaintanceship, with the fellow morning walkers. Every group tries to socialise and know each other better. As everywhere, ladies always segregate. There is a self-imposed constraint on the ladies talking to the men, lest they be misunderstood, or regarded too fast or too forward. The social interaction is generally confined to saying Hello, talking about the weather, or the current political issues, or the survival of the government. The current issues these days is the demolition of the Babri Masjid, which has led to the stalling of the proceedings of the Parliament. This is only a vote bank ploy indulged in by several political parties. Any excuse is good enough to politicise as long as it can procure votes. Nobody talks about the 100 killings and over 1000 injured in the Bombay blasts in 1992 organised by the fundamentalists to avenge the demolition of a structure called Babri Masjid. Nobody has talked about the massacres of 3000 Sikhs in October, November, 1984. The issue is the garnering of votes and not genuine sympathy with any person or any community.

A late night wedding

This week has been a week of marriages galore. Yesterday, I accompanied Surinder for a wedding in Janakpuri. For Surinder, it was a question of honouring an invitation from a bosom friend, of her late father. Dr. Sehgal, the grandfather of the bride, had travelled to Chandigarh to get our address, ring up Surinder and courier the invitation, as there is a postal strike. Postal employees are demanding from the government, as usual, higher wages and jobs for the people who are employed on a part-time basis. I told Surinder that even god listens to his devotees who want to see him or who ask for any blessings. I am duty bound to honour such an invitation, where the person inviting us has gone all out to invite us. A journey of 18 kilometres took 55 minutes due to pocky roads, confusing directions, fused street lights and almost no directional boards indicating which way to go. It is a common defect all over the country. These are small things totally ignored and never taken seriously. There are about seven lakh street lights in Delhi and each one of them costs Rs. 700 per year. My feeling is that such lights exist only on paper, and not on the ground like many other government supported projects. Huge cuts, kickbacks go on and the culprits get away with impunity. It appears that the system has become almost incurable. It is because those vested with authority do not discharge their duty of ensuring that people working under them also work, or they have vested interests in letting the matters at status quo level, for their personal cuts.

Meeting a king maker

I remain so busy, with nothing, even after retirement, that when I sit, at the end of the day, I find that I have not accomplished all that I should have. May be, I cannot quantify the work at the end of the day. The only thing which can be quantified is the number of words written by me. It is not possible to assess the net result of other work done. But on examining deeply, I find that I rarely waste time on the things I don't consider worthwhile. It is the only way of accomplishing all that I want to accomplish. I used to follow a practice of not picking up the telephone, as there used to be a number of wrong calls. For a change, I picked up the phone to answer every single call. I noticed that it not only wasted time on wrong numbers but also most calls were unproductive or those that should not have even been answered. A number of people telephoned to confirm whether my telephone number with them was the same I was speaking from. It may appear as something very small, but it interrupted the continuity of the task I was doing. A government servant, who has put in 35 years of service in the government knows primarily only the government work. My batchmate, Rohminthanga from Mizoram dropped in to see me and collect a list of the batch mates. He has got a six years tenure job, as the single member Election Commissioner, for Union Territories. This is almost an extension of service, for another six years. It is a periodic job, which becomes active when elections are to be held. In the evening, I visited a five star hotel to attend a wedding reception of the relation of a friend of mine. It was one of those obligatory attendance function, where a return visit was called both out of returning their attendance at my functions and courtesy. I met Harkishan Singh Surjeet, the General Secretary and the Supremo of Communist Party of India, Marxist. He is well past 75 and is both mentally and physically active. Being a doyen of Indian politics, he has commanded respect from all sections of politicians. He has never been a member of Parliament. But his standing is more than that of most ministers, and some former Prime Ministers. During the time of the previous United Front Governments, he was the king-maker. A number of Governors owe their jobs to him. Along with him was BS Ramoowalia, a pleasant and courteous member of the Parliament. He was a Cabinet Minister in the Devegowda and Gujral governments from 1996-1998. Always polite to a fault, and ever helpful, it is a pleasure to meet him. The wedding reception was full of well-fed, well-stuffed and highly ornamented ladies and bored gentlemen. It is strange but true that only those have the means and money to overfeed themselves and for whom food acts as a poison. These super rich people spend Rs. 5000 for one meal and then go to five star gymnasiums to shed the extra weight and calories gained from the hotel food. What some of these people spend on one day would be enough to feed a full family for one month. But that is how life goes on.

The saga of school admissions (December 15, 2000)

Yesterday, I addressed Amity Business School on personality development. Mr. Ashok Chauhan, the President of the Amity Institutions, has probably the best educational complex in fifteen acres of land in Noida. The group is doing a yeoman's service in providing excellent educational facilities, which compare very favourably with the best in the world. They provide Post Graduate Diplomas in Public Administration, Communication, the Behavioural Sciences, as well as Computers. Mr. Chauhan, at the rate he is devoted to the cause of education, would be the Educational Czar of India. Seeing is believing. What the private sector can do in the field of education can be seen in Noida Amity. My nephew Munish Tewari, who was the President of Indian Youth Congress, till a few months back, joined me for lunch at my suggestion. He wanted to meet me. Lunch is something which suits me to invite my friends and relatives. My wife is particular in providing proper food, whenever the guests come. The subject of discussion was the admission of children to the schools in Delhi. There are more children than the schools can cope and provide places for them. Best education is something, where even the lowest in society want the best for their children. It is at this time, the Principals of the schools throw their weight about. One cannot really fight with the educational authorities and the rising school bills. Best things cost money, in life and so if you want to get the best teachers and make your institution the best, you have to pay the best salaries. All this has to be paid for by those who want to avail of the best schools. It becomes a vicious circle and everything boils down to your capacity to pay. Munish told me that the current rate of capitation fee for admission of a child to Nursery/Primary class is Rs. 4 lakhs. The top private schools admit only those with money or influence. The bright children of the bureaucrats get admission, as they bring credit and merit to the School by their performance in the examination. I recalled a similar expedition in 1979. I had to visit a dozen schools for the admission of my two daughters. Most principals even refused even to meet me and my wife. Those who condescended to grant interviews said that they would let me know the fate of my request, for admission of my daughters. I had almost become a communist, because of the unjust treatment and lack of response. I later on saw the point of view of the educational authorities and was reconciled when my daughters got admission due to the efforts of my wife.

Shooting a film (Monday, December 18, 2000)

Yesterday, I reached Chandigarh for attending a seminar on corruption organised by Haryana Police. I came a day earlier to finish the shooting of a film based on my book, 'Outside CBI'. This book is an improved version of my autobiography first published as 'Without Fear and Favour'. The film producer has combined it with my book 'Inside CBI'. I had advised him to select a younger person to play the role of a hero. I do not act as the hero of the film. I am, as I am, in the film. The shooting for the telefilm was almost continuous from the time I arrived till at 11 A.M. 9.30 P.M. The film was partly shot, in Ebony departmental store. As part of the shooting and actually and really I gave an award of 100 grams of gold, to a lady, who had won a lucky draw, in a shopping competition. Ebony is the biggest departmental store of Chandigarh. It is a one-stop shop, where you can get anything you want, short of an elephant or a Mercedes car. Spick and span, neat and clean, it has created a niche for itself. I felt tired and remembered that drinking of plenty of water freshens one up. I drank half a dozen glasses of water and was fresh. Some body asked me a question as to who is the heroine of the film. I pleaded ignorance for the simple reason that I really did not know. Neither am I anxious for the fate of the film as the producer and director of the film are keen to complete and release it on the next Lohri day in 2001. It was a solid eight hours of acting without any rest or break. Late and overeating dinner was the next consequence. I slept off and by the time I got up, it was past 5 A.M. next day.

Haryana shows a desire to improve

The news about the film shooting and my interview and recording was there in three English newspapers of Chandigarh, that is, Hindusatan Times, The Indian Express, The Tribune and the Hindi paper, Dainak Bhaskar with my photograph. Almost everybody wrote about the telefilm about me in glowing terms. The seminar on corruption started at about 11.30 A.M. I had arrived about half an hour earlier. I utilised the time, in meeting old colleagues who had retired. There are about thirty retired Directors-Generals settled in Chandigarh. They meet once or twice, in a quarter either for lunch or dinner. The host police, Haryana, assured for them a place of pride by giving them prominent seats. I as a guest of honour was seated on the dais, along with the Chief Minister Om Prakash Chautala, the Central Vigilance Commissioner, N. Vittal, the Chief Secretary, Vishnu Bhagwan, Director General of Haryana Police and the host, Sh.M.S Malik. I suggested the simplification of rules and their implementation in a time-bound fashion. I also suggested that a healthy competition be allowed, between the government departments and private sector. Let the government partly privatise the work, pertaining to the licensing and fitness of the vehicles as well as passing of the construction and alteration plans of the building. Later on when I asked the Chief Minister as to how much of the suggestions given by me were meeting his approval, he replied that he would implement all of them. I rescheduled my programme and decided to return to Delhi as my work for the day was over. Mr. Vittal and I travelled by the Himalayan Queen, which brought us to Delhi within four and half hours at 10.10 P.M.

With an Indian, who made to the top in British Columbia, Canada

When my Secretary does not turn up the day, it leads to the accumulation of work of especially replying to the correspondence. I make it a point to reply to any letter received by me. I was doing the same when I was in government service. It at least gave an assurance to the person writing the letter, or petition, that his communication was not just thrown in to the waste paper basket. The absence of PA, was helpful in one way, that I was able to concentrate on my work, and finish some articles and reply to the phone calls, nearly 38 of them, in my answering machine. The answering machine enables me to reply to the phones, at my convenience. In the evening, there was a dinner cum meeting organised by the World Punjabi Organisation, to discuss the setting up of a Sikh section in Smithsonian Museum in Washington. The Sikhs of Delhi were represented by their intellectuals and intelligentsia, at the meeting in the India International Centre. I was also invited to the meeting presided over by the only Sikh Union Cabinet Minister, Sh. Sukhdev Singh Dhindsa. Dhindsa has an excellent track record and as the Minister in-charge of Sports, he was the one responsible for making the CBI report public. I suggested in the meeting that nothing useful ever emerges out of the meetings, and let a committee of half a dozen people do all the work on behalf of the entire community. The meeting was also attended by Ujjal Singh Dosanjh, the Prime Minister of British Columbia, Canada. Next day, that is 20th of December, was again a day dedicated to honouring Mr. Dosanjh. It started with a lunch hosted by LM Singhvi, MP, former High Commissioner of India in London, in the hotel Taj Man Singh, just two kilometres from my house. It was a formal affair and a sit down lunch attended by a number of politicians including the President of the Bhartiya Janta Party, Bangaru Laxman,

Deputy Chairman of Rajya Sabha Najma Heptulla, Former Prime Minister Inder Kumar Gujral. Normally, I have avoided Gujral, so that there is no unpleasant confrontation between me and him due to my having written in my book, Inside CBI about his role in the Bihar fodder scam. But I have no grudge, or grievance, against him. The choice with him was either to save his own job, or my job. Naturally, he preferred to save his own job. I greeted him and shook hands with him. I remembered the lesson from my own book "Be The Best", that courtesy does not cost anything. I could make it that my conduct visibly pleased him. Late in the evening I went to hotel Bristol to be guest of honour where Mr. Dosanjh was being lionised and honoured. It was well past midnight, when I hit my bed. In between, I went and addressed the officials of the Industrial Finance Corporation at the invitation of the Chairman, Mr. P.V.Narasimhan on the subject of motivating the staff to give their best to their organisation. IFCI is doing pretty badly in finance world, with one of the largest NPA.

Innovative ways of sticking to the job

My PA to whom I had given an advance of Rs. 3000 for the work done in December decided to go to his own village. I don't mind being cheated like this, as I have an unfailing faith in the goodness of human nature. The modus operandi of the then PA was to take advance money, so that one is obliged to continue him whether he works or not. I had to get rid of the previous secretary as every month he would ask for an advance. Not only I gave him advance for the month of December, but also extra Rs.2000 as he wanted to go to Simla for an examination for a better job. He had also taken an advance of Rs. 1000 yesterday for going to his home town. The moral for me is that in money matters, one should be correct and not over generous. This tends to make the people working for you, both negligent and careless. The same PA after taking the advance for his father's sickness was absent for 15 days in November, 2000 and for another 15 days in the month of December again. It is better not to have people, who will give tension. In fairness to myself, I replaced him. In the afternoon, I attended the annual lecture of the Intelligence Bureau to commemorate its establishment day. It was set up on 22nd December, 1887 by an order of the Secretary of the State of the United Kingdom. This year's lecture on the diplomacy, being the other side of the security, was delivered by Sh.L.M. Singhvi, MP, Former High Commissioner of India in London. It was a brilliant exposition by Sh. Singhvi. More than anything, it was an opportunity to meet a number of old colleagues, whom I had not seen for a long time. Surinder left for Beas, to the Radhaswami headquarters. It is a kind of a vegetarian sect of Sikhism, having followers from all denominations. I do not believe in any religion. As I was born a Sikh, I practise that religion. Sikhism is a very practical religion. It does not have any living Guru and the Holy Granth is enough to live a good life. I, in liberal traditions, have allowed my wife to practise, whatever belief she wants. She spends rather a disproportionate part of her time, in doing odd jobs for Radhaswami denomination. I, on my part keep my self busy, with my fairly large number of engagements. A large part is taken by the writing of articles, and completing books in the pipe line.

Education is better than stock and a sure money spinner

The weather is getting colder with the temperature ranging from 7 to 15 degree C. I go for a walk only at about 8.30 AM when the sun has been up for more than an hour. The room heaters keep the room temperature at comfortable 19°C. Some portion of the Lodi Garden gets sun and it makes the walk pleasant and enjoyable in the bitterest winter. The toilets in the garden are a model of filth and rubbish. It is partly due to the non-supply of the cleaning material, and partly due to the negligence of the staff and their supervisors. I recorded a talk, on All India Radio, about the security scenario in the country and it was broadcast thrice today. Later on I visited the Jagan Institute of Management and addressed the convocation and distributed MBA degrees there. The atmosphere was leisurely and casual during the function. The easy informality, has become the hall mark of the younger generation. Education has become a paying and commercially sound proposition in the big towns. For instance, in many places for admission a lot of money changes hands, under the table for admissions. The big engineering and medical colleges, especially in the south, have become money spinners. It is easier to pass the All India Services Examination, than to get admission for your children in schools. Influence, money and connections are required. When I was able to get admission for one of my daughters in 1980 without paying any money, which in any case, even if I could, would not have paid. I was told that it meant a loss of Rs. 20000. It is not that there is no corruption in private sector. It depends upon the opportunities available there.

About four hours were spent in the meeting of the DAV Management Committee, of which I was re-elected as the Vice President. I proposed the name of Sh.G.P. Chopra for the Presidency. Sh.Chopra has been an educationist of repute and has vast experience of administration. He was honoured with the award of Padma Shri by the government. He has a high standing both in the teaching and educational field. It has been achieved by him with a dedicated service of over four decades. Later on, I visited the road side book market on Asaf Ali Road and Darya Ganj, and picked up books for Rs. 76 which in a regular shop would have cost me Rs. 980. I missed my siesta, but did not feel that I had missed it. It was because I had not overstuffed myself with the lunch. It is the heavy meal which induces sluggishness and a desire to sleep. The day I want to keep myself awake and alert, I make it a point not to have lunch or have a very light lunch. I must confess that it is the love of spices and butter and not the food, which is at the bottom of overeating.

Christmas, just another day for me

The Christmas day was a home affair for me. I spent the entire day at home. My article on the editorial page of Pioneer, steering to bankruptcy, was published, as well as my article's first instalment, on Bofors also made its appearance in the Economic Times. I need to go out once a day only to break monotony. It is not necessary to go out because almost everyday with a few odd exceptions, I have one or the other speaking assignment, or some other programme for a dinner, or social engagement. In any case, my morning walk itself is a social activity. Occasional visits to a dispensary to get my periodical medicines, due to my bypass on 17th April, 1999 is also a way of interacting with others. Social interaction is one way of keeping oneself abreast, of thinking of others. One thing I hate is telling or accepting lies from others or cheating or being cheated. I had to dismiss my driver and PA for both lapses. May be, because they had been brought up in an atmosphere, where it was normal to cheat or defraud or tell lies. I find it difficult to deal with unreliable people. But it is human nature to get something for nothing if possible, and live off others. But if people know that you would not put up with any nonsense, they leave you free and accept you as you are. I tested some candidates, who came for secretary's job to me. But they cannot even type. I have kept the question of employing an alternate secretary open, till I find somebody suitable. Training a person itself takes a long time. Though the candidates said that they had done a course in computer, they could not handle any computer. It only shows that competent persons are difficult to come by. There is no dearth of opportunities or opening for skilled persons.

TV, no more an attraction

I quite often put on TV, while working on the computer, and once in a while I watch it. Most movie channels show the same movies which are all alike. They have the usual shooting, same rape and fight scenes. All heroes and heroines are almost alike, dancing either around the trees, or in gardens. They have the same hip shaking, gyrating, sex and suggestive scenes. Their figures and shapes are thin and skinny. Frankly, I can hardly distinguish one from the other. I have a feeling that they must be on perpetual diet to maintain slim and attractive figures, which is the envy of most well-fed and well-stuffed people, like me. The television channels have become an extension of the films. They have sounded the death knell of theatres. Ultimately, theatres will come back, as a two hour movie on a TV channel takes three to four hours. More than that, when the movie scene reaches a vital or strategic position, or plot, there is a commercial break. It takes the thrill out of watching the movie. When a mystery is about to be revealed or villain is about to meet his desserts, one has to watch a lot of advertisements of junk items, before one can see the rest of the movie. It is a totally deflating procedure. The only thing that can be said in justification of advertisements is that without them channels would not be able to survive.

A good-bye lunch

It was the second day of my new PA. He has to still get used to me and my method of working. The previous fellow had ruined one of my computers, which I gave him for working at home. I did it in good faith. He neither worked on it, nor took care of it. I have been rather too trusting in my nature. The result is that sometimes people take me for a ride or take me for granted. Before they realise that they have played a trick on me, they are thrown out by me. I had to dismiss two PA's and one driver for playing tricks and cheating me. Any amount of wailing had no effect on them. I always keep a soft exterior, but I am very strict otherwise. I do not take anybody for granted, nor allow others to take me for granted. Sometimes, politeness is misunderstood for weakness or being dumb. This is only a ruse to lure others to behave their natural self. Today, Mr. AS Dulat, Secretary RAW had hosted a big lunch, on the eve of his retirement from service from 31/12/2000 at the age of sixty. It was a kind of farewell lunch to all his officers along with some retired senior IPS officers who had served in the Intelligence agencies He had also invited me. I had an occasion to meet a lot of former colleagues, from my service. I cannot claim to belong to any service, now like other retired people. I have known Dulat from 1969, when I had joined as ADC to the Governor of Punjab in 1968. Dulat and his wife have been good friends. I had a second stint with him, as IG CRPF in J&K. Dulat was the head of the local Intelligence and we had to work in close co-operation to deal with the insurgency in Kashmir in 1990. Dulat has been an excellent professional, who has been doing his duty with a smile. All his colleagues and friends including myself grade him as a crown of his batch. One of the biggest satisfactions in life is to reach the top in one's profession, and retire from that height. Dulat has achieved that along with a few others of his batch. The top is never crowded. It normally has space for one man. May be one or two persons can stand near him. But the pedestal is meant only for one person. Of course, I have no complaints. I myself have been number one or the top person of Narcotics Control Bureau, Indo-Tibetan Border Police Force, Central Industrial Security Force, Bureau of Police Research and Development, Railway Protection Force and Central Bureau of Investigation. Only the last three months of my service were spent in a parking slot, where there was no work worth mentioning, given to me in the Home Ministry. This was a punishment posting given, for not agreeing to the then Prime Minister Gujral's orders to go slow in the fodder scam case. The then Prime Minister, Inder Kumar Gujral, told me, "Do you know that I am the Prime Minister"? My reply was "Yes Sir, I know. But you are not supposed to know what is passing between me and Patna High Court". This happened on 20th June, 1997, a day before I left for Interpol meeting, in Lyons, France. When I returned on 1st July, 1997, my number two man, RC Sharma had not only been posted, but had also assumed charge of the post of Director, CBI. When pressmen asked my reaction to my transfer, I replied "Same salary and no work". The then Prime Minister had his own sweet revenge on me. My regret is that he survived 18 days more after my retirement, as Congress had withdrawn support within three weeks of my retirement on 31st October, 1997. God has His own way of settling scores, and evening things out. One of the older colleagues was depressed and took me to a corner in the party. He expressed his unhappiness that a few days back he had gone to see a younger officer in his office. The official, who had worked under him, was rather officious and dismissed him politely by getting up and wearing a coat for going out. He told me that he realised that a polite hint had been given to him to leave. It was all done courteously and politely. He told me that one can be slighted without saying a word. He said that he never expected this from a person whom he had known for thirty years. I told him to follow the same policy, which I do. He asked me as to what my policy is? I told him that "the day I retired I made it a point not to ring up any government official, however junior or senior he may be. I said that the official may be genuinely busy or may not be there and I may be told as such. I would always get the impression that he avoided speaking to me. Moreover, even a junior official occupying the lowest position in the government always feels that he is the lord and master of all he surveys. For my peace of mind, I avoid having anything to do with any government office or government officials. A government official looks suspiciously at everything. Most are corrupt with a few exceptions. They would rather spend the time in cultivating people who matter, than on those, who may not be of any help to them. After retirement, one should learn to create one's own support group and do something, which would make him feel that he is still wanted. There is no such thing as permanent loyalty or a permanent friendship. Most relationships are relationships of convenience. My friend did not say anything. But I got the impression that the home truths told by me had sunk and he would not face any disappointments again, by following what I had rubbed in.

Everybody wants a short cut

Writing is a tough job and working on any book is still more difficult. If it is your own book, it is all the more difficult, because you are likely to by-pass, or ignore your own mistakes. I, like others also take an easy way out, of either attending to telephone calls, or periodically switching on the television. Editing your own book is still more difficult, because of the one track approach of the author, while writing a book. Simply because I have retired from service, I get all kinds of requests to intercede and take up cudgels on behalf of the people, approaching me. A young sweeperess approached me on the strength that her grandfather had worked for me thirty years back. I enquired about her problem. Her husband who was with her, was pushed to the background by her. She said that she wanted me to telephone a particular police station that they should take care of her. She also wanted me to tell the police station to thrash all those whom she wanted to be thrashed, because of personal enmity. I told her that I did not know who she was. Moreover, how could I ask anybody to be thrashed by the local police, when it is against the rules and laws. She would not take a 'no' for an answer. I told her that she should write down her complaint and I would send it to the person concerned. It is not in my nature, and nor do I intercede in any personal quarrel. She was disappointed, though her husband appeared happy at my reaction. Probably, she was under the impression that I would be at her beck and call. I told her whether in the government service or out of it, my approach to any problem or recommendations is the same. Another gentleman wanted me to speak to somebody in the Income Tax, so that he could get away with paying less income tax. I advised him to pay all the taxes, as otherwise how he could expect the government to function. I also told him that it is only through the taxes that government is able to provide electricity, water supply and other services. He was also disappointed at my response. He probably thought that my name and influence was for sale or use. I told him that my standards are the same, as a responsible citizen. Sahara television interviewed me on the kidnapping of the Kannada film star, Raj Kumar, by a brigand called Veerappan and the response of the local government to concede to all demands. My stand, which stood vindicated was that it is time the governments called a halt to yielding to the criminals and crooks. Incidentally, the Supreme Court of India rebuked the two governments of Karnataka and Tamil Nadu for their failure to apprehend the criminal.

Historical Gwalior

I had accepted an invitation from the Lions Club Gwalior to address them on 8th of August, 2000. I travel for the sake of convenience only to those places, which have good air or road connection. I also insist on those requesting on my visit to bear the travelling and hotel expenses. It is only to ensure that those who invite are serious about my accepting their invitation. Once on telephone I had accepted an invitation to be the Chief Guest of a function, near Bhatinda in Punjab. I was assured that I would be received and all transport arrangements would be made for the visit. But there was nobody to be seen at 4 AM, when the train reached Bhatinda. Fortunately, I had made alternative arrangements to rest before reaching the place of function at 11 AM. I concealed my bitterness but conveyed my polite displeasure to the organiser. Except for the usual sorry, there was no remorse or regret. Now, if the organisers know that they have to pay for my visit, they are serious, and do make arrangements.

I left for Gwalior by Shatabdi Express at 6 A.M. The standard breakfast of eggs and corn flakes was served. Shuffling through all the nine Delhi English newspapers, saw the end of 3.15 hours of journey. I read all the English newspapers published from Delhi. Each newspaper presents a different angle on any happening and incident. Sometimes, some papers miss some incidents, which are important. I also subscribe to all major English magazines. It is not out of any snobbery or love for English. It is simply due to the fact that the best analysts and writers are only with English publications. In any case, my education has been in English, having done Master of Arts or MA in English. My working language has been English for 37 years in government. So English is nearest to my mother tongue. I never fumble for written or spoken word in English, which sometimes I do in Punjabi. Whatever little time was left was utilised by me in working on the computer, in completing the articles which had a dead line. At Gwalior, there was just enough time to go to a hotel, and change into a suit as the three hours journey and sitting had crumpled the suit. People mostly judge you by the clothes you wear. After all all men look alike. The only visible and different part of men and women is their face while the rest of the body is clad in clothes. The second breakfast was at the house of a top businessman Mr. Davar. It would have been discourtesy to the organisers to have said a frank 'no'. I told politely to Mr. Prakash Sharma and the incoming Lions Club President, Mr. Mukesh Bhojwani that I had no space left for a repeat breakfast. But more out of obligation, that requirement for the food, I put everything on the plate, nibbled at a few items and put the plate back after a decent interval. Thoughtfully, a visit had been arranged to Bandi Chod Gurudwara. This Gurudwara is built in the fort, where the 6th Sikh Guru Hargobind Singh had been detained for 27 months by the Mughal Emperor Jahangir for alleged anti-Mughal activities. Jahangir is reported to have felt remorse at the unjust detention of the Guru and ordered his release. The Guru accepted the release, on the condition that along with him 52 unjustly jailed kings should also be released. On this a counter condition was put on him, that all who could catch hold of his shirt would be released along with him. The Guru got a garment stitched with 52 long hems. The result was that each king could hold on to one and walk out to freedom along with the Guru. These legends have been passed, from generation to generation, by word of mouth. It is essential to reduce them to writing at least for the next generations. But if any individual does it, he may be accused of twisting the tale. This kind of work is better done by a religious body, so that if there is a criticism, it cannot only be deflected, but also properly explained. Religious grounds are always delicate to tread on. No-body would like to indulge in a fight or arguments with any fundamentalist. There can be no victory over a mind set. I was honoured in the Gurudwara with a traditional Siropa or robe of honour and a sword. The sixth Guru had exercised temporal as well as spiritual authority. The arrest and detention of the sixth Guru in Gwalior showed that the policy of keeping people prisoners far away from their place of residence and influence was in vogue, in middle ages also. There is a considerable Sikh population, to the extent of nearly 10,000, in the Gwalior region, though nobody could give me the exact figure. There are a number of Institutions and Colleges, run by the Sikh community, in the area close by. In the evening, after about one hour of rest, I was taken to Scindia Museum. It is a palace, converted into a museum, where photographs, crockery, cutlery, paintings, ancient robes, weapons and coins are kept. This is a Royal family museum, containing family heirlooms. An interesting item, was a dining table, fitted with a mini train, for carrying food dishes for the 52 guests. The train would stop, from its almost crawling speed, till the guest picked up the dish in front of him, helped himself, and then put it back. It was an excellent show item. But Madhav Rao Scindia, the present ruler, and an important member of the Congress party, assured me that the train was a hit with the guests. Madhav Rao himself was a Congress man and his sister, Vijaya Raje and late mother, popularly called Rajmata, are/were in BJP or Bhartiya Janta Party. It is so in almost all important families. While Anil Shastri, one son of Late Lal Bhadur Shashtri is a Congressman, the other, Sunil, is the General Secretary of Bhartiya Janta Party. In other words, such an arrangement ensures that their bread remains buttered from both sides. Perhaps, it could also be a matter of conviction, and not necessarily a matter of convenience, as it may appear superficially. I really cannot hazard any conjecture on it. It is for the people, close to such families to make an accurate assessment.

In the night, the function at Gwalior started at 8 PM. I was the last speaker. This is generally so, with most of the organisers, that they keep the star speakers or star attraction as the last item. I could see that the audience was getting restive.

But they were too polite to find fault with me. I peppered my speech on the need for citizen's participation, for good governance with a lot of humorous incidents, so that the interest did not flag off. I had to use both Hindi and English, to emphasise that we get exactly that government which we deserve, and there are no free lunches in life. There was just enough time to pack my bag and catch the Grand Trunk Express train at midnight. It meant that I was without proper sleep, being up since 4 AM the previous night, to catch the train as well as this night, because the GT train brought me to Delhi at 5 AM. A programme like this necessarily means that one has to catch up on sleep, and recuperation the next day. Human body can stand some sleeplessness. But ultimately, one has to make up for the excess physical demands. My eldest daughter, Randeep, had come from Assam for a small operation, to get her post caesarean complications rectified. Her son and my grandson, named Danish, was born through a caesarean operation. Due to the negligence of the doctor, the stitches were carelessly fixed. The result was that she suffered and had to pay again to the hospital authorities, for the rectification of the stitches. I did not want her to get involved with the consumer courts. I went and saw her in Appollo Hospital, not for the sake of formality, but to make sure that my first born, my daughter was being looked after well. She was discharged in the evening. Her son just one year and four months old insisted on sitting in her lap. The medical advice was not to exert herself and not to pick up anything including her son. She explained this to her son. But children are children. As a compromise, she made him lie down with her. To keep Danish happy and diverted every morning, I would take him to Lodi Garden, where he would touch the fountains and water and try to catch crows. It was almost a repetition of what his mother used to do as a toddler. All children are alike.

On growing up, quite often we forget that we too were children once upon a time. One of the pleasures of having grandchildren is that the grandparents feel that they are indispensable to the grandchildren. The truth is that grandparents entertain their grandchildren for their own entertainment. No person, after growing up, remembers in any details as to how the elders of the family dotted on him or her. Danish, like his mother, has a very sweet and tingling voice. Lisping, broken sentences of children, are amusing. One has to guess, and to find out what the under three years children need or are saying.

I bang into another car

I get invited in a lot of social functions. Once, while going to M.P. Mr. Rudy's dinner, I had to drive, as the driver was on leave. I overtook and banged into a Cielo car. It was entirely my fault. I apologised and offered to compensate the loss, and pay the bills for any dents. But the other car owner, who was driving himself, appreciated my approach and said that anybody could have caused the dents. Though he told me not to bother, I gave him my name and address, that I would be willing to tell the truth to his insurance company so that my insurance company could pay. Since nobody had been injured, the matter was left there. I met a number of serving officials and confined myself only to shake hands and helloing them. My Secretary during the day spent all his time typing sixty congratulatory letters to the recipients of President's Police Medal from ITBP, CRP, CBI, RPF. I make it a point to send such letters to all persons whom I have known. I have either headed, or served, the above organisations in fairly senior capacities. These organisations still invite me for their major functions. There are some other organisations, where the idle rich come together for drinking and eating. However, when invited by such people, I either back out pleading other engagements or go only for an hour or so.

Predictable predictions

One of the biggest distractions is the telephones, which become active at the most inappropriate time. It may be a one minute call. But it distracts and diverts you from whatever you are doing, and disturbs the stream of thinking. I have a Cellular phone. But mostly, it is switched off and I use it only for emergencies. It is expensive, as all good things in life are. But it is useful. When Surinder, my wife, goes out of Delhi or I go out, the connectivity is always there. My cellphone does not work in Jalalabad. But it becomes active in Ferozpore. I plan in such a way that one of us is all the time in Delhi because of my mother, who is staying with us, as well as my daughter, Harveeen who had taken up a job after her MBA, in Delhi. This week was full of engagements, and there were one or two dinners everyday, followed invariably, by a series of speeches and functions. Even a patient person is likely to exhaust his patience in listening to the boring speeches, again and again. The pattern of speeches is sickeningly familiar, and repeated many times over. A few sentences are said in praise of the Chief Guest and then self laudatory references are made to the organisation, which had organised the event for the evening. I can predict to the last letter the content of the speeches, which are masterpieces of exaggeration and flattery.

I had agreed to address the installation ceremony of a Lions Club at Ludhiana. It was a packed day. I left Delhi by Shatbadi express and arrived in Ludhiana on time at about 11.30 AM. I straightaway went to DAV School for addressing the students. It was followed by lunch and meeting the pressmen. I was put up in the only five star hotel in Ludhiana, where I briefly relaxed in the afternoon. There was dampness in the brand new hotel and a musty smell. I went for tea to the house of Harbans Singh. It was another social gathering, where Harbans Singh had invited his other friends. My class fellows

Mohan Adya and Satish dropped into the damp hotel room. The function which was to start at 8 PM, started, after two hours of delay at 10 PM. It went on for two hours and finally the dinner was served at 12.30 AM. I left without taking the dinner, as I had to leave for Jullundur at 9 A.M. next day en route to Kapurthala with Pappu. I arrived there at 11 A.M. to address the students of a girls' college. Delay from one function kept on getting passed to the next. The lunch was served at 3 PM. As a place associated with the first Sikh Guru, Guru Nanak, Sultanpur Lodi was close. I felt that a pilgrimage could be combined with the visit. I visited Gurudwara Ber Sahib. I also visited his house, where his two sons Lakhmi Chand and Siri Chand were born. Guru Nanak was also jailed in Sultan Pur Lodi, for alleged shortage of funds. But when the accounts were checked, there was no shortage. The Guru had served there as the head of the Stores of the local chieftain. His sister Bibi Nanki was married there. At all these places, there are Gurudwaras to commemorate the Guru's association. I reached Jalalabad finally at about 8 PM.

The book bridegroom is absent

I have agreed to serve on the board of Directors of a few companies. The job is to see that such companies with which I am associated run properly. But in actual practice, any contribution by the non-share holder Directors is marginal. There was a book releasing function at India International Centre by my publisher of 'Outside CBI'. The author did not turn up on the ground of sickness in his family in Luknow. It was almost a marriage with the absentee bride groom, with myself, Commissioner of Delhi Police, Ajay Sharma and Director General, Central Reserve Police, MN Sabarwal acting as mid wives. As is customary, we heaped praise on the human rights book by a UP cadre retired DG, Dixit. I added, as a post script, that even the victims have human rights, about which nobody talks. I had agreed to join for tea with a political activist lady. Either she forgot or deliberately did not turn up. Fortunately, I had fixed the time for meeting near the book release function at Indian International Centre. I did not waste a minute and left the venue, as soon as the function was over. It happens that people invite you and forget about it. It can be very embarrassing. It has happened to me only once in my sixty years of existence. I really cannot crib much about it, as it is not a regular phenomenon. Even otherwise life would be dull and boring, if there were no misadventures. Sometimes, one gets a good feeling, when the work done in the past is still recognised. The Sports Industry almost lionised me when I joined them for their annual function dinner at Kanishka hotel for my contribution to their development, as Director, in Commerce ministry. They said that after I had left, nobody looked at them, as theirs was a tiny segment, of about Rs.50 crores exports in India's export basket of nearly Rs. 20,000 crores. They also said that but for my pushing the matters, the Sports Development Centres would not have come up in Meerut and Jullundur. I carried pleasant memories of the function, but not of the dinner, as I avoid all oil stuff prepared and served in hotels, including five star hotels.

Who is who, and where?

It has become a fashion to throw parties in five star hotels, at the slightest excuse by those who have money to burn. I attended a party, hosted by an influential TV anchor person, who is highly connected both in official and political circles. A dozen Union Ministers, more than two dozen Members of Parliament, three Chief Ministers, a number of would-be Union Ministers and scores of bureaucrats were present in strength. Those of us, who had participated in her programmes were also invited. I attended the programme for an hour and then quietly slinked away, when I saw the photographers trying to click me with a former Chief Minister, who had been chargesheeted by the CBI, when I was heading it. It was to embarrass me so that my photograph could be published to show that I had a soft corner for such people. It had happened to me, when I was heading the CBI. An evening newspaper made a headline story of my talking to a former Prime Minister, PV Narasimha Rao and travelling in his car to his house. Not that meeting anybody, or talking to a person, involved in any case, actually confirms any compromises. But it is good enough to spoil the public image. Even after retirement from the service, the press and people expect from me exactly the same conduct I had while in service. Hosts of most dinners in the five star hotels, practically try to collect the 'Who is Who', of the country, by roping in a few film stars, ministers, models, or other minor celebrities. It is a one-up game, as to who can collect bigger crowds, or a larger number of ministers, or media mughals or TV personalities. Money is the least of the problems for such hosts. More opportunities mean more money and more money can be impressive only if it is flaunted. After a certain level, some people do not feel satisfied, unless they can ignite their cigarettes with bank notes. One of the civil servants in the party told me that he had endless troubles from Government officials. He himself was a serving secretary to the Government of India, who did nothing to improve the departments he had served. I reminded him that he had to ensure others that his department did not give troubles to others. This is the only way in which the system can be improved. Those in the system want it to improve, without trying to improve their part of the system. Despite having a system of financial advisers in the government at every step, the financial position of the country has deteriorated. Despite being almost an unwritten requirement, that financial advisers should be totally negative, except for acting as brakes to development, the system has not been able to attain or come near the objective, for which it was set up. Bureaucracy has been multiplying at a faster rate than inflation. Instead of alleviating the poverty of the common man, those becoming bureaucrats manage to alleviate their own poverty first. The CBI had organised a lecture in memory of the first Director of the CBI, DP Kohli. A guest speaker Prof. Indersasean spoke about the criminal justice system. It appeared from his talk that he was totally innocent of the existing legal system. Many persons attain eminence, because it is thrust on them. It is more so in academic circles.

The Federal Bureau of Investigation of the United States of America has been wanting to open an office in Delhi for a long time. A debate has been going on, as to the merits and demerits of opening an office. I visited Sahara TV Channel, for an interview on the subject. I explained that for increasing co-operation, on a reciprocal basis, India should welcome the move and open a similar office in the USA. In fact, it is the Indians, who siphon off money to America and Europe and it is never vice versa. The setting up of an FBI office would not be a great deal to bother about. It will be a one-man office, whose main objective would be guard the American interests, not only in India but also in neighbouring countries. It is up to us to make use of the FBI, to expedite our own cases pending in America. Social occasions become the vehicles of social interaction and catching up on old friends. My batch-mate RK Takkar had invited us for the wedding of his daughter near Gurgaon. Takkar and I are from the same college. Moreover, Surinder and he were course mate in the Advanced Professional Programme in Public Administration (APPA) in the Indian Institute of Public Administration in 1980-1981. Weddings are late night affairs. I had a dinner of fruits and desserts. Takkar has served as Chief Secretary, Jammu and Kashmir and Delhi Administration with distinction. When I was in the Commerce Ministry as Chief of the Vigilance, Takkar was also there as

Textile Commissioner based in Bombay. We have been in touch with each other and friends for a long time. So I did not feel like backing out, as I would have done, for somebody not known to me, or vaguely known. Normally, a last minute excuse is given that I am out of Delhi, or somebody has died or not feeling well. But most of the time, the real reason is that either it is inconvenient to go, or the place is too far and the route is not familiar or the visit will be socially insignificant and incompatible. I also visited Ebony departmental store of Noida for the programme to promote my books. So far, I have written ten books. Noida Ebony had almost all my books in stock. It is a well displayed store, having all kinds of goods. It is just like the European departmental stores like the Selfridges, British Home Store, or Woolsworth in London. It has excellent decor making it very expensive looking. I told Mr. Nirula, that as it is one of the best looking stores, with smart sales men and women, the first impression a customer might get would be that of the store being expensive, and beyond the reach of an ordinary middle class person. Somehow, the customers want to purchase their requirements from those, who look like them in dress and deportment. Of course, there are a few shops especially in Bombay, which sell jewellery or clothes by appointment. It is strange but true, that some people wait for days together to visit such shops. Nobody argues in such places, even on the day light price robberies. Prices charged are sometimes atrocious, and beyond the reach of middle class people. Only people, having money to throw away, go to such shops, where the price asked for and the value or worth of the item have no relationship. Expensive look inhibition does not apply to such people. Mr. B.S. Nirula and Mr. Lalit of the Ebony are the forces behind the Ebony Chain. One of the benefits of a neo liberalised economy has been the increase in the business opportunities and increase in the purchasing power of ordinary persons.

These days the tailor makes you a celebrity

At the suggestion of Ebony chief I have also agreed to visit Chandigarh Ebony for the promotion of my books. Book promotion is a two-way traffic. Apart from promoting the book, it also promotes the shop. A lot of publicity had been done to announce my visit. The store was willing to meet all my expenses, for travelling and hotel in Chandigarh. I declined on the ground that it would not be fair to put them to heavy expenses. The hosts had arranged for a lunch in one of the top hotels of Chandigarh. Lunches and dinners have become part and parcel of any programme. In fact, without eatables, we feel something has gone amiss. In any case, according to Indian traditions, food is a part of anything, whether it is a life or death function or a celebration of a festival or engagement or a marriage. Lunches and dinners are an accepted part of government, official life. It is more so in the Ministries of Commerce, Industries and Finance.

All foreign visitors are dined and wined at the cost of government. When our government officials go abroad, similar arrangements are made for them by their hosts. A few lunches and dinners, at the cost of the government by the senior officials, are part of their duties. All meetings and conferences have invariably a packed agenda, which takes care of their meals. I had a stint as a Director in the Commerce Ministry of the Government of India in the early 1980's. I could never afford to go on my own to the five star hotels in Delhi. But official lunches and dinners made the visits almost a routine. The dinner had a price tag of listening to self praises and long boring speeches. After some times the visits to five star hotels ceased to hold any charm for me. After the initial gusto was over, I realised that quite often the food served was hardly tasty. The same curry was used for the vegetarian as well as non-vegetarian items. A top chef confirmed that condiments are the same. Only their proportion is different. Once I contracted food poisoning as a result of eating fish in a five star hotel. I gave up eating fish. Only when I was assured in Australia that the food and fish would be of the best quality, I resumed eating fish. Five star name does not always mean five star food.

Pay, Your Honour

Many a time, honours conferred are managed. I asked one of the organisers as to how they selected people for honouring them. He replied that they go by the recommendations made by the people known to them, as they have no independent means of verifying the claims made on behalf of such people. Such people render a tremendous service by recognising merit. Sometimes, even those who have done nothing but have tons of money manage to purchase honours. Money absolves all sins, and is a sure route to popularity. It can be seen by the city pages of newspapers, like the Times of India and The Hindustan Times and some others, where city page is devoted only to those who hosted some social party and to what people were wearing. The pages are also devoted to the best or so called designer clothes available in the market, and also to the best tailor. It has become an age, where a tailor maketh the man, as Shakespeare would have put it. For the rich and famous, the problem is not of making both ends meet, but how to flaunt wealth and prove to their rivals, neighbours and friends that they are more successful. It is the one-up-manship game, which is in vogue. It has been so for ages. One of my colleagues, a Deputy Secretary in the Railways, GS Gill had been insisting on my having dinner with him. I had been avoiding it so as not to put him to expenses. Ultimately, I had dinner with him at the Curzon apartment's old restaurant, now made into the Civil Services Club. Somehow, I always feel guilty, if I am the cause of money being spent on me. It is more so for dinner, which I feel takes a lot of time, which can be better spent on the things which matter in life. In any case, food has ceased to be the main attraction in life, which it was thirty years back. I remember having tried all the different restaurants in Delhi and Bangalore to decide where the best food was available. Now I relish only the home food and nothing more.

I went for a TV recording in Rajat Sharma's programme, on Thursday, 06 April 2000 on the opening of an office of the Federal Bureau of Investigation in Delhi. Rajat Sharma is one of the top anchors in the country. He had hosted the programme, Aap Ki Adalat, where the poor accused, generally a public figure, was grilled, often reducing him to a pulp. It is a battle of wits between him and his guests. He would be respectful, polite and courteous and still make his point. He is one of the best in the country. He has trained his staff also very well. Woe to anybody, who goes unprepared to face him.

Choosie in hospital

My daughter Choosie (Gagandeep) is very affectionate and soft-spoken. She cannot say anything harsh to anybody. Affection oozes out of her. She was not feeling well and was admitted to a hospital. I went to see her and offered to pay her bills. She declined, as her office would take care of her. One advantage of the government or even private service is the medical reimbursement. Somehow, it has been put in the rules of both the private sector and the government that your health and consequently your sickness is also the responsibility of your employer. The rationale is that it is your productivity, which lets the employer make all his money or profit. So he owes a social, moral and a legal responsibility for your well-being. This provision has been misused in the government, where some officials made false claims in collusion with unscrupulous government doctors and chemists selling medicines. Some officials are still facing prosecution. I noticed that my PA, who was with me for one year, started cheating. He was using my postal stamps, making phone calls during the working time I was away. His output was not even one tenth of that which was there, when he had initially joined. One thing I cannot stand is cheating. I do not mind if I am told the truth. It is more palatable than falsehood. I had to recruit his substitute. I interviewed two candidates and found that they could not type even one paragraph correctly. I hired one person, who after one day of working would take two days of leave. I had to tell him to find an employer, who would suit him. I had no time to convey my displeasure to him again and again. His trick was to ask for one months salary in advance and then not turn up. Next month again, he would give an excuse of some serious sickness in the family and beg for an advance. I have always tried to be liberal with my personal staff. But there is a limit to the extent of ride I permit myself to be taken for. I just told him one day that his services were not needed.

Actual users, actually absent

I attended in the evening a programme, organised by Akhil Bhartiya Sahitya Parishad, as Chief Guest on terrorism and human rights. It was a business-like meeting. More than anything else, it showed that people were interested in fighting and giving a helping hand in vanquishing terrorism. The two MPs, DN Misra and Vijay Kumar Malhotra, who were present came fully prepared. Unfortunately, no official agencies tap such enthusiasm. Instead, the organisers are dubbed as communal, or glorifying themselves. There is hardly any public involvement in any of these programmes, for the simple reason that the administration is self-centred and corrupt, with a few honourable exceptions. It has to be drilled into the bureaucracy by the political masters that they owe it to the country to attend such meetings, so that they come to know what is the ground reality. At present, the ministers officially get to know only that much, which the officials want them to know. The political masters should have their independent sources, instead of all the time relying on what is given as an official version on the file. Of course, the practice and way of approach with a fixed mind-set by the bureaucracy will have to change. While a private person does not expect any reward for his patriotism and nationalism, he expects some consideration, respect and recognition from the administration. One of the most difficult jobs is to change the mind-set. With nearly 1.94 crores states and central employees, the government faces a herculean task of making people think in a straight line, especially when there are no rewards for doing your job well and no retribution for not working or delivering results.

Farmhouses or Palaces?

I get invited to several lunches and dinners which I try to avoid. But some are unavoidable. One such was a lunch at Ashok Sawhney's farm. People have built almost palaces on open agricultural land. These huge houses are used as weekend retreats or for hosting parties for hundreds of people. In fact, some people stay at their farms to avoid pollution in Delhi. These farm houses have all the conveniences of water supply, electricity, central heating or air conditioning. My late father was the first to build a garage for our tractor at our farm at Jalalabad. He built a room on its roof. He had kept a bed and a few old chairs for his rest and visitors. The electricity from the tubewell was available to run a pedestal fan. As the land was less than three kilometres away, he could be back to the house in five minutes. He never stayed there for the night. The servants working at the farm made use of the living room. My late father, Mahant Kartar Singh, could see the entire farm land of 50 acres from the roof. In Delhi, the so-called farm houses have about one to three acres of land. I spent four hours in travelling by car due to the traffic congestion. In the evening, I was invited for a TV recording on cricket match fixing on the Doordarshan channel. The only problem with recording is that most studios are located in Noida. A minimum of two hours has to be reserved for travelling alone, for a five minutes interview. I feel uncomfortable when I am not able to work on my computer for a few hours. I try to keep a balance between the outdoor activities and writing. This is the only way to be happy and satisfied as far as I am concerned. It might be changed tomorrow. But for the present this makes me happy.

Again, there was an interview recording on Jain Television on cricket fixing. One of my batchmates and friends Sh. R.K. Puri is heading the association of the top hoteliers of the country. He had hosted a reception in honour of the delegates and specially invited me to join. I went at the appointed time in the evening to Maurya Sheraton, a five star hotel. Most people were still to come. The trouble with punctuality is that sometimes you are left by yourself and even the hosts do not turn up thinking that guests are bound to be late. One of the top hoteliers told me how a top minister had received ten and a half crore rupees in his hotel. When I asked him whether he would be willing to say the same in a court of law, he simply told me that it was for my consumption only. I told him that such information keeps floating all over. Unless it is converted into evidence, it has no value. I also told him that a person like him should be public spirited and come out openly. It was to no avail. I have not written their names, because I feel that I cannot and should not write anything till I can prove it. It will lead to unnecessary litigation. He also said that, in the complicated transfer of money from and to India then minister showed it as a receipt of the amount from his relations abroad.

In the Mecca of academic excellence

I left for Manipal for a programme organised by Manipal Deemed University, on Indo-American co-operation in the wake of the visit of the then President of the United States, Clinton. I normally do not travel except by the highest class. The Vice-Chancellor of the University made a request to me to travel Y or economy class and accept the fare as such. I had written to him that the University could re-imburse to me whatever it could. But I would travel by the highest class. On his appeal and the appeal of Mr. MD Nalpat, a good journalist, I travelled by Y class to Bombay. From Bombay, in any case, there was no class in the plane except Y category. The plane was filthy-looking from outside. It appeared that it needed a coat of paint badly. But being a part of the government company, it had fallen on bad days, maintenance-wise. Most air hostesses had passed the prime of their youth. Instead of looking Miss India, they appeared to be Mother India. Passengers preferred to be looked after, but definitely not by grandmother-type of airhostesses. Younger people feel that they have a world to conquer, whereas the old have already been conquered by the world. Some passengers were too demanding even from the old airhostesses. Airhostesses by their expressions conveyed, being harried and harassed. Most passengers, in spite of their third rate behaviour, expect first class service. As the service of liquor has been stopped, during the domestic flight, nobody had a license or any excuse to misbehave or sexually harass the airhostesses on the ground of being drunk. It had happened in the past where some legislators and ministers misbehaved and blamed it on too many drinks served to them. The economy class is rather cramped and uncomfortable. Of late, some deaths have been reported, on long distance travel of the economy class passengers. I make it a point to walk down the aisle of the aircraft in every flight to stretch my legs. I have been doing it, since I first travelled by air in September, 1965 from Hyderabad to Delhi to see my bride, who is now my wife. The airfare then was Rs.250, by AVRO or Fokker Friendship aircraft. But at that time, air travel had such a tremendous charm and thrill that I did not notice anything wrong with the seats. During the fifties and sixties till the eighties, there used to be only one class on all domestic flights. As there was a monopoly of the Indian Airlines and Air India, occasionally one needed influence and recommendations to get air tickets. Once I had to seek the recommendations of the then minister, Minister for Civil Aviation or Flying, to get a ticket for travelling abroad. One of the top hoteliers in the country travelling with me told me as to how a former Union Minister accepted a bribe of Rs. Twenty Crores in his presence and in his hotel. But when questioned by me, whether he would be willing to lodge a complaint and fight corruption, he said that he was in the business of making money and not a sanitary inspector to clean society of the corruption. He said that he was the victim of bureaucracy and throttling laws at every step. He was not prepared to wind up his shop by waging an unequal fight, where everybody accepted and demanded kick-backs. He said that the Indian system is such that either you have to be influential or have a lot of money to buy any sanction or approval or just to be left to work in peace. He said that he had become rich by enriching others, and he did not mind bribing others. His bottom line was that you could purchase respectability with a heavy purse, and be in the photographs of magazines and newspapers. It is almost true because corrupting others or being caught in corruption is considered an acceptable social crime and not a thuggery of the worst order. The political and social leaders have to see that it becomes easier for the citizens to do right, and difficult to do wrong. On arrival at Manipal, we were effusively welcomed by Dr M.M. Pai, the President or Chancellor of the University. He hosted a reception dinner for the delegation at the sea beach cottage. We had been put up at the only five star hotel of the Manipal Academy. I had a light-hearted chat and a joke session with the Indian Ambassador to Kuwait, who was also participating in the seminar. Dr. Pai told me as to how some retired officials, including judges and former Ministers and Prime Ministers, had tried to pressurise him either for admission or for passing failed candidates in MBBS or MD examinations. He stood his ground, and faced a lot of flaks. But he never compromised on excellence in education. He told me that he was proud to find his students all over the world. Manipal is one of the top centres of excellence in education, and the credit for this goes to the Pai family. Karnataka State has provided the maximum number of Doctors and Engineers to the country. There used to be a system, where irrespective of your merit, but with the basic requirement, you could get admission to a Medical or an Engineering College and pass out as a Doctor or an Engineer. Money or influence could get you admission. This system has been rectified now. Now only a few seats for sale or influence are at the discretion of the management. Manipal has one difference with other places. It has not compromised on the quality of education. It is located far away from metropolitan towns, leaving little scope for students to do anything other than their studies. Ideally, the educational institutions and all organisations, striving for excellence in any field, should be located far away from any distractions.

It was a comfortable stay in the five star hotel Valley View International at Manipal. But whereas the best coffee is available in the South, the tea preparation is not the best. Since I carry my own tea-making kit, I did not face any problem of making and having the tea of my taste. The main inaugural function was in the afternoon at 3.30 P.M. As I had already planned to leave on 13th of April, I delivered my oration as the principal speaker in the main function itself. It was well received and I received a thunderous ovation for it. The forenoon had been left free for the tour. Manipal being a small place did not have any monuments to be seen. I had seen all the buildings in the campus during my one hour morning walk. All said that they had liked my speech. But this is what everybody says to everybody who speaks. Nobody says that he spoke badly. I ate a heavy dinner and had to have a post-dinner walk, so that I could sleep comfortably. One can never sleep with an overfed and overstuffed stomach.

A five star hotel, is a hotel not home

I had told the organisers that I would not be able to stay for more than two days. A hotel is a hotel and, despite the best of facilities, cannot beat your own pad, however small or ill organised it may be. One's home runs as per one's own convenience, and the hotel runs mechanically, with no human touch, either in services or in general approach. The objective of the house is to cater to all your needs. The object of the hotel is to cater to general needs, and for specific services one has to pay extra. Many a times one avoids asking anything extra on the sole ground that for a day or two one can adjust to anything. 13th April is the birth day of the Khalsa. On this day, Guru Gobind Singh gave birth to the present Sikh philosophy. Most people practise a religion, because they were born into it. Being a Hindu or a Sikh or a Muslim is a matter of accident, because a particular person's parents happen to be either Hindus or Muslims or Sikhs. Only later on, people develop any fantatical attachments. I respect all religions. The result is that I am equally happy in visiting any place which is holy and which gives me peace of mind. It does not make me less of a Sikh, of which I am proud of. My entire day was spent in travelling first by road from Manipal to Mangalore airport (90 minutes). The plane was late by one hour from Mangalore to Bombay. But still I could catch the flight at 7 PM and reach Delhi by 9 P.M. For covering this much distance, the Mughals would take three months by horses, on foot and elephants. Modern gadgets have shrunk the distance dramatically. Manipal was a new experience for me, as I had visited this place more than 25 years ago, as a Director of Youth Services in 1975. It was a small town at that time with nothing to write home about. It has changed beyond recognition and attained a position in its own right on the world's educational map.

Punjabian the shan (Pride and jewel of Punjab)

I had accepted to address the Baisakhi mela organised at Ghaziabad. I combined it with addressing a management institute and a dinner along with the function. My address on how to excel in life was appreciated by the teachers and the taught. Afterwards, I received an award of the Samaj Rattan, from a social organisation, followed by an other award of Pride of Punjab or Punjabian the Shan. I confined my speeches to the minimum, lest the audience felt bored. I said that nobody was interested in long boring speeches and I would prefer to join them in seeing the good variety programme put up on the occasion. I cannot say whether the thunderous clapping was because of the speech being appreciated, or the audience feeling relieved at being spared the agony of another set of didactic lectures. I have seen that some speakers go on speaking, without assessing the reactions of the audience. I can instantly judge whether the audience want me to stop, or continue speaking. I also attended the wedding reception of a 55 years old TV anchor of a regional language channel. Almost everybody in the political sphere had come to pay homage to the old doddering couple, who control guests TV appearances in their slot on a popular channel. It was good to see that the old man had not lost his zest for life and lust in marrying his 45 year old colleague. It confirms again and again that God ensures sunshine and rain on every field, however barren it may be. I had been invited, as I had appeared in his programmes. Otherwise, I had no reason to be there, as I hardly knew the couple. It was a treat to see how many old men, including tottering politicians, felt encouraged to take similar steps. Old foes and friends were generous in congratulating the couple and said within everybody's hearing, that they would be glad to participate in their programme. This was the real reason for the presence of most people. Since I was delayed, I decided to drop my driver near his house in Noida and drove back home. It is unfair to the driver but cannot be helped. I always tell my driver, that I am engaging him for my convenience and if it does not suit him, he is welcome not to work with me. I also tell him, that his working hours would depends on my engagements which may not necessarily be from 10 AM to 5 or 6 PM.

Despite my best efforts, sometimes with a view not to displease others, I succumb to the requests, which are nothing but a waste of time. I do so once in a while to keep up the enthusiasm of others. I admire the enthusiasm of Mr. Aggarwal, who is keen to solve the problems of Delhi. But unfortunately, the people in the Capital are too busy to look into and help in solving the problems of others. I attended a meeting convened by him in another person's office in Malcha Marg, Chankya Puri. Unfortunately, I was the only person, apart from the organisers, attending the meeting. My efforts to ask my colleagues to join had not evoked any response. It is a natural phenomenon of the impersonal metropolitan life. I had to drive the vehicle, as my driver had not turned up. When the driver drives the vehicle, I use my time in reading or completing one of the pending chores. I lost time in driving as well as in the unproductive meeting. Things may be expensive in Delhi, but they are available. My daughter, Randeep, wanted me to send her an electric kettle so that her husband could use it during his tours. I went and purchased a kettle as per her specifications from Khan Market. One may stint for oneself, but never for one's children. Parents always do more for their children, than what their children do or care for them. I remember, my late father almost on his death bed used to say that he was all right, to save me, from the trouble of going to be with him. He probably knew that his end was close by. But he never wanted to inconvenience me, even in his last earthly moments. Probably, I am no different, like million of other fathers. My class fellow and a good friend, Manohar Singh Prem, came to my house for lunch. Manohar is an excellent host and has acquired British citizenship. He had a job in the Environment Department in the United Kingdom, from where he has retired. He always looks after me well, when I am in London.

Life goes on

I visited Jalalabad again with Surinder and Harveen from Delhi for three days. Invariably on the morning of arrival from Delhi, the morning walk is the causality. But I compensated for it by going to the field in the evening. Though we travelled by air conditioned first class, still the early arrival of the train disturbs your sleeping rhythm. I caught up on the sleep during the day. It was more difficult for my friend Om, who had to reach Ferozpore at 5 AM. He has never grudged in receiving and seeing me off. The stream of visitors has been reduced to a trickle. Only those who want me to make recommendations on their behalf come. In any case, whether in or out of service, most people came to me for recommendations to get their work done. I meet everybody, and do forward their applications to the concerned. I tell people that nothing can be guaranteed, as all officials have to work within certain parameters. I also tell them that I would not recommend any wrong doing or illegal action, harming anybody else. Once in a while, I am advised that since I have retired, I should not hesitate in recommending all the cases, which come to me. I tell them that this would amount to undoing and undermining all the values I had stood for in my life.

There are plenty of such times when I am invited for meals. My marked preference is for lunch, as I avoid any meals and definitely heavy fatty meals, which make one uncomfortable and guarantees a restless night even with the help of antacids, churan or anything of that nature. I love good food and hog it. But now, I have to be careful with my weight and health. It is again a circle that when you eat more, you exercise more to balance it, and probably spend more on the doctors to ward off the illnesses gained as a result of greasy and fatty food. The traditional Indian way of showing hospitality by feeding, whether required or not, has not changed. This had led to the development of the food industry in a big way, without any minimum health or quality food checks. The host does make an effort to check the food. But his examination is confined only to the visual part. He has no means to detect, whether the meat served is from diseased animals or whether the best of vegetables are used. One salesman told me that they have the maximum profit from mixed vegetables. They can mix all kinds of vegetables. Nobody can detect the stale ingradients. The only condition he ensures is that the food is well presented. Sometimes, a conscious hostess adds a few home cooked dishes. I invariably ask as to what is the home item and go for that. One of the things I check up on is whether my pension is being credited regularly to my account. It must be said to the credit of the government that the system of crediting pension to your bank account has ended many hassles. Of course, the bank has to satisfy itself every year that the person getting the government pension is alive. The time in Jalalabad is mostly spent on socialising or in condoling somebody's death or congratulating on a child's birth. I do this only to the extent my mother tells me. It is more to please her, and occasionally because of my personal relations with the person.

I left Jalalabad on 23rd, with Surinder and Bibban for Ferozpore to catch the train to Delhi. My cousin Inderjeet Singh Madan, a good host, extends his hospitality, not only for excellent lunches and dinners, but also sends his air conditioned Esteem car to pick me up from Ferozpore and drop me to Ferozpore for catching the train. On this particular day, he was out and so we travelled in my late father's Maruti 800 to Ferozpore. My father had invested in this car, just four months before he passed away. It has not done even 19000 kilometres and is always left in Jalalabad. It is very decent of Inderjeet to send the car all the way. But sometimes, I feel that it is unfair. So I insist that he must make sure that his own work should not suffer because his luxury car is with me. Only when I accept engagements near Jalalabad and if he is free, he comes with me. Otherwise I use my small family car. Once I had to go for a function. He insisted that I take his car, which he also needed. I thanked him for his consideration but told him that if the invitation was for me, means of transportation would make no difference. I do not go to any place or show, which is only for a show-off. On the way to Ferozepore, once my car got punctured. It was dark and there was no torch with us. Om, the expert car doctor and a person who will find a solution to any problem, hit upon the new innovative idea, of using the head lights of the vehicles coming on the road to change the tyre. We could reach fifteen minutes before the departure of the train. My mother appear to be happy in Jalalabad, as the house ran according to her convenience. She spends sometime in Delhi. When she gets bored, or wants a change, she comes to Jalalabad and this circle continues. She is hard of hearing and does not like to use any hearing aids. Nobody, however old, (she is more than 84 years of age) wants to admit that age is not on his or her side. The infirmities of the age, or old age, are a part of life. The stationing of a personal car at Jalalabad is something, which gives me a feeling of mobility and independence.

Good governance, a universal requirement

On arrival at New Delhi, I joined for dinner at the residence of Sardar Harbhajan Singh in Defence Colony. Harbhajan Singh is the President of All India Small and Medium Newspapers Federation for the last 20 years as well as the Editor of the Indian Observer, a weekly. He has given me a permanent column in his magazine and I am duty bound to send it to him. He is both politically and socially active. Though his leanings are towards the Congress, he has friends in every walk of life. His pre-dinner snacks are so good that by the time dinner starts, most guests have eaten so much that unless they have an additional stomach, they cannot eat any more. His snacks are as good as a dinner. But Harbhajan Singh is a poor eater himself. It is for this reason that he and his son Gurinder are slim and trim. Other guests at the dinner included ND Tewari, a Congress stalwart, a former Chief Minister of UP as well as Central Minister. Those who have worked with him, always speak well of him. He said that he has read my books and conveyed his appreciation. Mohinder Singh Sathi and Industry Minister of Delhi, Narinder Nath were also present. I told them that good governance is the direct result of sustained, honest and responsive follow up. I told the Finance Minister that he must make it easier, to pay sales tax. I told him that if he made it transparent and easy the corruption will die, or be reduced to the barest minimum. Another friend and Editor of Dainak Bhaskar, Alok Mehta, told me that he has kept my photo on his table for my services rendered to the Nation.

Harveen, my daughter, during the campus interview, had earlier been selected for the job of Finance officer, subject to her getting a first class and the minimum marks. Her results declared by her Institute, that is, International Management Institute showed that she had scored more than adequate marks for her job in ONGC, and she would join there in due course. I felt satisfied that at least the good education invested in three daughters had paid off. Two of them are working for government organisations, and the third picks up the same amount of money, by being an international consultant. She consciously took up casual work, because her son Danish born on 10th June 1998 is not even one year old. She is devoted to him and marvels at his smallest gesture and words, as all parents and grand parents do, for their first born. We ourselves are no less thrilled at his smallest utterances, and interpret it, in our own light. Little children are a source of delight, fun and play, as long as they listen to us. The same child, when he or she grows, defies what and whom he had meekly accepted. One of my retired friends says that the reason for his devotion to his grandfather is the stark truth that he is the only one, who listens and cares for him in his family. He told me that neither his sons nor daughters care whether he is dead or alive. During the leave of my driver, I do the driving. I have been driving since 1962 and have a license since then. But the fact remains that shrinking parking place, and more than forty lakh vehicles in Delhi for a population of 1.20 crores, make driving a nightmare. It is not only that you should be driving well and following the rules. It is equally important that the others should also follow the rules of the game, which most often is not the case. The return of the driver from leave is welcome, as it enables me to be more mobile and adds one to two hours to my productive time, which otherwise would be spent in driving. One has to concentrate on driving and seeing the road ahead, to make sure that neither I bang into somebody, nor somebody else bangs into me. Match fixing, which in plain language means underplaying for huge money, has been the hot news. Interviews on several channels, including Sahara, Jain and

Doordarshan kept me busy on most evenings in the month of April and May 2000. Like military or para military, which have their own uniform, the saints or sadhus have the saffron colour clothing as their uniform. The sadhus classify themselves, depending upon the visage they present or what their followers tell about them. I have been attending a number of functions, where sadhus have been either chief guests or presiding officers. The desire for trapping of importance, and being photographed or be on TV has not left such worthies. They also like to be photographed with the Ministers or have people touching their feet. This is one thing which I religiously avoid. Many want to do it to me on the ground that I am a Mahant. I tell them that I am an ordinary person like millions of other Indians. I am as much a part of god, as any body else. I visited my bank, which I do periodically, to withdraw money. A fact which has been neglected is that government itself has ceased to be a model citizen. The government offices do not vacate the buildings taken on rent on the expiry of their lease. They continue sticking to the buildings at the old rates and vacate the same after a long protracted court trial. My bank, with whom I have been having an account for over 30 years, had to vacate its premises after it had lost the court case. When I questioned the manager as to why they cannot keep up their word, he replied that it is the head office policy to hang on to the buildings at the old rent. It is financially cheaper. I told him that it is taking shelter under tenancy laws not to pay the rent commensurate with the market rates. He said that constitution guarantees equal rights to everybody, and so the bank has the right to fight the case right up to the Supreme Court. My reply was all government or public sector employees expect the government to be a fair employer. But when it comes to redressing people's grievances, or being fair to them, it is essential that government organisations do the same to the people, for whose sake they supposedly exist. One should be even-handed to all.

Sacking though unpleasant, is at times necessary

I had an efficient secretary for over one year. I noticed that he felt that working with me was like working with the government, where you get your salary, as long as you mark yourself present. I had to terminate his services and tell him that I would like to manage on my own. I had a mind to tick him off and dismiss him. I felt that I must give him a face-saving sack. I had also noticed that he was using my postage for his work. I also noticed that he would spend all the time in talking on the telephone, or watching TV, whenever I had to go out. His output had come down in less than six months. As it is, he was coming only for four hours, as I had originally felt that my work load did not need more than half a day's dedicated work. I had engaged him earlier on the recommendation of a steno from The Pioneer, the best newspaper of Delhi. I feel that he was sacked from there. I do not believe that a person cannot reform himself. Hence I did not even inquire about his past. But when he got up to his old tricks, I just told him to find another job, as I did not need his services. However I was clear that I did need a secretary to attend to all routine correspondence, type material or scan it for the magazine and books. I had an interview for selecting a new PA. Unfortunately, the new candidates could not type even one sentence correctly. Ultimately, I agreed to keep a new secretary, recommended by my publisher, Sanjay Jha. He worked with me exactly for five months and out of this period, he was either late or absent on one excuse or the other. I gave him a salary raise of Rs. 500 and gave him even two months advance salary. This made him further unpunctual. He felt that I was obliged to continue with him, having given him advance salary. He would tell me that he was going out for three days or fifteen days and wanted to be paid for his absence. I had to tell him, when he returned after fifteen days absence, that I had kept him for my work and my convenience. Since he did not work as per the schedule, I did not need his services. He could return the advance given to him, at his convenience. My peace of mind was more important to me, than fighting with him, for not having done his job properly. He did not expect to be fired off so politely. I told him to go to the person who had recommended him for the job. However, I made sure that all new secretaries sit away from the telephone and TV. This particular PA was caught by me on a number of occasions playing games on the computer. I pointed out to him that I was paying for my typing work, and not for any time he spent on playing games on the computer. I had a busy week of interviews on Jain and Sahara television networks on cricket match fixing. According to the allegations, the cricket players had accepted money to underplay and lose the match. My point of view was that the Prevention of Corruption Act does not recognise any corrupt practice, except by a government servant and so the players were not guilty of corruption. They might be guilty of gambling or cheating, only if proper evidence was available, but nothing more.

Every trade has its uniform and the usual dress of a mendicant is saffron dress. I have attended a number of functions, presided over or blessed by sadhus. There are no sadhus in Sikh religion. The sadhus or priests have a serious look about them, as if they were carrying the burden of the entire universe. They are always expected to be serious, glum and better if they have a reasonable paunch. It is a difficult existence, where one is always at the mercy of the householders for their meals or other bare necessities. I suppose, a sadhu is always expected to be in constant communication with God and always begging either for His blessings or forgiveness for some or the other for imaginary or real sins. I was also the chief guest for a function of the World Brotherhood Organisation as I had agreed to be its patron.

Some glimpses, some functions, some home truths

It was a programme of World Brotherhood Organisation to honour the heroes of the Nation. As the patron of the organisation, I was invited to give awards at Hotel Meridien. I suggested that MP RL Bhatia and Kuldeep Nayar should give away a few prizes. As a patron of the organisation, I felt that in all fairness, we should also involve others in honouring other guests, so that they take interest in the activities of the organisation. It was a late night, as next morning I had to get up at 3.20 AM to catch the Jaipur flight to address the May Day Conference. The trouble with getting up so early is that you cannot sleep again for fear that you might miss the flight, at 6 A.M. I willy-nilly kept on lying on the bed, but got up in time to be ready to receive the former Governor, Satyanarayan Reddy, who came to my house to pick me up as both of us had to go for the same function. We were using the same vehicle provided by the organisers, who had also arranged for our air tickets, as well as hotel accommodation in Jaipur. We reached the airport in time and checked in. There was a last minute announcement of the delay of the plane. Obviously it compounded on the sleep, as one could not sleep at the air port. I gulped a few cups of tea to stay awake. The plane left after a delay of two hours, for a flight of fifty minutes. It almost amounted to the same amount of time taken by a fast train like Shatabdi to Jaipur. The organisers had put me in hotel Ashok Classic. The hotel is part of the Ashok group owned by the ITDC. It is a well maintained hotel. A programme had been organised to discuss the role of the media, in the changing milieu of society. Rajasthan press has been fairly vocal in exposing evils in the state. The state has more than 800 big and small newspapers. The function was attended by Rajasthan Information Minister Jitendar Singh, as well as Sh. Harbhajan Singh, All India President of Small and Medium Newspapers Federation. Sh. Harbhajan Singh is based in Delhi and brings out a magazine called Indian Observer. In fact, it was at his invitation that I had come to Jaipur. A meeting had been arranged with the Chief Minister of Rajasthan, Ashok Gehlot. I told the Chief Minister that, if he wanted to succeed, he had to make sure that the bureaucracy did not sabotage what it did not agree to. I also complemented him for not yielding to the black mail of 74 days strike by the government employees, who wanted almost the entire budget to be spent on them. He told me that people were happier, when the employees were on strike. They did not have to bribe anybody. There was no interruption in the power supply. He felt helpless in weeding out the dead wood and the corrupt from the service. He also admitted that the corrupt were most influential in pressurising him to get plum postings. He also said that he had displeased many by not agreeing to their atrocious demands. Before meeting any VIP, I always inquire to in what language he would prefer to be talked to. I was advised that though the CM of Rajasthan could understand English, it would be better, if I spoke in Hindi. I talked to him in Hindi only. There was a function in the evening organised by a voluntary organisation to honour the heroes of the society. The heroes were ordinary persons like teachers, doctors, social workers, and small government officials, who had done extraordinary work. It was distinctly better than government honours. For any government honour or an office, a lot of lobbying, pleading and begging, is almost a must. Nothing moves in the government, unless it is moved. It is true of any award. Moreover, the government awards only go to government supporters, or those who have a soft corner for it or extend indirect support. I also found time to purchase two Jaipuri mattresses. These special mattresses are very light and are adequate for most of the part of the year. Rajasthan is extremely hot in May and June. It was a full day, which extended up to 11 P.M.

Pressure tactic pays

I got up early, as I had to catch the flight at 8 A.M. Just before I left for the airport, I was told that the flight had been cancelled. I was given the option of travelling either by the evening flight or return to Delhi by train. While I was contemplating as to which will be the better of the two options, I was told that the flight would leave on time. We reached the airport and boarded the plane. I was curious to know as to how the cancelled flight materialised. During the flight a lady, who was sitting next to me, told me that the flight had been almost cancelled at Udaipur, as the private airline wanted to divert the flight to some other place. Half a dozen lady passengers went on Dharna, protesting against the cancellation of the schedule and upsetting their programme. The private airline had no option but to yield to the women power. The airline had its revenge, by serving stale snacks. You have the option of either leaving them or taking them. I preferred to ignore the snack tray. There is nothing the airhostesses can do about. Their job is only to serve. The only contact in the aircraft is through the airhostesses. The job of an airhostess may appear to be glamorous. But people, including women, have different views about it. When, in London, I asked a receptionist of my hotel whether she ever wanted to be an airhostess, she replied that she never wanted to be a waitress in the air. I know a friend of mine, who fell for an airhostess on Delhi-Bombay route and married her. An airhostess told me that her aim was to hook a rich young man as her husband. She also said that only the rich and affluent travel by air. There is nothing wrong in using your job as a stepping stone for marrying the rich. Marriage for convenience is not unusual. People end up marrying in their closed circle, or acquaintances, or casual friends. Being an airhostess and marrying a passenger is the same as a hotel receptionist marrying a guest. Even most IAS and other class one lady officers when under training never forget that they must hook a suitable husband, when the going is good. There is a good rationale, because in any case it is easier for men at any age to get married. But in the case of women, finding a suitable match even when they are young and desirable can be a problem. That is why sometimes one finds the ugliest of men having the most ravishing of wives.

Some partying

Mr. Amar Singh M.P. very rich in his own right is an excellent host. He threw a party in honour of a visiting Australian tycoon, Kerry Paker in Ashoka hotel. The 'Who's Who' of Delhi including myself had been invited. Amitabh Bachan and a host of film actors and actresses were present. I did not recognise most of them and read next day in the papers that film actresses like Sridevi and the Kapoor clan were present. This is due to the reason, that one has an image of the film folks, as they are dressed in films. Their dress is not the same as they wear in parties. Some newspapers in Delhi have a supplement to report as to who has given what party and who were present there. The only qualification for getting into the social pages is the money you can spend and the celebrities you can herd for such occasions. The talk in such gatherings veers around helloing and complementing each other. My boredom level for such parties, depending upon the interesting and interested people one meets, ranges from half an hour to one hour. It is also a chance to cultivate new friendships and renew the old ones. In most parties, the snacks served are so heavy and tempting, that there is no place in the stomach for dinner. I rarely stay for dinner, as I generally and generously feed myself on the comparatively gheeless and tandoori snacks. Amar Singh has a knack of making himself pleasant, and pleasing and making each one of his guests feel that he is their best friend. I have always enjoyed meeting this pleasant young man, who has more friends than enemies.

During the month a seminar had been organised at the Constitutional Club on the role of the Print Media. Out of the five persons invited, as many as three persons, like Dr. Kidwai, M.P., Bhisam Narain Singh, former Governor and Mani Shanker Iyer MP, were absent. Only two of us that is myself and Madan Lal Khurana were left in the field to speak. It would have been impolite for me to enquire about the absence of the big names. I kept wondering whether sometimes the organisers, to attract a crowd, print big names without the consent of the concerned, to catch attention. Or even if an earlier consent is there, the speaker is not able to come for good reasons, which might have been explained to the organisers. But such reasons are not shared with the audience.

Convocation : then and now

My youngest daughter, Harveen nicknamed Bibban, had her final convocation of finishing her MBA in the International Management Institute in Qutab Institutional Area. There is a sea change in the scenario of formal convocation or awards day during my times in the 1950's and in 2000. There was a very casual atmosphere. Gone were the days of strict discipline and being over deferential. American culture, of easy informality, has come to stay everywhere and no institution, except may be the armed forces, have remained immune to it. The students were respectful, but not obsequious. Mr. Nitish Sen Gupta, MP is heading the Institute, which has a high standing in the B-Schools. Nitish has been a civil servant all his life, having joined IAS in 1957 and retired as a Secretary to the Government of India. Thanks to the standing of the Institute, all students who have done their MBA's from IMI have been picked up by good companies during the campus recruitment. Campus recruitment is a unique concept, where organisations pick up talented students and offer them jobs, subject to their passing the final examination with a minimum percentage. Here is a case of a thirsty man, coming to the well and having his fill with the best.

Working couples

Ms. Jija Hari Singh, IPS, a lady officer from my former Karnataka cadre, now working at the Airport Authority of India, had invited us for a dinner. She is married to an IAS Officer, Subir Hari Singh of the same cadre. The posting of working couples is always a hat trick, especially in Government of India. A number of couples have to try to stay together. I have also seen that some couples prefer not to be posted together, so that they can avoid the tension of staying together. In fact, one of my friends who is no more told me that he preferred this arrangement of casual and infrequent meetings, as it enabled him to have husband-wife relations, and still gave him space to live. Differences are natural, when two almost independent persons with separate good income are to live together. Money is the source of all relationships and less dependence means more independence. I stayed for an hour and met every guest and left without eating any dinner on the truthful ground that I normally do not eat any dinner. Most people accept and value my approach. I myself do not insist on my guests to eat more than what they want. In any case, at the fifty plus age, the food loses its attraction and lure for most people. But it does not mean that temptation is any the less. When there is attractively packaged and presented food, most of us fall for it, irrespective of what the body needs, demands or should avoid.

Sharing my views

During the week, I also addressed the monthly meeting of Noida Rotary Club on the present scenario in the country. Most people were fed up with corruption. I said that charity should begin at home and they should pledge not to give bribes. As long as there is a giver, there will always be a receiver. I also told them it is our country and the onus lies on us. I addressed another meeting, on the role of citizens, in Hotel Connaught, during the week. It was only to remind the countrymen that they had certain duties also and not only rights, under the constitution. I believe that this is the only way to remind people that they must take an active interest in the country's affairs. It is essential to develop a spirit of 'Never Die'. It is a joint effort by the print media to carry such messages. It is surprising that the visual media, like TV, devote nearly 80% of its time and almost all its prime time only to political stories of what a particular politician said and the reactions of others to it. The news has become politician-centred rather than issue-centred. The CBI had organised a seminar to discuss, whether the confessions made before the CBI and police officers should be admissible. It is strange but true that this law was introduced in 1863 and continues to be so, as laid down by the British rulers. The British did not trust their own police, because of the awful reputation it enjoyed. The position has not changed much even now. Left to himself, any citizen would like to keep the police of the present day also at an arms length and have nothing to do with them, if he could manage. I attended the function for sometime and left to meet the publisher of my autobiography to collect a cheque of royalty. There is no way an author can know, whether the account rendered to him is correct or errs on the side of favouring the publisher, who has to shell some royalty to the author. Except for one, my publishers have been fairly decent. I feel that the message of my books is more important than the money which the books bring me. In any case, whatever is received is spent on paying the salary of my secretary and my driver. In the evening, I briefly went for a dinner to a five star hotel, much against my nclination. It was a dinner organised by a businessman from my village Jalalabad, who had made tons of money. He felt that my presence, however brief it might be, would enhance his prestige. Tons of money does not mean tons of 'class', which was conspicuous by its absence. In any case, the definition of 'class' is a relative affair and there are no hard and fast measurements for it. A rich man can afford to create and sustain a class of his own. Riches have excused the crass behaviour of many.

❑❑❑

Index